全国跨境电商"十三五"系列教材

国际商法

韩永红 李婷婷◎编著

INTERNATIONAL COMMERCIAL LAW

双语版
第2版

人民邮电出版社

北京

图书在版编目（ＣＩＰ）数据

国际商法：双语版：英汉对照 / 韩永红，李婷婷
编著. -- 2版. -- 北京：人民邮电出版社，2024.5
全国跨境电商"十三五"系列教材
ISBN 978-7-115-63288-3

Ⅰ．①国… Ⅱ．①韩… ②李… Ⅲ．①国际商法－双
语教学－高等学校－教材－英、汉 Ⅳ．①D996.1

中国国家版本馆CIP数据核字(2023)第238233号

内 容 提 要

本书涵盖四部分内容：国际商务法律环境、国际货物买卖法、国际知识产权转让和国际商事争议解决。为培养读者直接用英语思考、分析和解决法律问题的能力，本书摒弃了中英文对照的写作方式，代之以每章的"导读"和"小结"用中文写作，正文及"课后练习"用英文写作，对于正文中重要的法律概念、规则和制度则采用脚注的方式，以中文给出较为全面、精练的介绍。

本书配有电子课件、习题、习题答案等教学资料，用书教师可登录人邮教育社区（www.ryjiaoyu.com）免费下载。

本书适合作为本科、高职院校经济管理类、法学类、商务英语、法律英语等专业相关课程的教材，也适合作为国际商法从业者的自学用书。

◆ 编　　著　韩永红　李婷婷
　　责任编辑　刘向荣
　　责任印制　胡　南

◆ 人民邮电出版社出版发行　　北京市丰台区成寿寺路 11 号
　　邮编　100164　电子邮件　315@ptpress.com.cn
　　网址　https://www.ptpress.com.cn
　　固安县铭成印刷有限公司印刷

◆ 开本：787×1092　1/16
　　印张：11.5　　　　　　　　2024 年 5 月第 2 版
　　字数：310 千字　　　　　　2025 年 3 月河北第 2 次印刷

定价：49.80 元

读者服务热线：(010)81055256　印装质量热线：(010)81055316
反盗版热线：(010)81055315

前　言

党的二十大报告指出，必须完整、准确、全面贯彻新发展理念，坚持社会主义市场经济改革方向，坚持高水平对外开放，加快构建以国内大循环为主体、国内国际双循环相互促进的新发展格局。本书第 1 版自出版以来有幸得到使用者的青睐，这也鼓励我们再接再厉，继续为我国涉外法治人才培养事业贡献点滴力量。同时，在过去数年间，国际商事交易所处的环境发生了一些重大变化，与国际商事交易有关的国际条约、国际商事惯例、国内法都有新的进展：如 2020 年 1 月 1 日，《国际贸易术语解释通则》（Incoterms 2020）生效；2020 年 9 月 12 日，《联合国关于调解所产生的国际和解协议公约》生效；《中华人民共和国民法典》于第十三届全国人民代表大会第三次会议通过，自 2021 年 1 月 1 日起施行等。

为及时反映国际商事交易的新形势、新规则，我们对原书做了全文修订。

本书保持了第 1 版的体例和内容结构。全书设四部分。第一部分：国际商务法律环境；第二部分：国际货物买卖法；第三部分：国际知识产权转让；第四部分：国际商事争议解决。

本书每章包括"导读""热身问题""小结"和"课后练习"。"导读"是对本章内容和结构的简介。课前对"热身问题"的讨论则可以帮助读者获取必要的背景知识，激发读者的学习兴趣和探索热情。"小结"是对本章讨论的主要理论、规则和观点的简要归纳，以帮助读者回顾本章的主要内容。"课后练习"包括"正误辨析""问答题""案例题"等多种形式，以帮助读者巩固所学知识。

本书在具体内容上对第 1 版做了全面补充和修订，以反映不同国际商事交易领域的国际条约、国际商事惯例、国内法，特别是我国国内法及司法实践的新进展。在国际货物买卖合同部分，本书重点补充了《中华人民共和国民法典》中与合同相关的规定，以更新第 1 版中与《中华人民共和国合同法》相关的规定；在国际货物运输保险部分，本书补充了《国际贸易术语解释通则》中的新规则；在知识产权国际转让部分，本书介绍了我国知识产权立法和司法实践的新进展，对相关内容进行了更新；在国际商事争议解决部分，本书进一步强化了对国际商事仲裁问题的讨论，并对国际商事调解、国际商事仲裁领域制度的新进展进行了重点介绍。

为培养读者直接以英语思考、分析和解决法律问题的能力,本书仍采用"非传统"双语形式——正文以英文写作,"导读"和"小结"以中文写作,对于正文中重要的法律概念、规则和制度则采用脚注的方式,以中文给出较为全面、精练的介绍。

在本书编著过程中,编者参考了国内外的一些相关著作和研究成果,在此对这些作者致以谢意。

编者秉承认真、负责的态度写作本书,但鉴于时间和精力的限制,本书可能难免有错漏之处,谨请读者不吝指正。

韩永红

广东外语外贸大学教授、博士生导师

目　录

Part Ⅰ The Legal Environment
of International Business

Chapter 1
International Business and the Risks

 导读

本章主要介绍和讨论：（1）国际商务的一般知识，包括国际贸易的内容、历史和主要参与主体等；（2）国际商务的经济环境、政治环境、文化环境和竞争环境；（3）国际商务中可能存在的3类主要风险，包括政治风险、交易风险和法律风险。学习本章的目的在于了解国际商务及其国际环境，为后续国际商法的学习奠定知识基础。

 ## Warm-up Questions

(1) What is the impact of international business on your daily life?

(2) How does international business differ from domestic business?

(3) What are the risks of doing business internationally?

1.1　What Is International Business

International business[1] consists of the import and export of goods and services. Exporting is the shipment of goods out of a country or the providing of services to a foreign buyer located in another country. Importing is the entering of goods into a country or the receipt of services from a foreign provider. Exporting is often the first choice when businesses decide to expand abroad. It may provide businesses an opportunity to reach new customers and to explore new markets. Importing is also a regular and necessary part of international business. It involves purchasing goods or services on a worldwide basis to reduce production costs. Such a process is often described by the term of **global outsourcing**[2].

International business may be conducted among individuals, businesses, and even governments in multiple countries. Businesses include very small firms that export (or import) a small quantity to only

---

1. international business：国际商务。国际商务是一种跨越国界的商业活动，是在不同国家间进行商品、劳务、资本、技术和信息等资源的国际转移，其主体活动是进出口贸易，包括货物贸易和服务贸易。

2. global outsourcing：全球采购。全球采购是指利用全球的资源，在全世界范围内去寻找供应商，寻找质量最好、价格合理的产品或服务，从而降低整体生产成本。全球采购的对象包罗万象，既有原材料、配件、成品、设备，也有房屋、市政及环境改造等工程，还有教育、金融、互联网等服务。

one country, as well as very large **multinational corporations (MNCs)**[1]with integrated operations and strategic alliances around the world. It is reported that exports by MNCs account for one-third of world exports, and one–third of the world's production of goods and services.

International business is different from domestic business because the environment changes when a firm crosses national borders. An individual traveling from his home country to a foreign country needs to have the proper documents to carry foreign currency, to be able to communicate in the foreign country, to be dressed appropriately, and so on. Doing business in a foreign country involves similar issues and is thus more complex than doing business at home country. States generally have different economic environments, government systems, laws and regulations, currencies, taxes and duties as well as different cultures and practices. Companies doing business in a foreign country would encounter the greater distances, communication problems, language and cultural barriers, differences in ethics and religions, different currencies, and exposure to strange foreign laws and government regulations. Typically, a company understands its domestic environment quite well, but is less familiar with the environment in other countries and must invest more time and resources to understand the new environment. The following considers some of the important aspects of the environment that changes internationally.[2]

1.2   The Environment of International Business

A. The economic environment can be very different from one nation to another. Countries are often divided into three main categories: the developed or industrialized countries, the developing countries or emerging economies, and the least developed countries or third world. These distinctions are usually made based on **gross domestic product (GDP) per capita**[3]. Better education, infrastructure, technology, health care, and so on are also often associated with higher levels of GDP.

Within each category, there are major variation. Overall, the developed countries generally have a high GDP per capita, a high standard of living, and are in the later stages of industrialization. They are characterized by advanced technology, modern production, management methods, and advanced research facilities. They have diversified economies rather than only dependent on agriculture, oil or mining alone. Today it can be said that many developed countries are entering a postindustrial economy, with declining manufacturing but a growing service sector. The best examples of developed countries may include the United States, Canada, the European nations, Australia, New Zealand and Japan. Developing countries usually have a lower GDP per capita than developed countries. Many have large agrarian populations, densely populated cities, and unskilled labor. However, the typical developing

---

1. multinational corporation, MNC：跨国公司，又称 transnational corporation, multinational enterprise。跨国公司主要是指以本国为基地，通过对外直接投资，在世界各地设立分支机构或子公司，从事国际化生产和经营活动的大型企业。
2. 以下将分别介绍影响国际商务的重要内容（经济环境、政治环境、文化环境和竞争环境）。
3. GDP per capita：人均国内生产总值，指一国在一定时期内（通常为1年）实现的国内生产总值按人口取平均值。人均国内生产总值是衡量一国经济发展水平的重要指标。

country is hard to describe. Some are newly emerging economies like China[1],Brazil, India, Russia, and South Africa. The least developed countries (LDCs) are the world's most impoverished and vulnerable countries. The criteria are based on GDP per capita averaged over three years, The list of LDCs covers 48 countries including Laos, Afghanistan, Bangladesh, and so on.

In addition to the level of economic development, countries can be classified as free-market economies, centrally planned economies, or mixed economies. Free-market economies are those where the government intervenes minimally in business activities, and market forces of supply and demand are allowed to determine production and prices. Centrally planned economies are those where the government determines production and prices based on forecasts of demand and desired levels of supply. Mixed economies are those where some activities are left to market forces and some, for national and individual welfare reasons, are government controlled.

Clearly, the level of economic activity combined with education, infrastructure, as well as the degree of government control of the economy, affects virtually all aspects of business, and a company needs to understand this environment if it is to operate successfully internationally.

B. The political environment is another important aspect of the international business environment. It refers to the type of government, the government's relationship with business, and the political risk in a country. Doing business internationally thus implies dealing with different types of governments, relationships, and levels of risk.

There are many different types of political systems, for example, multi-party democracies, one-party states, constitutional monarchies, and dictatorships (military and nonmilitary). Also, governments change in different ways, for example, through regular elections, occasional elections, death, or war. Government-business relationships also differ from country to country. The business may be viewed positively as the engine of growth, or may be viewed negatively as the exploiter of the workers, or somewhere in between as providing benefits and drawbacks. Specific government-business relationships can also vary from positive to negative depending on the type of business operations involved and the relationship between the people of the **host country**[2] and the people of the **home country**.[3]To conduct a business successfully in a foreign country, a company needs to have a good understanding of all these aspects of the political environment.

C. The cultural environment is one of the critical components of the international business environment. It seems more difficult to understand because the cultural environment is essentially unseen. The "culture" has been described as a shared, commonly held body of general beliefs and values that determine what is right for one group. National culture is described as the body of general beliefs and values that are shared by a nation. Beliefs and values are generally seen as formed by factors such as history, language, religion, geographic location, government, and education; thus, firms begin a cultural analysis by seeking to understand these factors.

Companies need to understand what beliefs and values they may find in countries where they do business. In fact, several models of cultural values have been proposed by scholars. The most

---

1. 中国国家统计局 2022 年 2 月 28 日公布的经济数据显示，2021 年中国全年国内生产总值（GDP）114.36 万亿元，人均 GDP 为 8.09 万元。

2. host country：东道国，一般指国际直接投资的所在国。

3. home country：母国，一般指国际直接投资的来源国。

well-known one is that developed by Hofstede in 1980. This model proposes four dimensions of cultural values including individualism versus collectivism, uncertainty avoidance, power distance and masculinity versus femininity[1].Individualism is the degree to which a nation values and encourages individual action and decision making. Uncertainty avoidance is the degree to which a nation is willing to accept and deal with uncertainty. Power distance is the degree to which a nation accepts and sanctions differences in power. And masculinity is the degree to which a nation accepts traditional male values or traditional female values. This model of cultural values has been used extensively because it provides data for a wide array of countries. Many academics and managers found this model helpful in exploring management approaches that would be appropriate in different cultures. For example, in a nation that is high on individualism (such as the U.S.), individual goals, individual tasks, and individual reward systems are effective, whereas the reverse would be the case in a nation that is low on individualism.

D. The competitive environment can also change from country to country. This is partly because of the economic, political, and cultural environments. These environmental factors help determine the type and degree of competition that exists in each country. Competition can come from a variety of sources. It can be the public or private sector, come from large or small organizations, be domestic or global, and stem from traditional or new competitors.

The nature of competition can also change from place to place: Competition may be encouraged or discouraged in favor of cooperation; relations between buyers and sellers may be friendly or hostile; barriers to entry and exit may be low or high; regulations may permit or prohibit certain activities.

An important aspect of the competitive environment is the level and acceptance of technological innovation in different countries. The last decades of the twentieth century saw major advances in technology, and this is continuing in the twenty-first century. Technology is often seen as giving firms a competitive advantage. Hence, firms compete for access to the newest in technology, and international firms transfer technology to be globally competitive. It is easier than ever for even small businesses to have a global presence thanks to the Internet, which greatly expands their exposure, their market, and their potential customer base. For economic, political, and cultural reasons, some countries are more accepting of technological innovations, others are less accepting. To do international business effectively, companies need to understand these competitive issues and assess their impact.

1.3   History of International Business

International business is as old as the oldest civilization. Throughout the history of mankind, countries traded to obtain needed items from silk to spices that were not readily available in their own countries. Asia, the Middle East, Africa, and Europe have been the major marketplaces of trade for hundreds of years. In history, there were famous "Silk Road", which linked the market of China with the

---

1. 此处讨论的是"霍夫斯坦德的国家文化模型"理论。吉尔特·霍夫斯泰德（Geert Hofstede）是荷兰文化协会研究所所长，他在问卷调查数据的基础上，撰写了著名的《文化的结局》一书。在此书中，霍夫斯泰德认为：文化是在一个环境中具有相同的教育和生活经验的许多人所共有的心理程序。这种心理程序在不同群体、区域或国家存在差异。这种文化差异可分为四个维度：权力距离（power distance），不确定性避免（uncertainty avoidance），个人主义与集体主义（individualism versus collectivism）以及男性化与女性化（masculinity versus femininity）。

Middle East and Europe, and the first international sea trade route established by the Europeans in the sixteenth century. With the advent of great naval power, Portugal and Spain opened the Americas, India, and the Pacific to trade. For more than three hundred years, trade in cotton, corn, horses, weapons thrived among Europe, America, and Africa.

Since the end of World War Ⅱ, much has been changed in the field of international business. The General Agreement on Tariffs and Trade (GATT) negotiation rounds resulted in trade liberalization, and this was continued with the formation of the World Trade Organization (WTO)[1] in 1995. At the same time, worldwide capital movements were liberalized by most governments, particularly with the advent of electronic funds transfers.

The world today is economically interdependent. It is fair to say that **globalization**[2] continues to represent the historical trend of the world. Phenomena such as climate change and free trade agreements demonstrate the continuing relevance of global cooperation and interconnectivity.

In effect, globalization is not only an economic concept with significant legal meaning. It is an economic process, which appears to be unstoppable. Undoubtedly, with the increasing globalization of the economy, we will experience more cross-border activities. Many economists and business experts believe that no trade can be purely domestic in such a globalization process. The reality of the increasing economic interdependence among countries makes all trade international. No longer can an economic or policy change in one country occur without causing reverberations throughout the world's markets. For example, the deterioration in trade relations between the United States and China can affect the manufacturing plants in Canada or Mexico. The Mad Cow disease affected far more than the English cattle and the beef trade worldwide.

Globalization can be attributed to many factors. Natural resources and raw materials are unevenly located around the world. Technology advances in communications have brought people closer than ever and made the world, to some extent, a village on the earth. Most nations have moved away from pure protectionism of trade and increasingly moved toward free trade. Recent decades have seen a steady and robust movement towards regional integration, for example, **EU**[3] and the development of free trade areas such as **China-ASEAN**[4] and **NAFTA**[5]. Technologies of patents, copyrights, trademarks, and

---

1. GATT and WTO：关税与贸易总协定与世界贸易组织。为推动国际贸易的自由化，1947 年多国签订了《关税与贸易总协定》。1994 年 4 月 15 日，在摩洛哥的马拉喀什市举行的关税与贸易总协定乌拉圭回合部长会议决定成立更具全球性的世界贸易组织，以取代成立于 1947 年的关税与贸易总协定。1995 年 1 月 1 日，世界贸易组织成立。世界贸易组织是当代最重要的国际经济组织之一，截至 2024 年 2 月，拥有 166 个成员。

2. globalization：全球化。目前全球化有诸多定义。通常意义上的全球化是指国与国之间在政治、经济、贸易上的互相依存不断增强，人类生活在全球规模的基础上发展及全球意识的崛起。

3. EU（European Union）：欧洲联盟，简称欧盟。欧盟是欧洲地区规模最大的区域性经济合作的国际组织，现拥有 27 个成员。成员之间关于货物贸易、服务贸易、货币、金融政策等的基本政策和法律已实现统一或协调。

4. China-ASEAN：中国—东盟自由贸易区，是中国与东盟十国组建的自由贸易区。2010 年 1 月 1 日中国-东盟自由贸易区正式全面启动，成为一个涵盖 11 个成员、19 亿人口、GDP 达 6 万亿美元的巨大经济体，是目前世界人口最多的自由贸易区，也是发展中国家间最大的自由贸易区。

5. NAFTA（North American Free Trade Area）：北美自由贸易区。由美国、加拿大和墨西哥 3 国组成。1992 年，三国正式签署《北美自由贸易协定》；1994 年 1 月 1 日，协定正式生效，北美自由贸易区宣布成立。自由贸易区内的国家货物可以互相减免关税，并削减非关税壁垒，而贸易区以外的国家则仍然维持原关税及贸易壁垒。在长达数年的讨论和协商之后，《美墨加协定》（USMCA）于 2020 年 7 月 1 日生效，正式取代了《北美自由贸易协定》。

know-how are transferred by licensing agreements around the world, as freely as goods and services are sold. Greater political stability in newly emerged economically powerful countries has led to increasing trade volume around the world.

Globalization is also a legal event, as evidenced by the spread of the rule of law among nations. Greater economic interdependence has required countries to reach an agreement on important legal issues. The global economy has been affected by the development of widely accepted international conventions and practices, which provide a reliable and consistent legal environment for international business. Meanwhile, national laws are required to be harmonized and adjusted to new development in international business.

1.4   Risks of International Business

Factors such as differences in language, culture, economics, politics, and laws bring barriers. No company can make a strategic business decision or enter an important business transaction without a full evaluation of the risks involved. To a great degree, the management of international business is the management of risk. In this part, we will discuss just two types of international business risks: political risk and the risk of exposure to foreign laws and courts.

A particular concern of international companies is the degree of political risk in a foreign location. **Political risk**[1] is generally defined as the risk to a company's business interests resulting from political instability or civil unrest, political change, war, or terrorism in a country in which the company is doing business. For example, political decisions made by governmental leaders about taxes, currency valuation, trade tariffs, wage levels, labor laws, environmental regulations and development priorities can affect business conditions and profitability. Similarly, political disruptions such as terrorism, riots, civil wars, international wars, and even political elections that may change the ruling government, can dramatically affect businesses. Generally, political risk is associated with instability.A country is seen as riskier if the government is likely to change unexpectedly, if there is social unrest, and if there are riots, revolutions, war, terrorism, and so on.

Companies naturally prefer countries that are stable and that present little political risk, but the returns need to be weighed against the risks, and firms often do business in countries where the risk is relatively high. In these situations, companies seek to manage the perceived risk through **political risk insurance**[2], ownership and management choices, supply and market control, financing arrangements, and so on. Handling political risk requires planning and vigilance. Firstly, the company must understand the domestic affairs of a country. Typical questions might include: Is the country subject to religious or ethnic strife? Is the country politically stable? Can the government of the country rule effectively? The firm must also understand regional politics. Is the region stable? Are neighboring countries in the region

---

1. political risk: 政治风险。一般是指企业在进行对外投资决策或对外经济贸易活动时，因东道国政治环境发生变化、政局不稳定、政策法规发生变化给投资企业带来经济损失的可能性。政治风险通常包括战争、内乱、恐怖主义、征收、征用、没收、国有化、汇兑等风险。

2. political risk insurance：政治风险保险。政治风险保险是一种比较新的专业险种，主要承保外国投资者因东道国征用、国有化、外汇转移限制、战争致使贸易中断等情况给企业造成的财产损失。政治风险保险的保险期分为短期和长期两种。短期保险期限为 1 年，长期保险期限为 3~15 年。

hostile? Finally, it is well advised that managers of the company should keep abreast of all political affairs that could affect their business interests worldwide.

Exposure to foreign laws and courts is another risk for international business. Laws vary from country to country depending on social, political, cultural, and historical traditions. Some acts that are perfectly legal in one country may be illegal in another. For example, under Islamic law in many Middle East countries, there is a prohibition against charging interest on a loan. However, in other parts of the world, it is almost taken for granted.

Settling disputes among companies can be much more difficult in international business than in domestic business. It may involve complex procedural problems: What country's court should hear the case? What country's laws should apply? Should the case be submitted to **arbitration**?[1] and so on. **Litigation**[2] in a foreign court is both costly and time-consuming. The laws of a foreign country can differ greatly from those laws that are accustomed to at home. In addition, language and logistical issues can be problems as well. A company may respectively need representation by attorneys in its own country and in the foreign country. Frequent court appearances could cost a lot of time and travel expenses.

 ## Chapter Summary

本章是关于国际商务及国际商务环境的介绍。国际商务是一种跨越国界的商业活动，是在不同国家之间进行商品、劳务、资本、技术和信息等资源的国际转移，其主体活动是进出口贸易，包括货物贸易和服务贸易。个人、企业乃至政府（在某些情况下）都可以从事国际商务活动，其中最活跃的主体当属跨国公司。

相较国内商务活动，国际商务因跨越了国境而更为复杂。他国的经济环境、政治环境、文化环境和竞争环境等情况都将对国际商务活动产生重要影响，可能会给国际商务活动带来政治、经济和法律风险。

国际商务的历史悠久。"二战"之后，国际商务发展迅速，全球化加剧了国家之间的经济依赖，有力地促进了国际商务的繁荣，也对国际商务相关的法律规制产生了重大影响。

 ## Exercises

Part Ⅰ. True or False Statements: Decide whether the following statements are True or False and explain why.

1. International business consists of the import and export of goods.

2. In international business, exporting is more important than importing.

3. Only multinational corporations can conduct international business transactions.

4. Based on GDP per capita, countries are often divided into three main categories: the developed countries, the developing countries, and the least developed countries.

---

1. arbitration：仲裁。一般指当事人根据他们之间订立的仲裁协议，自愿将其争议提交由非司法机构的仲裁员组成的仲裁庭进行裁判，并受该裁判约束的一种制度。仲裁和法院的审判一样，是解决民事争议的方式之一。通过仲裁解决国际商事争端已得到各国法律的普遍认可。

2. litigation：诉讼，是指有管辖权的法院根据纠纷当事人的请求，运用审判权确认争议各方权利义务关系，解决纠纷的活动。诉讼必须遵循诉讼程序（法定的顺序、方式和步骤）。

5. China is a newly emerging country and has graduated from the group of developing countries.

6. It seems more difficult to understand the cultural environment because the cultural environment is essentially intangible.

7. According to Hofstede's model of culture, China is a country of individualism.

8. International business began to exist after the end of World War Ⅱ.

9. With the increasing globalization of the economy, we will experience more cross-border international business transactions.

10. Terrorism, riots, and wars occurring in one country are political risks, which may affect international business.

Part Ⅱ. Chapter Questions: Discuss and answer the following questions according to what you have learned in this chapter. You are encouraged to use your own words.

1. Describe a real-life example of international business.

2. What are the factors that contribute to globalization?

3. What is the influence of globalization on international business?

4. How do you understand the cultural environment of international business? Can you give an example illustrating the impact of culture on international business?

5. What methods a company may rely on to reduce or avoid the political risks in international business?

6. How do you understand the statement in the text that "Even the small local companies are affected by global competition and world events"?

7. Give an example of political risk in international business.

8. What are the possible methods to avoid or reduce the business losses resulting from political risk?

9. Can you give a real-life example for the statement in the text "Most travelers to a foreign country could conceivably break laws but not even be aware of it"?

10. What are the problems that may arise from litigation in a foreign court?

Part Ⅲ. Case Problem

Frigaliment (Plaintiff), a Swiss corporation, entered contracts to purchase chicken from BNS International Sales Corporation (Defendant), a New York corporation. The English language contracts between them stated: "US Fresh Frozen Chicken, Grade A, Government Inspected, 75,000 lbs. 2 1/2-3 lbs at $33.00; 25,000 lbs. 1 1/2-2 lbs at $36.50." When the chickens were shipped to Switzerland, Plaintiff found 2-lb sizes were mature stewing chickens or fowls, but not young broiling chickens as they had expected. Plaintiff protested and claimed that in German the term "chicken" referred to young broiling chickens. Defendant pointed out the reference to "US fresh frozen chicken, grade A." The USDA defined the term "chicken" as subsuming different grades of chicken, including broilers and fowl, as well as other types such as capons, stags, and roosters.

1. What's the focus issue in this case?

2. If you were the judge, what kind of chicken did Plaintiff order? Was it "broiling chicken" as the Plaintiff argued, or any chickens weighing 2 lbs as the Defendant insisted on?

3. What would the parties have done to avoid this ambiguity?

4. What can you infer from this case?

Part Ⅳ. Further Reading

Now more businesses are striving to go international and crack foreign markets. When dealing with businesses outside of your region, knowing the economic and technical differences in your target area is surely sufficient. So why is it that many individuals are experiencing pushback when it comes to their lack of cultural sensitivity and awareness? It's just as important to prepare for and familiarize yourself with your target country's cultural differences.

Do you know that Mexican businessmen prefer to avoid explicit disagreements and that their way of saying "no" is often disguised as a "maybe" or "I'll get back to you". Are you still waiting to hear back from a potential business partner in Mexico? Perhaps you've had their answer all along. Other cultural differences to note when doing business in Mexico include the 10-minute rule for punctuality, working hours, avoiding the use of aggressive paper or hand movements and ensuring that you do not stare for too long. Take note of these differences, for although your technical knowledge of Mexico's economic and tax rules may be exemplary, being unaware of their working culture may ultimately be your pitfall. Be sure to cry "Salud!" when toasting your business success in Mexico.

On the cultural side of things, the British are an interesting bunch with several peculiarities that those looking to do business with us should be aware of. For some cultures, making your introductions is standard, however, most British feel far more comfortable being introduced by a mutual party – be sure to take this into account if you find British lingering on the edge of the group uncomfortably.

Chapter 2
International Business Law and International Organizations

 导读

本章的主要内容是介绍规制和影响国际商务活动的法律框架。希望读者通过本章的学习和讨论，能够了解（1）国际法的基本概念和特征；（2）国际公法和国际私法的区别和联系；（3）国际商法的基本概念和法律渊源；（4）对国际商务和国际商法的发展具有重要影响的一些国际组织。

 Warm-up Questions

(1) Can you name some laws of China?

(2) How does international law differ from domestic law or national law?

(3) Can you name some international organizations, which play a role in regulating international business?

2.1 International Law

International law can be defined as the body of rules regulating activities beyond a country's border. International law has several characteristics that distinguish it from a country's domestic or national law. Firstly, instead of being enacted by a national legislative body, international law consists of rules that countries agree to follow. It is lawmaking by consent. In fact, international law exists because nations agree that it is in their interests to cooperate and to conform to commonly accepted norms. Secondly, there is no global authority for enforcing international law, although some commonly misunderstand the power of the United Nations and other international bodies. It is true that international courts and tribunals such as the International Court of Justice or the dispute body of the WTO do issue judgments against nations. But it is based on the precondition that nations must agree to be a party to these cases, and enforcement mechanism like in the national law does not really exist. The enforcement mechanisms in international law may include diplomacy, the withholding of foreign aid or assistance, trade sanctions and retaliation, or war. In certain cases, where individuals are convicted of having committed international crimes, prison sentences and the death penalty will be used.

In a broad sense, international law traditionally falls into two categories: public international law and private international law. **Public international law**[1] deals with those rules affecting the relationships between nations. It might cover the rules for resolving territorial disputes, for conducting diplomacy or war and for how human rights are protected and so on. **Private international law**[2] deals with the relationships among individuals and corporations beyond the border of one country. It might include the rules for enforcing the wills of deceased persons who have owned property in more than one country, for settling disputes arising from international sales and so on.

2.2 International Business Law

A. Defining International Business Law

It is generally agreed that **international business law** is the body of rules and norms that regulates the cross-border transactions in goods and services between parties. Here "parties" include natural persons, **legal persons**[3], and international organizations. In some circumstances, states may also be a party to international transactions in the capacity of commercial not sovereign entity. Besides, states also play a unique role in regulating and supervising the international business between private parties in the capacity of a sovereign.

B. History of International Business Law

At the beginning, the rules and norms governing international business are basically the creation of merchants. In the 12th century, medieval Europe experienced a renaissance of trade and commerce. Merchants met at trade fairs to exchange goods such as wine, fruit, and porcelain. To meet the demand of trading over long distance, primary banking systems and new legal instruments were created to facilitate the payment. Over time, the merchants developed a set of customs for exchanging goods, and it is an unwritten code on how to bargain, barter, and sell goods at trade fairs or in city markets. For example, it is a widely accepted consensus that if one bought the goods at the trade fair and later discovered the goods had been stolen, the innocent buyer will incur the loss anyway. By relying on these customs, merchants would know what was expected of both parties to a transaction and how to avoid and resolve a dispute. Formally these customs became known as the *lex mercatoria* or **law merchant**[4],

---

1. public international law：国际公法。国际公法是那些主要调整国家、国际组织间关系，有法律约束力的原则、规则和制度的总称。具体而言，国际公法包括国际条约法、国际海洋法、外层空间法、国际人权法、战争法和国际人道主义法、国际争端解决等内容。

2. private international law：国际私法。国际私法主要调整私人主体间的涉外民商事法律关系，主要解决适用哪方法律的问题。由于涉外因素又称国际因素，民法和商法在西方传统上称为私法，国际私法因而得名。在英美普通法系则更多地被称为"冲突法"（Conflict of Laws）。

3. legal person：法人。通俗地说，法人即法律拟制的人，不是生物学意义上的人。准确地说，法人不是人，是组织。《中华人民共和国民法典》第五十七条规定："法人是具有民事权利能力和民事行为能力，依法独立享有民事权利和承担民事义务的组织。"法人分为3个类型：营利法人、非营利法人和特别法人。常见的有限责任公司和股份有限公司就属于营利法人。事业单位、社会团体、基金会、社会服务机构等属于非营利法人。机关法人、农村集体经济组织法人、城镇农村的合作经济组织法人、基层群众性自治组织法人，为特别法人。

4. lex mercatoria（law merchant）：商人（习惯）法，是中世纪时期逐渐形成的国际"商业惯例"。其特点是：发展不成体系，从习惯性做法发展为惯例，再到法律。随着欧洲中央集权国家的兴起，欧洲各国都以不同的方式使之成为国内法的一部分。

and they were "enforced" by the merchants themselves. Considering their reputation and the importance of maintaining permanent good business relationships, merchants will follow these customs in transactions. As trade spanned greater distances and involved more complicated skills, merchants took on greater risks, and transactions required more complex legal rules. By the eighteenth century, the courts recognized the law merchant and made it a part of the common law in England. In the continent of Europe, the law merchant was incorporated into stricter legal codes, for example, *the French Civil Code* of 1804 and *the German Civil Code* of 1896.

As the business world became more complex, and with the dawn of air travel and worldwide communication, a clearer and uniform set of modern rules governing international business is needed in the twentieth century. In fact, international business law has grown and shaped significantly in the twentieth century, especially after World War Ⅱ. The leaders of the nations fighting against Germany, Italy, and Japan realized a push to arrange a comprehensive network of multilateral agreements to settle the world's political and economic problems. In July 1944, they met in Bretton Woods determining to create a system of rules and obligations that would promote trade liberalization and multilateral economic cooperation. Under the Bretton Woods system, the **International Monetary Fund (IMF)**[1] and the International Bank for Reconstruction and Development (**IBRD or World Bank**)[2] were established. However, the International Business Organization, an institution planned to establish, only resulted in the General Agreement on Tariffs and Trade came into effect in 1947 (GATT 1947). Its articles established rules governing customs procedures, quantitative restrictions, subsidies, anti-dumping and countervailing duties, and state trading. A small secretariat (the GATT Organization) was set up in Geneva, Switzerland to oversee the operation of the GATT Agreement.

The contracting parties to the GATT 1947, which were most of the states allied with the United States and Europe during the Cold War, regularly participated in multilateral trade negotiations (or "Rounds") to negotiate trade concessions. And finally "**The Final Act Embodying the Results of the Uruguay Round of Multilateral Trade Negotiations**"[3] which provided for the establishment of a World Trade Organization (WTO), which came into existence on January 1, 1995.

The Uruguay Round Final Act is made up of three parts. The first part, the formal Final Act itself, is a one-page "umbrella" that introduces the other parts. The second part of the final Act is the WTO Agreement and its annexes. The 14 Agreements on Trade in Goods (including GATT 1994), the

---

1. IMF: 国际货币基金组织。根据 1944 年 7 月在布雷顿森林会议签订的《国际货币基金协定》，于 1945 年 12 月 27 日在华盛顿成立。其职责是监察货币汇率和各国贸易情况，提供技术和资金协助，确保全球金融制度运作正常。

2. World Bank: 世界银行。成立于 1945 年，参加世界银行的成员必须首先是国际货币基金组织的会员国。世界银行总部设在美国首都华盛顿，在全世界有 120 多个办事处。

3. The Final Act Embodying the Results of the Uruguay Round of Multilateral Trade Negotiations: "乌拉圭回合多边贸易谈判结果最后文件" 以下简称 "最后文件"。该 "最后文件" 包括:《马拉喀什建立世界贸易组织协定》；附件 1A: 货物贸易多边协定。该附件涵盖《1994 年关税与贸易总协定》(它是对原来的 GATT 1947 的修改版本)、《农业协定》《技术性贸易壁垒协定》《海关估价协定》《装运前检疫协定》《原产地规则协定》《进口许可程序协定》《实施卫生与植物卫生措施协定》《补贴与反补贴措施协定》《保障措施协定》等 14 个协定；附件 1B:《服务贸易总协定》；附件 1C:《与贸易有关的知识产权协定》；附件 2:《关于争端解决规则与程序的谅解》；附件 3:《贸易政策审议机制》；附件 4:《诸边贸易协定》。

General Agreement on Trade in Services (GATS), the Agreement on Trade-Related Aspects of Intellectual Property Rights (TRIPs), the Understanding on Rules and Procedures Governing the Settlement of Disputes (DSU) and the Trade Policy Review Mechanism (TPRM) are binding on all members of the WTO. The Four Plurilateral Trade Agreements (Agreement on Trade in Civil Aircraft, Agreement on Government Procurement, International Diary Agreement and International Bovine Meat Agreement) are only binding on those members that have accepted them. The third and final part consists of the Ministerial Declarations and Decisions. (See Exhibit 2-1: Outline of the Uruguay Round Final Act)

Exhibit 2-1: Outline of the Uruguay Round Final Act

Ⅰ. FINAL ACT

Ⅱ. AGREEMENT ESTABLISHING THE WORLD TRADE ORGANIZATION (WTO AGREEMENT)

Annex 1A: Agreements on Trade in Goods

1. General Agreement on Tariffs and Trade 1994
2. Uruguay Round Protocol to the General Agreement on Tariffs and Trade 1994
3. Agreement on Agriculture
4. Agreement on Sanitary and Phytosanitary Measures
5. Agreement on Textiles and Clothing
6. Agreement on Technical Barriers to Trade
7. Agreement on Trade-Related Investment Measures
8. Agreement on Implementation of Article Ⅵ[concerning antidumping]
9. Agreement on Implementation of Article Ⅶ[concerning customs valuation]
10. Agreement on Preshipment Inspection
11. Agreement on Rules of Origin
12. Agreement on Import Licensing Procedures
13. Agreement on Subsidies and Countervailing Measures
14. Agreement on Safeguards.

Annex 1B: General Agreement on Trade in Services

Annex 1C: Agreement on Trade-Related Aspects of Intellectual Property Rights

Annex 2: Understanding on Rules and Procedures Governing the Settlement of Disputes

Annex 3: Trade Policy Review Mechanism

Annex 4: Plurilateral Trade Agreements

Annex 4(a): Agreement on Trade in Civil Aircraft

Annex 4(b): Agreement on Government Procurement

Annex 4(c): International Dairy Agreement

Annex 4(d): International Bovine Meat Agreement

Ⅲ. MINISTERIAL DECISIONS AND DECLARATIONS

The principles and rules established by the WTO have been an integral part of modern international business law.

C. Sources of International Business Law

Modern international business law is derived from several sources. Before determining the sources of this law, it is necessary to know the meanings of "**sources of law**"[1]. Strictly speaking, the concept of sources of law has two meanings: substantive sources and formal sources. The former refers to the substance of the principles and rules of law —what the law is; the latter denotes the forms of law—constitution, treaty, statute, or customs that provide authority for legislation and judicial decisions. The latter meaning is more often used in legal literature. In this sense, sources of international business law include international treaties and conventions, international business customs and usages, national law, and other sources such as resolutions of international organizations and soft law.

1. International Treaty and Convention

A treaty is an agreement between two or more parties to solve an issue that affects the countries signing the treaty. A convention is a set of rules for the parties agreeing to the convention to solve an issue that affects a larger part of the world. In the field of international business, the purpose of some treaties is to liberalize trade between the contracting parties such as the GATT. Another group of treaties or conventions aims at the unification of law. They introduce common substantive rules for regulating the transactions between individuals and companies in some fields of international business, e.g., international transportation or international sale of goods. The provisions of the treaties or conventions become part of the national law of the contracting parties. For a specific treaty or convention, only the contracting parties are bound by it. Several treaties are, for instance, not yet in force or are at present only applied by a limited number of parties. For that reason, many unifying law treaties or conventions achieve only a limited or a regional unification.

There are some important international treaties or conventions as the sources of international business law, including but not limited to *the United Nations Convention on Contracts for the International Sale of Goods* (CISG 1980) in the field of international sale of goods, *International Convention for the Unification of Certain Rules of Law Relating to Bills of Landing* (Hague Rules 1924), *the Convention for the Unification of Certain Rules for International Carriage by Air* (Montreal Convention 1999) in the area of international transportation, *the International Convention on the Protection of Industrial Property* in 1883 and revised in 1979 (Paris Convention 1979) in the field of trade in intellectual property, and the *Convention on the Recognition and Enforcement of Foreign Arbitration Awards* (New York Convention 1958) in the sphere of international commercial arbitration.

2. International Business Custom and Usage

International business customs and usages stem from the tradition of law merchant or the *lex mercatoria* in the history of international business. They refer to the general rules and practices in international business activities that have become generally adopted through unvarying habits and common use. In fact, each sector of the industry has developed its practices and usages, which are adapted to the needs of the sector. Thus, there are specific usages in the bank sector, grain trade, the oil

---

1. sources of law：法律渊源。法律渊源可以指法的实质渊源，即什么是法；法律渊源也可以指法的形式渊源，即法的各种具体表现形式，如宪法、法律、法规、国际条约、惯例等。现今，法律渊源更多在形式渊源的意义上使用。本部分内容讨论的即国际商法的具体表现形式，包括国际条约、国际惯例、国内法、示范法等形式。

industry, etc. International business customs and usages, in their nature, are not law, but they are undeniably important in international business. Since trade customs and usages are usually widely recognized in the specific industry, they are often incorporated into international sales contracts to specify the rights and obligations of the parties.

International business customs and usages used to be oral rather than in writing. In recent decades, some non-governmental organizations, with the view to facilitating the use of trade customs and usages, have collected and compiled them into sets of rules in a written form. *The International Rules for the Interpretation of Trade Terms* (***Incoterms***) published by the International Chamber of Commerce is a good example. *Incoterms* is an acronym for "International Commercial Term" and was first published in 1936. It had been updated periodically since that time. *Incoterms* underwent major revisions in 1953 and 1990, and it was republished with new terms in 1967, 1976, 1980 and 2000. The current version of *Incoterms* was published in 2020 and is known as ***Incoterms 2020***[1]. *Incoterms* provides rules for determining the obligations of both seller and buyer when goods are to be carried from one location to another as part of the sale transaction. They state what acts the seller must do to deliver, what acts the buyer must do to accommodate delivery, what costs each party must bear, and at what point in the delivery process the risk of loss passes from seller to buyer. Each of these obligations may be different for different commercial terms (e.g. F.O.B. and C.I.F.). The International Chamber of Commerce has also published *Uniform Customs and Practice for Documentary Credits* (***UCP***)[2], the widely accepted rules and guidelines for handling letters of credit in the international sale of goods. This document was newly revised in 2006 (known as *UCP* 600) and took effect in 2007.

3. National Law

Although there is an increasing number of international treaties or conventions and trade usages, national law is and will still be an important source of international business law in the foreseeable future. Every state has established its legal system governing domestic transactions. For instance, on sale of goods, there are *Civil Code of the People's Republic of China* in China, the Uniform Commercial Code in the United States and Sale of Goods Act in Britain.[3] The international cross-border transaction leads to the possibility that different legal systems will govern the transaction. In the absence of a governing uniform law, **conflict of laws rules**[4] will be used to determine which legal system will apply

---

1. *Incoterms 2020*：《国际贸易术语解释通则》（2020）。国际商会为统一各种贸易术语的不同解释于 1936 年制定的一套解释通则，随后，为适应国际贸易实践发展的需要，国际商会先后于 1953 年、1967 年、1976 年、1980 年、1990 年、2020 年进行过多次修订和补充，旨在准确界定国际货物买卖过程中之运输环节买卖双方的权利和义务。具体内容参见本书第五章的相关内容。

2. *Uniform Customs and Practice for Documentary Credits*（*UCP*）：《跟单信用证统一惯例》，旨在明确信用证有关当事人的权利、责任、付款的定义和术语，减少因解释不同而引起各有关当事人之间的争议和纠纷。其具体内容参见本书"国际支付"一章。

3. 关于国内法的具体介绍请见本书第三章。

4. conflict of laws rules：冲突法规则（又称法律适用规则）。指由境内法或国际公约规定的，指明某一涉外民商法律关系应适用何种法律的规则。它们是国际私法规则的主要组成部分。各境内法对同一问题有不同的规定，当该问题的案件有涉外因素时，就会发生法律的冲突，因此需要冲突法规则来指明应适用何种法律。例如，《中华人民共和国涉外民事关系法律适用法》第四十一条规定：当事人可以协议选择合同适用的法律。当事人没有选择的，适用履行义务最能体现该合同特征的一方当事人经常居所地法律或者其他与该合同有最密切联系的法律。

to the transaction in question. For example, the conflict of law rules on contracts run parallel, to a great extent, in different legal systems. All systems recognize the possibility of choice of law. If there is no express **choice of law clause**[1] in the contract, under most legal systems the rule of most significant connection will apply.

4. Other Sources

Resolutions of international organizations are sometimes binding. For example, all members of the United Nations are bound by the resolutions of the Security Council by virtue of the UN Charter. Resolutions and recommendations of the International Labor Organization are binding on the members if the members are obliged by a treaty to give effect to these resolutions and recommendations in their national legislations.

Some international organizations drafted rules and norms on international business for the free choice of nations. These rules and norms are often embodied in an **international model law**.[2] In the field of international business, typical examples of model law are *the UNCITRAL Model Law on International Commercial Arbitration* and *Principles of International Commercial Contract*. The former was drafted by the UNCITRAL in 1985 and the latter by the International Institute for the Unification of Private Law (UNIDROIT) in 1994. In the preamble, the Principles of International Commercial Contract states: "These Principles set forth general rules for international commercial contracts. They shall be applied when the parties have agreed that their contract be governed by them." And Article 1 (1) of *the UNCITRAL Model Law on International Commercial Arbitration* provides: "This law applies to international commercial arbitration, subject to any agreement in force between this State or any other States or State."

2.3   International Organizations

International organizations, including **intergovernmental organizations (IGOs)**[3], and **non-governmental organizations (NGOs)**[4], are very important to the shaping and development of international business law. In the following, the functions and structures of some selected international organizations are discussed.

---

1. choice of law clause：法律适用条款。合同的一项条款，内容为合同当事人指定适用某一国家法律以解决因该合同产生的争议。

2. international model law：国际示范法，是指一些国际组织为规范或便利某些国际活动（主要是国际商务活动）而制定的一些准则和规则。国际示范法对国家和国家内的个人和组织没有强制性的法律约束力。

3. intergovernmental organizations：政府间国际组织。从国际组织的成员构成性质看，国际组织可分为政府间（官方）国际组织和非政府间国际组织。政府间国际组织是若干国家为了特定目的以条约形式建立的一种常设机构。其基本法律特征包括：在条约和章程规定的范围内，享有参与国际事务活动的独立地位，具有直接承受国际法权利和义务的能力，而不受国家权力的管辖。在当今国际社会中，活跃着许多著名政府间国际组织，例如联合国、世界贸易组织、欧盟、上海合作组织、亚投行等。

4. non-governmental organizations：非政府间国际组织。非政府间国际组织是为了促进在政治、经济、科学技术、文化、宗教、人道主义及其他人类活动领域的国际合作，由不同国家的民间团体、政党或个人建立的一种非官方的国际联合体。随着国际关系及全球化的进一步发展，非政府间国际组织得以迅速发展，其在国际事务和国际法上的地位和作用日益受到重视。

A. Intergovernmental Organizations

Intergovernmental organizations are permanent organizations set up by two or more parties to carry on activities of common interest. Some intergovernmental organizations, which play an important role in the development of international business law, belong to or are affiliated with the most important intergovernmental organization — The United Nations(UN). The goals of the United Nations are the maintenance of peace and security in the world, and the promotion of economic and social cooperation to improve, among other things, living standards and economic and social development. The UN operates in the economic and social field and in other areas through its own bodies and specialized institutions. In the following, some IGOs affiliated with the UN, which play an important role in governing international business, will be discussed.

The United Nations Commission on International Trade Law **(UNCITRAL)**[1] devotes itself to the creation of uniform law for international business. UNCITRAL, located in Vienna and established by the General Assembly of the UN on December 17, 1966, consists of delegates from 60 parties now. The main task of UNCITRAL is the harmonization and the unification of legal rules in the field of international business by promoting the use and adoption of legislative and non-legislative instruments in several key areas of commercial law. Those areas include the sale of goods, dispute resolution, international contract practices, transport, insolvency, electronic commerce, international payments, secured transactions, and procurement. These instruments are negotiated through an international process involving a variety of participants, including members of UNCITRAL, which represent different legal traditions and levels of economic development, non-members, intergovernmental organizations, and non-governmental organizations. Thus, these texts are widely acceptable as offering solutions appropriate to different legal traditions and to parties at different stages of economic development. In the years since its establishment, UNCITRAL has been recognized as the core legal body of the United Nations system in the field of international business law.

As such, it has drawn up conventions and model laws, inter alia, of *United Nations Convention on Contracts for the International Sale of Goods* (CISG 1980), *United Nations Convention on Carriage of Goods by Sea* (the so-called Hamburg Rules 1978), and *UNCITRAL Model Law on International Commercial Arbitration* (1985,with amendments as adopted in 2006). Considering the rules will be applied everywhere in the world, UNCITRAL has been trying to avoid the use of technical legal terminologies which are not widely used.

Within the framework of the UN, several other organizations play a role in the sphere of international business, such as the World Bank, and the World Intellectual Property Organization. They will be discussed in the later chapters of this book.

Outside the UN, there are some other very important IGOs for the development of international

---

1. UNCITRAL：联合国国际贸易法委员会。该国际组织是联合国系统在国际贸易法领域的核心法律机构，其宗旨是促进国际贸易法的逐步协调和统一。该国际组织由联合国大会选出的 60 个成员方组成。成员的构成代表了世界各个不同地理区域及其主要经济和法律体系。迄今，该国际组织在国际商事仲裁和调解、国际货物销售、破产、国际支付、国际货物运输、电子商务、采购和基础设施发展等众多国际贸易领域的法律协调和统一方面取得了重要进展。

business law such as the **WTO**[1]. The WTO serves four basic functions: (1) To implement, administer, and carry out the WTO Agreement and its Annexes, (2) to act as a forum for ongoing multilateral trade negotiations, (3) to serve as a tribunal for resolving disputes, and (4) to review the trade policies and practices of members. Additionally, the WTO is to cooperate with the IMF and the World Bank to achieve greater coherence in global economic policy-making. Simply speaking, the WTO is a set of rules governing global trade, a forum for multinational trade negotiation, a tribunal for dispute settlement, and an institution to review trade policies.

The WTO is structured in three tiers. One tier is the Ministerial Conference, which meets biennially and is composed of representatives of all WTO members. Each member has an equal voting weight, unlike the voting in the IMF and World Bank where there is weighted voting, that is finally powerful states have more voting in the decision-making process. The Ministerial Conference is responsible for all WTO functions and can make any decisions necessary. Ministerial Conference, by a two-thirds vote, has the power to adopt the interpretations of the WTO agreements. And by a three-fourths vote, it is authorized to grant waivers of obligations to members in exceptional circumstances. When Ministerial Conference is in recess, its functions are performed by the General Council.

The second tier is the General Council, which has executive authority over the day-to-day operations and functions of the WTO. It is composed of representatives of all WTO members, and each member has an equal voting weight. It meets whenever it is appropriate. The General Council also has the power to adopt the interpretations of the WTO agreements.

The third tier comprises the councils, committees, and bodies, which are accountable to the Ministerial Conference or the General Council. Ministerial Conference committees include Committees on Trade and Development, Balance of Payment Restrictions, Budget, Finance, and Administration. General Council bodies include the Dispute Settlement Body (DSB), the Trade Policy Review Body (TPRB), and Councils for Trade in Goods, Trade in Services, and Trade-Related Intellectual Property Rights. The councils are all created by the WTO Agreement and are open to representatives of all members. The councils also have the authority to create subordinate organizations.

The process of decision-making in the WTO Ministerial Conference and General Council relies upon "consensus" as the norm (there are some exceptions which will be discussed below), just as it did for decision-making under GATT 1947. Consensus is the making of a decision by general agreement and in the absence of any voiced objection. Where a decision cannot be arrived at by consensus, the matter at issue shall be decided by voting, except where otherwise provided.

For **the structure of the WTO**, see Exhibit 2-2.

---

1. 世界贸易组织的组织结构。（1）第一层是部长级会议。部长级会议是世界贸易组织的最高权力机构，至少每两年举行一次。部长级会议可以就任何多边贸易协议所涉及的所有问题做出决定。（2）第二层是总理事会。在两届部长级会议期间，日常工作由总理事会负责处理。总理事会由全体WTO成员组成，代表部长级会议处理WTO的所有事务，它分别以争端解决机构和贸易审议机构的形式召开会议，监督解决成员间的争端，并分析成员的贸易政策。（3）第三层是理事会、委员会及工作组或专家组。理事会包括货物贸易理事会、与贸易有关的知识产权理事会和服务贸易理事会。理事会由全体世界贸易组织成员组成，并没有下属机构。上述三个理事会分别负责处理与各贸易领域协议或协定相关的工作。委员会是上述三个理事会的下属机构，包括市场准入委员会、农产品委员会、动植物卫生检疫措施委员会、技术性贸易壁垒委员会、补贴与反补贴措施委员会、反倾销措施委员会、海关估价委员会、原产地规则委员会、进口许可程序委员会、与贸易有关的投资措施委员会、保障措施委员会等。另外，在总理事会一级，争端解决机构也有两个下属机构，即对争端进行裁决的争端解决专家组，以及处理上诉的上诉机构。

Exhibit 2-2: the structure of the WTO

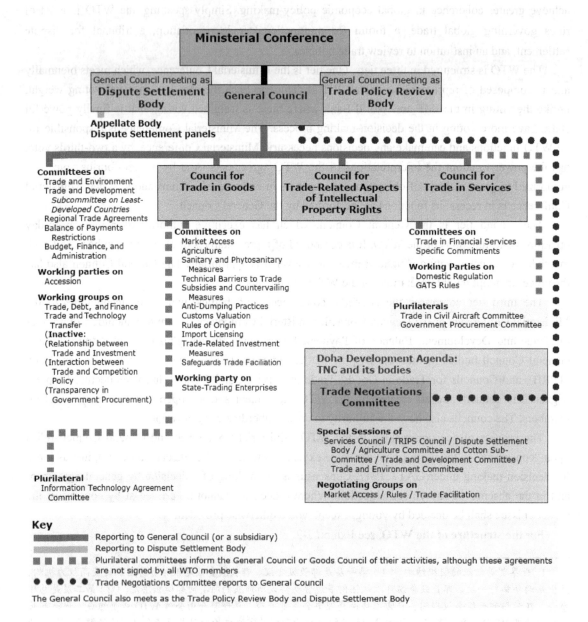

WTO structure

All WTO members may participate in all councils, committees, etc, except Appellate Body, Dispute Settlement panels, and plurilateral committees.

Ministerial Conference

General Council meeting as **Dispute Settlement Body**

General Council

General Council meeting as **Trade Policy Review Body**

Appellate Body
Dispute Settlement panels

Committees on
Trade and Environment
Trade and Development
Subcommittee on Least-Developed Countries
Regional Trade Agreements
Balance of Payments
Restrictions
Budget, Finance, and Administration

Working parties on
Accession

Working groups on
Trade, Debt, and Finance
Trade and Technology
Transfer
(**Inactive:**
(Relationship between Trade and Investment)
(Interaction between Trade and Competition Policy)
(Transparency in Government Procurement)

Plurilateral
Information Technology Agreement Committee

Council for Trade in Goods

Committees on
Market Access
Agriculture
Sanitary and Phytosanitary Measures
Technical Barriers to Trade
Subsidies and Countervailing Measures
Anti-Dumping Practices
Customs Valuation
Rules of Origin
Import Licensing
Trade-Related Investment Measures
Safeguards Trade Faciliation

Working party on
State-Trading Enterprises

Council for Trade-Related Aspects of Intellectual Property Rights

Council for Trade in Services

Committees on
Trade in Financial Services
Specific Commitments

Working Parties on
Domestic Regulation
GATS Rules

Plurilaterals
Trade in Civil Aircraft Committee
Government Procurement Committee

Doha Development Agenda: TNC and its bodies

Trade Negotiations Committee

Special Sessions of
Services Council / TRIPS Council / Dispute Settlement Body / Agriculture Committee and Cotton Sub-Committee / Trade and Development Committee / Trade and Environment Committee

Negotiating Groups on
Market Access / Rules / Trade Facilitation

Key

▬▬▬ Reporting to General Council (or a subsidiary)
▬▬▬ Reporting to Dispute Settlement Body
■ ■ ■ ■ Plurilateral committees inform the General Council or Goods Council of their activities, although these agreements are not signed by all WTO members
● ● ● ● ● Trade Negotiations Committee reports to General Council

The General Council also meets as the Trade Policy Review Body and Dispute Settlement Body

Another important intergovernmental organization is the **European Union (EU)**[1], which began to take shape in 1951 with the establishment of the European Coal and Steel Community. Two

---

1. European Union（EU）：欧洲联盟，简称欧盟。欧盟是由欧洲共同体发展而来的，创始成员国有6个（分别为法国、德国、意大利、荷兰、比利时和卢森堡）。该联盟现拥有27个成员方，正式官方语言有24种。欧盟内部建立了一套较为完善的组织机构：包括欧盟理事会、欧盟委员会、欧洲议会、欧洲法院、欧洲审计院、欧洲中央银行等。

additional "communities"—the European Economic Community and the European Atomic Energy Community—were created in 1957. In 1965, common institutions (see below) were established for the three communities and the three communities became known collectively as the European Community (EC). In 1993, the Maastricht Treaty renamed the EC as the European Union.

The EU is important because—unlike most other IGOs—EU possesses supranational powers. That is, EU law within its scope of applicability is superior to the laws of the members. This "supremacy principle" has two consequences: First, the members are required to bring their internal laws into compliance with EU laws; second, EU law is directly effective within the members.

The EU Consists of many institutions. (1) The European Commission, which is the administrative and executive branch of the EU. Its primary responsibilities are to see the EU rules are respected and EU policies are implemented. (2) The European Council is the principal EU rule-making institution. It is made up of ministers of the EU members. (3) The European Parliament is the principal EU deliberative and supervisory body. It must give its opinion of EU legislation before it can be adopted by the Council. (4) The European Economic and Social Council is an EU consultative body made up of a wide range of special interest groups. (5) The European Committee of Regions is an EU consultative body made up of representatives from local and regional governments. (6) The European Court of First Instance is the EU's trial court with jurisdiction over (a) disputes brought by private persons against EU institutions and (b) employment disputes between EU institutions and their employees. (7) The European Court of Justice is the EU's supreme tribunal. (8) The European Central Bank is responsible for carrying out the EU's monetary policy. (9) The European Court of Auditors is responsible for overseeing the EU budget.

B. Non-governmental Organizations

Non-governmental organizations (NGOs), as their name indicates, are not established by states, but by private persons or associations. They are not governed by international law but by national law. Nevertheless, they are international in composition because they group members from different regions. NGOs are active in the field of international business. Indeed, many branches of business or profession have an international organization with which the respective national association is connected. For example, the well-known IATA (International Air Transport Association), the international association of airline companies, formulates extensive air transport regulations and tariff regulations. Some NGOs deserve a more extensive description, for example, the International Chamber of Commerce (ICC).

The International Chamber of Commerce located in Paris associates 45 million companies in more than 170 regions, making it easier for businesses to trade internationally. It is an association under the French law. The ICC may discuss the problems of international business with its members and then draw up statements and recommendations on the problem. It represents the position of the business world. Businesses and organizations have little power to make their viewpoint known on an international level. Through the ICC, businesses and organizations can make their voices heard. The ICC has a National Committee in about 90 countries, including China as direct members, who can, if necessary, contact the local government to voice their opinion. Moreover, the ICC has consultative status with the institutions of the UN so that it can also make its opinion known at the UN level.

The main activities of the ICC are the drafting of "private codifications" for certain matters related to trade law. The international practices are generally applied in these matters. The application of the "private codifications" drafted by the ICC depends on the recognition by the communities concerned. Thus, in this way, the *Uniform Customs and Practice for Documentary Credits* (*UCP*) and the *Incoterms* enjoy universal application. The ICC has offered enterprises the opportunity to introduce an international code of conduct in respect of fair publicity or environmental protection. The ICC also has its Arbitration Rules and a Court of Arbitration, which allows enterprises from various parties to settle their trade disputes efficiently by arbitration.

Chapter Summary

　　本章旨在帮助读者了解规制和影响国际商事活动的法律框架。在对国际法（国际公法和国际私法）做一般性介绍的基础上，本章重点讨论国际商法的相关问题。国际商法是调整超越一国国界或地区的国际商事交易活动的规范的总称。从事国际商事交易活动的主体包括自然人、法人、其他组织、国际组织和国家或地区（在某些场合）。国际商法是国家或地区间商事交往发展到一定规模后产生的。随着欧洲商业的复兴和发展，一些国际性的商业中心城市在中世纪的地中海沿岸出现了。这些城市中的商人用他们在商事交往中形成的习惯规则调整商事交易关系，由此而形成商人习惯法（商人法）。商人习惯法后来得以推广使用。随着欧洲中央集权国家的兴起，欧洲各国都采取不同的方式将其纳入国内法的范畴。"二战"后，重建国际经济法律秩序的一系列努力也催生了大量影响国际商事交易活动的国际条约和国际贸易惯例。国际商法包括：国际条约、国际贸易惯例、国内法和国际示范法等。国际组织（政府间国际组织和非政府间国际组织）在国际商法的发展过程中发挥着重要作用，例如，联合国国际贸易法委员会在协调和统一国际商业交易规则并使之现代化方面做了卓有成效的工作。

Exercises

Part Ⅰ. True or False Statements: Decide whether the following statements are True or False and explain why.

　　1. International law is not enacted by a national legislative body. Instead, it consists of rules that countries agree to follow.

　　2. *Lex Mercatoria* or law merchant, formed in medieval Europe, was a written law and enforced by states.

　　3. International business customs and usages are not binding on parties unless the parties have incorporated them in the contract.

　　4. *UNCITRAL Model Law on International Commercial Arbitration* is an international treaty.

　　5. The ICC and the UNCITRAL are nongovernmental organizations with the task of unifying the national law on international business transactions.

　　6. The WTO is a set of rules governing global trade, a forum for multinational trade negotiation, a tribunal for dispute settlement, and an institution to review trade policies.

　　7. International treaties and conventions have unified the rules and norms governing international business, thus national law plays a little role in international business law.

　　8. International business customs and usages take the form of oral rather than writing.

　　9. Within the EU, if the law of a member is regarded to be against the European Commission

Treaty, the European Commission will initiate a lawsuit in the European Court of Justice to enforce the member to bring its law into conformity with the EC Treaty.

10. The International Court of Justice can settle the disputes arising from the international sale of goods between two companies.

Part Ⅱ. Chapter Questions: Discuss and answer the following questions according to what you have learned in this chapter. You are encouraged to use your own words.

1. How does international law differ from national law?

2. What is international business law? How do you understand its use for international business?

3. Unlike the other IGOs, the EU has a supranational power. How will you understand its supranational nature? Can you find any other organization that is parallel to the EU in this aspect?

4. What's your understanding of the statement that *Incoterms* is not law but important to international business?

5. What are the four basic functions of the WTO?

6. How do you understand "treaty"? Name a treaty regulating international business tractions.

7. Give an example of international business customs and usages and discuss how it differs from an international treaty?

8. Give an example of international model law, and discuss the use of it for international business.

9. What is the role of the International Chamber of Commerce in promoting international business?

10. Briefly talk about the structure of the WTO.

Part Ⅲ. Case Problem

Colorado Fuel sold caustic soda to a buyer in Mumbai under an international sales contract in which a trade term of CIF is used. And the contract contains a statement "All the trade terms in this contract shall be interpreted according to the *Incoterms 2020*." The soda was fully loaded aboard a ship when a labor strike made it impossible for the vessel to sail. As a result, the soda arrived in Mumbai 6 months later. The buyer sued for the late shipment.

1. Was Colorado Fuel liable for damages?

2. Did it matter that Colorado Fuel had known that a labor strike was imminent when loading the goods?

Part Ⅳ. Further Reading

The legal framework of international business law consists of laws and policies from all parties engaged in international commercial activity. Early trade customs centered around the law of the sea and provided, among other things, for rights of shipping in foreign ports, salvage rights, and freedom of passage. During the Middle Ages, international principles embodied in the *lex mercatoria* (law merchant) governed commercial transactions throughout Europe. Although laws governing international transactions were more extensive in some members than others, the customs and codes of conduct created a workable legal structure for the protection and encouragement of international transactions.

The other main sources of international commercial law are the laws of individual members, the laws embodied in trade agreements between or among members, and the rules enacted by a worldwide or regional organization—such as the United Nations or the European Union. Countries improve economic relations through trade agreements that cover a variety of potential commercial problems. This helps the investment and trade climates among members. For example, the North American Free Trade Agreement (NAFTA) is a treaty that was ratified by the legislatures in Canada, Mexico, and the U.S. and went into effect in 1994. It reduces or eliminates tariffs and trade barriers among those nations. Although some tariffs were eliminated immediately, many were phased out through the year 2009. The industries most affected include agricultural products, automobiles, pharmaceuticals, and textiles. NAFTA includes a variety of issues not usually found in trade agreements, such as the protection of intellectual property and the environment, and the creation of special panels to resolve disputes involving unfair trade practices, investment restrictions, and environmental issues.

There is no international regulatory agency or system of courts universally accepted for controlling international business behavior or resolving international conflicts among businesses or members. International law can be enforced to some degree through (1) international arbitration, (2) the courts of an individual members, or (3) the International Court of Justice(ICJ). Certain disputes may be taken to the ICJ for resolution. The ICJ is headquartered in The Hague, Netherlands, and is a part of the United Nations. Only members have standing to go before the Court; individuals and businesses have no standing to initiate a suit. The members decide whether to pursue claims on behalf of their citizens. ICJ decisions providing monetary judgments or injunctive relief may be referred to the United Nations Security Council for enforcement. However, the decisions of the above tribunals in resolving international business disputes can be enforced only if the members involved agree to be bound by them.

Chapter 3
National Laws and Legal Systems

 导读

本章主要介绍和讨论:（1）世界两大主要法系——普通法法系（英美法系）和民法法系（大陆法系）的概况和主要特点；（2）境内法——代表性成员方关于货物买卖的法规。旨在帮助读者具体了解作为国际商法的重要渊源之一的境内法。

 ## Warm-up Questions

(1) Can you find any differences in the laws of the two members?

(2) Do you know any law in China governing the sale of goods?

(3) What is the role of national law (the law of one members) in international business law?

3.1   Major World Legal Systems

Just as we have mentioned in the previous chapter, national law is an important source of international business law. Although many achievements have been obtained in the unification or harmonization of national legal systems in the area of international business, great differences still exist from one member to another. Those differences may exist in the role of legislatures in enacting codes, the role of judges, the courts in applying the law, and in legal procedures. Although it would be impossible to describe the legal system of every nation, it is possible to describe the basic systems or "family-groupings".[1] These systems may be classified in many ways: For example, by origin, cultural similarity, political ideology, etc. However, the two most widely recognized modern legal systems found in the world today are the **Civil Law system**[2] and the **Common Law system**[3].

---

1. 法系是根据若干国家和地区基于历史传统原因在法律实践和法律意识等方面所具有的共性而进行的法律分类，它是这些具有共性或共同传统的法律的总称。

2. Civil Law system：大陆法系，又名民法法系。其起源可追溯到古罗马皇帝查士丁尼下令编纂的《民法大全》(Corpus Juris Civilis)。欧洲国家继受了古罗马法的法典化特点。近代欧洲的对外扩张使得大陆法系的影响及于拉丁美洲和亚洲、非洲等其他地区。该法系中，法律的标准渊源是法典，司法判例尽管也很重要，但不像在英美法系中那样成为创制法律的主要方式，这也是两大法系的重要分界点。

3. Common Law system：英美法系，又称普通法法系。英美法系起源于中世纪的英格兰。同大陆法系偏重法典相比，英美法系在司法审判原则上更"遵循先例"，即作为判例的先例对其后的案件具有法律约束力，成为日后法官审判的基本原则。

A. Civil Law System

The civil law system, also called the continental legal system, is the oldest and most influential of the legal families. It is derived from the Roman Empire, or more particularly, the *Corpus Juris Civilis* issued by Emperor Justinian. The civil law system is characterized by the use of detailed codes that establish both basic principles and detailed rules for regulating the conduct of individuals. The grounds for deciding cases are found in these codes. In other words, the purpose of codes is to provide all citizens with manners and a written collection of the laws which apply to them, and which judges must follow.

Prominent examples and models for much of the civil law world are the *French Civil Code* of 1804 and the *German Civil Code* of 1896. They were models for most contemporary civil codes in countries such as Italy, Netherlands, Spain, Portugal, Switzerland, and Japan. The *French Civil Code* of 1804 is often referred to as the Napoleonic Code (1804), named after the French emperor Napoleon (1769-1821). Most scholars regard it as the first modern code. The code comprises three components: the law of persons, property law, and commercial law. It incorporated the principal idea of the French Revolution, including the right to possess private property and the freedom to contract. The style and form of the *French Civil Code* of 1804, which was intended to be a handbook for the citizen are easy to read, and understandable to everyone, The *German Civil Code* of 1896 was enacted almost a century later. Because Germany first had to unify itself and take shape as a nation, and the drafting project itself was enormous, taking more than 20 years to complete. The organization and form of the *German Civil Code* are incredibly precise and technical. Some special terminology was used, for example, the "real right". Legal concepts were defined and then used in the same way throughout the entire code. Unlike the *French Civil Code*, the *German Civil Code* lacked accessibility to the average people and was meant for the use of trained experts.

The civil law codes, which must be noted, only deal with the law of persons, family law, property law, inheritance law, law of obligations, commercial law, labor law, and criminal law. Public law, i.e., constitutional and administrative law is uniformly governed by separate rules and many civilian lawyers still regard it as a form of political science not really amenable to legal regulation.

China can be described as a civil law country, not because of received tradition, but because its legal system is statute based.

B. Common Law System

The common law system, also named the Anglo-American law system, is much less widely distributed than the civil law system. It is developed first in England, and later in English-speaking countries of the world. The common law system is based on the system of case law that originated in medieval England around the twelfth century and then was carried to England's colonies. Today, countries and regions that belong to the common law system include (but are not limited to) Australia, the UK (except Scotland), India (except Goa), Cyprus, Nigeria, Ireland, Singapore, USA (except Louisiana), Canada (except Quebec), New Zealand, Pakistan, Malaysia, and Bangladesh.

The common law's basis is a court decision, or precedent, which is also the principal factor distinguishing it from the civil law. That means the principles or rules of law on which a court rested a previous decision are authoritative in all future cases in which the facts are substantially the same.[1] The term of common law is used to describe the part of English law that is not based on **statutes**[2].

Nowadays common law has developed to be a matrix of case law and statutes, and in case of discrepancy, the statutes will prevail. It is concluded by some scholars that the civil law and common law systems are sharing more similarities.

In fact, civil law and common law systems today have many differences and similarities. Firstly, both systems regard the statute as a primary source of law. However, the legal codes in civil law members are more comprehensive than the statutes in common law members. Where there are gaps in the legal codes, judges will draw from the codes' general principles to decide a case. Secondly, the courts in both systems issue judicial decisions. While civil law judges may often cite earlier court decisions, they are not bound to follow them. Civil law judges do not render opinions that make new law in the form of binding precedent, as do common law judges.

3.2   National Laws Governing International Business Transactions

Despite the great influence of international treaties and international trade customs on international business, national law is still an important source for rules. It is partly due to the incomplete coverage of international treaties and international trade customs, and partly attributed to the legal and cultural traditions of different members.[3]

In common law members, traditionally the principles and rules governing business transactions are embodied in case law. However, in recent decades, in order to relieve the complexity of case law and facilitate the uniformity of commercial law, statutes have been adopted. In 1951, a new commercial law was proposed by the American Law Institute and the National Conference of Commissioners on Uniform State Laws in the United States. It is *The Uniform Commercial Code* (**UCC**)[4], the primary commercial law for domestic transactions in the United States. The purposes of the UCC are as follows: (1) To simplify, clarify, and modernize the law governing commercial transactions; (2) To permit the

---

1. 英美法以判例法为主要特征。其基本原则是 "遵循先例"，即法院审理案件时，必须将先前法院的判例作为审理和裁决的法律依据；对于本院和上级法院已经生效的判决所处理过的问题，如果再遇到与其相同或相似的案件，在没有新情况和提不出更充分的理由时，就不得做出与过去的判决相反或不一致的判决，直到将来某一天最高法院在另外一个同类案件中做出不同的判决为止。

2. statute：制定法。在英美法中，制定法专指由立法机关所制定的法律，表现为条文形式的规范性法律文件。其制定机关不一定为议会或国会，例如在美国，联邦、州、市或县的立法机关均可制定。该词在使用时专指以立法的形式创设的法律，故与由法院判决所形成的判例法相对。

3. 尽管有关国际货物买卖的国际公约、惯例正日益增多和完善，但离国际货物买卖法的统一还有相当的距离。各国法院或仲裁机构在处理国际货物买卖合同争议时，仍需借助国际私法规则选择适用某个成员方的境内法。因此，各方有关货物买卖的境内法仍是国际货物买卖法的重要渊源之一。例如《联合国国际货物销售合同公约》并未覆盖国际货物销售合同涉及的所有法律问题，关于合同效力等问题则留给各国境内法调整。

4. *The Uniform Commercial Code* （UCC）：《统一商法典》，是美国商事领域的基本法。该法分为 11 章（Article），以总则（General Provisions）和各分则的形式，对现实中的商事规则和商事惯例进行了归纳。它基本消除了各州商法对州际交易因规定不同而造成的障碍，实现了美国商法在州际交易范围内，关于销售、票据、担保、信贷各领域规定的统一。

continued expansion of commercial practices through custom, usage, and agreement of the parties; (3) To make uniform the law among the various jurisdictions (states). (See UCC 1-102). The UCC was drafted as a model law to be enacted by a particular state. Now it has been adopted by all U.S. states, only partially in Louisiana. It covers many areas of commercial laws including sales of goods, leases, commercial paper, bank deposits and collections, L/C, bulk transfer, warehouse receipts, B/L, investment securities and secured transactions. It does not, however, cover the sale of real estate or services, insurance, intellectual property, etc. Article 2 of the UCC applies to "sales and contracts of sales". Many early principles of the law merchant are still found in Article 2 in a modern, codified form such as trade terms. Contracts not covered by the UCC or other statutes are governed by the common law. That is, where the UCC is silent, the case law of contracts applies to the transaction. Since the United States has been a contracting state to CISG since 1988, for many international sales involving U.S. companies, the UCC has been supplanted by CISG.

In England, the *Sale of Goods Act* 1893 had codified many rules for law merchants. And this law was revised in 1979[1]. This act provides rules for a variety of contractual issues related to the sale of goods. As for the form requirements for the sales contract, it provides "Subject to this and any other Act, a contract of sale may be made in writing (either with or without seal), or by word of mouth, or partly in writing and partly by word of mouth or may be implied from the conduct of the parties." For the passing of risk, this act states: "Unless otherwise agreed, the goods remain at the seller's risk until the property in them is transferred to the buyer, but when the property in them is transferred to the buyer the goods are at the buyer's risk whether delivery has been made or not." In recent years, new statutes related to the regulation of contracts such as the Supply of Service Act have been passed to adapt to new social and technological changes.

In civil law countries, the principles and rules governing business transactions are usually found in codes, supplemented with some newly passed statutes. For example, in France, there are the *French Civil Code* of 1804 and the *French Code of Commerce* of 1807 and in Germany, there is the *German Civil Code* of 1896.

In China, the laws governing business transactions have undertaken great changes since 1978. These laws witnessed China's transition from a planned economy to a market economy. On January 1, 2021, the ***Civil Code of the People's Republic of China***[2] came into effect, which repealed the *Contract Law of the People's Republic of China*. In this code, the Book Three Contracts, which provides detailed principles related to contracts, is a combined achievement made by legislators and legal scholars. Book Three Contracts has drawn on accepted legal concepts and principles from both civil law and common law legal systems, as well as international conventions such as CISG, and then adapted them to the

---

1. Sale of Goods Act 1979：英国《货物买卖法》(1979)。该法对买卖双方的权利和义务、违反契约的补救办法、所有权和风险转移等问题做出了较为详细、全面的规定。

2. *Civil Code of the People's Republic of China*：《中华人民共和国民法典》。该法被称为"社会生活的百科全书"，是新中国第一部以法典命名的法律，在法律体系中居于基础性地位，也是市场经济的基本法。《中华人民共和国民法典》共 7 编，1260 条，各编依次为总则、物权、合同、人格权、婚姻家庭、继承、侵权责任，以及附则。2020 年 5 月 28 日，十三届全国人大三次会议表决通过了《中华人民共和国民法典》，自 2021 年 1 月 1 日起施行。《中华人民共和国婚姻法》《中华人民共和国继承法》《中华人民共和国民法通则》《中华人民共和国收养法》《中华人民共和国担保法》《中华人民共和国合同法》《中华人民共和国物权法》《中华人民共和国侵权责任法》《中华人民共和国民法总则》同时废止。

economic, political, and cultural situations of China.

Chapter Summary

　　虽然有关国际货物买卖的国际公约、惯例正日益增多和完善，但离国际货物买卖法的统一还有相当的距离。各国法院或仲裁机构在处理国际货物买卖合同争议时，仍需借助国际私法规则选择适用某个成员方的境内法。因此，各成员方有关货物买卖的境内法仍是国际货物买卖法的重要渊源之一。因此，本章重在帮助学习者理解境内法在国际商法中的重要作用。

　　为方便读者快速了解各国境内法的特征，本章首先介绍了当今世界两大主要法系：民法法系（大陆法系）和普通法法系（英美法系）。大陆法系最重要的特点就是以法典为第一法律渊源。使用大陆法系的国家主要包括欧洲大陆及受其影响的其他一些国家。如欧洲大陆上的法国、德国、意大利、荷兰、比利时、西班牙、葡萄牙、瑞士等国和拉丁美洲、亚洲的许多国家。英美法系是承袭英国中世纪的法律传统而发展起来的法律制度。在英美法系，判例法占主导地位，近几十年来，英美法系国家也制定了大量制定法作为对判例法的补充。目前世界上大约有 26 个国家属于英美法系国家，主要包括英联邦国家，如英国、美国、澳大利亚、新西兰等。两大法系下还存在其他一些差别，如法官的角色不同。大陆法系强调法官只能援用制定法中的规定来审判案件，法官只能适用法律而不能创制法律。英美法系强调法官既可以援用制定法也可以援用已有的判例来审判案件，而且，也可以在一定的条件下运用法律解释和法律推理的技术创造新的判例。因此，法官不仅适用法律，也在一定的范围内创制法律。随着国际交流与合作的广泛开展，两大法系出现了相互借鉴、融合的趋势。

　　本章还介绍了美国（《统一商法典》）、英国（《货物买卖法》）和中国（《中华人民共和国民法典》）等国家关于调整货物买卖法律关系的国内法。本章的拓展阅读部分简要介绍了合同纠纷法律冲突时应适用的主要冲突法规则。

Exercises

Part Ⅰ. True or False Statements: Decide whether the following statements are True or False and explain why.

　　1. Common law and civil law systems share no similarities and totally differ from each other.

　　2. Civil law system is characterized by the use of detailed legal codes and decisions made by the judges are not treated as precedents.

　　3. Nowadays common law consists of case law and statutes, and in case of discrepancy between case law and statutes, the former will prevail.

　　4. International treaties are the most important source of international business law, and national law plays a little role in regulating international business transactions.

　　5. Under the *Civil Code of the People's Republic of China*, a contract must be made in written form, otherwise it will be not valid.

　　6. Since the United States has been a contracting state to CISG since 1988, for many international sales involving U.S. companies, the UCC has been substituted by the CISG.

　　7. The legal system of China belongs to the civil law system, and the common law system does not influence China.

8. In common law countries, judges in deciding cases must follow precedents.

9. The *Contract Law* is now the law governing the sale of goods in China.

10. Book Three Contracts in the *Civil Code of the People's Republic of China* has drawn on accepted legal concepts and principles from both civil law and common law legal systems.

Part Ⅱ. Chapter Questions: Discuss and answer the following questions according to what you have learned in this chapter. You are encouraged to use your own words.

1. What are the differences and similarities between civil law and common law systems?

2. In your opinion, which legal system is better—The common law system or the civil law system? Give your reason.

3. What is the role of national law in governing international business transactions?

4. How do you comment on the characteristics of China's legal system?

5. Compare the form requirements for contracts between the *Civil Code of the People's Republic of China* and *Sale of Goods Act* of the U.K.

Part Ⅲ. Case Problem

The Sterns entered into a surrogacy agreement with Mary Beth Whitehead in which she agreed to bear the child of Mr. Stern (through artificial insemination) in exchange for costs plus $10,000 and to terminate her rights as a mother even before the baby was conceived. Upon the birth of the baby (Melissa) and the subsequent handover to the Sterns, as agreed, Mrs. Whitehead "became deeply disturbed, disconsolate, stricken with unbearable sadness." She persuaded the Sterns to give her one last week with the child by telling them that she was suicidal. So the Sterns handed their child over to the suicidal woman. It turned out that the suicidal woman (Mary Beth Whitehead) fled to Florida with her husband and the baby. There, they took evasive maneuvers to avoid detection before being ordered to turn over the child. The Sterns filed suit, seeking possession and ultimate custody of the child and enforcement of the surrogacy contract in which the child would be placed permanently in their custody and Mrs. Whitehead's parental rights would be permanently terminated. After a lengthy trial, the court ordered that Mrs. Whitehead's parental rights be terminated and that sole custody of the child be granted to Mr. Stern. The court also entered an order allowing the adoption of Melissa by Mrs. Stern, all in accordance with the surrogacy contract. Mrs. Whitehead appealed.

1. Is the surrogacy agreement a valid contract? Decide the case under the law of China and give your reason.

2. How will this case be addressed by courts in a country where its law permits surrogacy?

Part Ⅳ. Further Reading

Conflict of laws is a set of rules of procedural law which determine the legal system and the law of jurisdiction applying to a given legal dispute. In civil law, lawyers and legal scholars refer to conflict of laws as private international law. They typically apply when a legal dispute has a "foreign" element.

For the laws applicable to contracts, no element of the law is more confusing than that under the conflict of laws and the conflict between the places of making and performance of a contract where such places are not the same. To resolve the issue, courts have established the rules.

1. Choice-of-Law Clauses. A choice of law clause is a provision in a contract in which the parties stipulate that any dispute between them arising from the contract will be determined in accordance with the law of a particular jurisdiction. Many contracts and other forms of legally binding agreement include such a clause. Then, if the dispute is litigated, the clause is normally honored by the court hearing the lawsuit.

2. The Significant Relationship Rule. The significant relationship rule provides that the rules regarding the rights and duties of the parties with respect to an issue in the contract are determined by the local law of the party which has the most significant relationship to the transaction and the parties. In addition to being referred to as the "significant relationship" rule, this is also referred to as the center-of-gravity theory, the interest weighing or choice-influencing theory, and the grouping of contacts theory. According to this rule, courts apply the law of the state with the most significant contacts with the parties and the transaction underlying the lawsuit in the absence of a valid contractual choice of law. Rather than mechanically apply the law of the place of contracting or the place of performance, courts apply the law of the party with the most significant contacts with the parties and the transaction underlying the lawsuit. The main intention behind the application of the significant relationship rule is to identify the party most significantly related to the particular issue and to apply its law to resolve the same. The following factual contacts have to be considered when applying the significant relationship rule to determine the law applicable to an issue: The place of contracting; the place of negotiation of the contract; the place of performance; the location of the subject matter of the contract; and the domicile, residence, nationality, place of incorporation, and place of business of the parties.

Part Ⅱ International Sale of Goods

Chapter 4
Overview of International Sale of Goods

 导读

本章介绍国际货物销售的基本内涵、主要程序和期间可能面临的风险，以便读者在具体学习国际货物销售的相关法律之前大致了解国际货物销售的概况。

 Warm-up Questions

(1) In your opinion, what is the international sale of goods?

(2) As far as you know, which stage is the most important one in the procedure of international sale of goods?

(3) List as many as possible the risks that the parties may face in the international sale of goods.

4.1　Fundamentals of International Sale of Goods

We can have a better understanding of the international sale of goods with the help of the *United Nations Convention on Contracts for the International Sale of Goods* (CISG), which is now the principal law regulating the sale of goods between parties in different countries.

According to CISG Article 1, the Convention is applicable if the following three conditions are met: **(1) The contract is for the sale of goods; (2) the contract is between parties whose places of business are in different countries; (3) the places of business are located in parties that have ratified CISG.**[1] The convention itself does not expressly define "sale" or "goods". However, according to the cases decided under CISG[2], generally, it is understood that a "sale" is the passing of title from the seller to the buyer for a price. "Goods" are assumed to be things that are movable and tangible. Nevertheless, CISG does expressly define what is "international". Article 1 requires that a contract of

---

1. 《联合国国际货物销售合同公约》第 1 条：（1）本公约适用于营业地在不同成员方的当事人之间所订立的货物销售合同：（a）如果这些成员方是缔约方；或（b）如果国际私法规则导致适用某一缔约方的法律。

2. 《贸易法委员会关于〈联合国国际货物销售合同公约〉判例法摘要汇编（2012 年版）》。

sale of goods be deemed to be "international" if the places of business of the parties are located in different contracting parties to CISG. In other words, it does not require that the goods be shipped between different states, nor that the negotiations of the contract occur in different nations. Neither the location of the goods themselves nor the citizenship or nationality of the parties, is necessarily decisive. Instead, the "place of business" of each party must be located in a different contracting party to CISG. Therefore, in a contract involving two Austrian citizens one of whom had his place of business in Italy, the court held that CISG applied, and not Austrian law.

Then, what is "a **place of business**"? This term in CISG refers to a permanent place of business. And the drafting history of the convention suggests that **a permanent establishment is required and neither a warehouse nor the office of a seller's agent qualifies as a "place of business".** This interpretation has been adopted by the courts. A seller's "liaison office" in the buyer's nation was held by the Paris Court of Appeal not to be a "place of business," because it was not an autonomous legal entity. (See Case 4-1)

【Case 4-1】

Fauba France FDIS GC Electronique v. Fujitsu Microelectronik GmbH
CLOUT 158

BACKGROUNDS AND FACTS

A French buyer ordered electronic components from a German seller through the seller's liaison office ("bureau de liason") in France. The order specified that the final purchase price, previously indicated by the seller, would have to be revised taking into account a possible decrease in market prices and that the goods would be delivered at certain dates, upon confirmation by the seller. The seller replied, specifying that the purchase price would have to be revised according to both the increase and decrease in market prices. In its statement, the seller also declared that it was not yet able to confirm the order with regards to some components ("item 5" of the order). Shortly after, the parties agreed to modify the "item 5" of the order, specifying the price and dates of delivery. Later, the buyer canceled the order involving some other components. The seller objected to such partial cancellation, alleging that it had already dispatched the goods concerned for delivery. Upon delivery, the buyer rejected the goods in excess and requested the seller to take back the said goods. The seller refused to take back the goods rejected by the buyer and demanded payment. Before the appellate Court (Cour d'Appel de Paris, 22-04-1992) the seller argued that the contract was not governed by CISG as it was concluded between the French buyer and the seller's "bureau de liason" in France, and that therefore both parties had their places of business in France.

DECISION

The appellate Court rejected the argument, stating that the seller's "bureau de liason" was not an autonomous legal entity but rather a branch of the German seller in France. Therefore, the contract was to be considered an international sales contract governed by CISG as the parties had their places of business in different states.

4.2　Procedure of International Sale of Goods

Before we go into detailed legal knowledge related to international sales transactions, it is better to have a brief overview of the procedure of international sales transactions. Even though it is recognized that there are variations in the procedure of actual transactions, international sales transactions generally undergo the following 4 stages.

A. Preparation for Transaction

The preparations may include finding a profitable market, selecting a creditworthy partner, and applying for an export or import license.

B. Negotiation of Sales Contract

Four main steps are generally involved in the negotiation of a sales contract: Enquiry, offer, counter-offer, and acceptance. An **enquiry**[1] asks for the possibility of having a sales transaction and can be an invitation to offer, which is different from an offer. Chapter 6 will have more details related to the formation of the sales contract.

C. Performance of Contract

This stage is important but complicated, with many variations resulting from different choices of transportation and payment methods. As most international sales contracts are concluded with sea transportation and L/C (Letter of Credit) payment, we use this type to illustrate the procedures as follows:

1. Opening and examining L/C

The buyer applies for the issuance of L/C and forwards it to the seller. The seller examines and ensures all terms and conditions in L/C are in strict conformity with those in the sales contract.

2. Seller's getting goods ready

The seller should prepare the goods in the exact quantity and quality as stipulated in the contract, and should also pack and mark the goods in line with the requirements in the contract.

3. Seller's obtaining mandatory inspection certificates

If required by the law or the contract, the seller should apply for mandatory inspection and obtain the relevant inspection certificates from authorized institutions before shipment.

4. Arranging for shipment

According to their agreement in the contract, the seller or the buyer may arrange for the shipment of the goods.

---

1. **enquiry**：询盘，又称询价。当事人一方为洽商交易向相对人提出的有关交易条件的询问。其目的是询问对方是否有买进或卖出该项商品的意图，以便磋商交易条件,但并非对方做出回答后就立即能签订合同，只是期待对方向自己提出条件。这是试探市场动态、联系客户的一种手段，因此，询盘又称邀请发盘（要约邀请），对询盘人没有法律约束力，它虽能引发交易，但并非交易磋商的必经步骤，其与发盘（要约）的主要区别在于询盘的主要交易条件不全。

5. Buyer's inspection of goods at the port of shipment

The buyer or its agent will inspect the goods at the port of shipment before loading.

Clearing goods for export

Most frequently (except under the trade term EXW, see Chapter 5), the seller, instead of the buyer, should carry out the customs formalities for export.

6. Getting goods loaded for shipment

According to their agreement in the contract, the seller or the buyer may get the goods loaded for shipment.

7. Obtaining insurance

According to their needs and agreement, the seller or the buyer may obtain insurance for the goods.

8. Seller's presentation of documents to the bank for negotiation

The seller presents all necessary documents specified in L/C to the bank for negotiation of payment.

9. Buyer's examination of documents and making payment to the bank

The buyer receives and examines the relevant documents and then makes payment to the bank.

10. Clearing goods for import

Most frequently (except under the trade term DDP, see Chapter 5), the buyer, instead of the seller, should carry out the customs formalities for import.

11. Buyer's taking delivery and inspection of goods

With the payment made and shipment documents obtained, the buyer can take delivery of the goods from the carrier. The buyer should inspect the goods, or cause them to be inspected, to check whether the goods conform to the contract.

D. Settlement of Disputes

If any disputes arise in international sales transactions, it is better to settle them through negotiation or mediation. If that does not work, the disputes can be submitted to arbitration as agreed in the contract (if any). Otherwise, litigation will be necessary.

4.3   Risks in International Sale of Goods

An international sales transaction, no matter how straightforward it may seem at the start, is not completed until the buyer has taken delivery, the seller has received payment and other related obligations have been fulfilled. This may seem obvious; however, even seemingly simple transactions can, and sometimes do, go wrong.

For buyers and sellers that are engaged in international sales transactions, they may experience one or more of the following risks.

A. Contract Risks

Greatly owing to the spread of the rule of law, contract plays an increasingly important role in everyday life. A person, from the cradle to the grave, may never commit a crime; however, it is hard to imagine the person has not ever entered into a contract.

Nowadays, the contract is a basic way of conducting business transactions. For example, in a sale of goods transaction, the parties usually rely on the contract to provide the rights and obligations of the parties including the transfer of title to the goods, the arrangement of transportation, payment and insurance, the way to settle any potential dispute and many other matters agreed on by the parties.

All forms of transactions contain elements of risk, but when it comes to international sales transactions, the risks may enter a new dimension. Internationally, you seldom have common laws and regulations that can support the transaction, as would be the case within one country. Instead, established trade practices and conventions are used to guide the transactions and settle the disputes. The key to successful international sales transactions, therefore, depends on a knowledge of these practices and conventions and ensuring that the undertakings in the individual contract are in line with such practices and conventions. That is why we will cover the laws and practices on international sales contracts in detail in Chapter 5 and chapter 6.

B. Transportation Risks

Once the buyer and seller have negotiated the contract for the sale of goods, and how those goods will get from point A to point B, a carrier must actually transport those goods. In international sales, goods are usually transported by sea, air, rail or truck. And with the wide use of containers, sometimes two or more than two modes are combined to accomplish international transportation of goods, i.e., multimodal transportation of goods.

A typical process of international transportation of goods by sea is as follows. Goods are transported from a seller in Country A to an inland carrier and are carried to a seaport for transportation abroad. The inland carrier will deposit the goods in a warehouse or port depository for examination by customs officials and for consolidation with other goods if the load is not large enough to occupy a ship. A stevedoring company or the ship's crew will load the goods and then stow the goods aboard the ship, mark the goods and issue a bill of lading on behalf of the carrier to the **shipper**[1]. At a seaport in Country B, the ship will be directed by port authorities to tie up at a pier or to anchor in the harbor. When the buyer presents the bill of lading, the ship's crew will unload the goods onto the dock. The crew or a stevedoring company will then deliver the goods to a customhouse or a bonded warehouse for inspection. Once the customs of Country B have inspected the goods and their related documents, and collected import duties, the goods will be released for entry into Country B. A local inland carrier may be employed to transport the goods to the buyer's place of business. When goods are transported by air, rail, or truck, much the same procedure is followed except that the carrier will issue an air waybill or similar nonnegotiable receipt instead of a bill of lading.

The risks in the physical movement of the goods from the seller to the buyer have to be evaluated, based on aspects such as the nature of the goods, the size of the delivery, the buyer and their country, and the actual transportation route. Most goods in international sales transactions, apart

---

1. shipper: 货主、发货人、托运人。船运货物的货主，广义上也包括陆运、空运货物的货主。在运输契约上，指将货物交付承运人运输的托运人。

from smaller and non-expensive deliveries, are covered by cargo insurance, providing cover against physical loss or damage during transportation, either by sea, air, land, or by a combination of these modes of transport.

Transportation of those goods is governed by a private contractual relation. In many instances, it is also enhanced by the international conventions concerning the carrier's liability for loss, misdelivery, and monetary damages. In fact, an independent body of rules has been established for governing the international transportation of goods, which will be covered in Chapter 7.

C. Payment Risks

Payment risk for the seller is often defined as the risk of the buyer going into bankruptcy or being in any other way incapable of fulfilling payment obligations. At the same time, any advance payments before the delivery of the goods may be risky for the buyer. This is particularly true for the transaction with an unknown foreign seller for the first time. One of the best ways of managing risk in international sales transactions in such a situation is to use the international Letter of Credit as a payment instrument, instead of transferring money directly through the bank. Chapter 8 will provide more information related to this payment mode, other payment modes and related conventions and practices.

 ## Chapter Summary

根据《联合国国际货物销售合同公约》，国际货物销售就是营业地在不同成员方的当事人之间的货物销售。

国际货物销售的主要程序包括四个部分：贸易准备、合同谈判、合同履行、争议解决。其中，以采用海洋运输方式和信用证支付方式的国际货物销售为例，合同履行部分大致包括以下步骤：开立和审核信用证、卖方备货、卖方办理出口商品检验证书（必要时）、安排装运、买方在装运港检验货物、货物装船、购买保险、卖方提示单据给银行以收取货款、买方审核单据后付款给银行、办理进口通关手续、买方收取并检验货物。

国际货物销售中的风险主要包括合同风险、运输风险和支付风险三方面。

 ## Exercises

Part Ⅰ. True or False Statements: Decide whether the following statements are True or False and explain why.

1. The United Nations *Convention on Contracts for the International Sale of Goods* (CISG) is the principal law governing the international sale of goods. Here "international" means the nationalities of the parties are different.

2. In international sales transactions, the seller always has to carry out the customs formalities for export.

3. In international sales transactions, the buyer always has to carry out the customs formalities for import.

4. Cargo insurance only covers loss or damage during sea transportation.

5. Letter of Credit is a kind of payment instrument.

Part Ⅱ. Chapter Questions: Discuss and answer the following questions according to what you have learned in this chapter. You are encouraged to use your own words.

1. Before sales negotiation, what preparations should be made by the parties?
2. What are the main steps involved in the negotiation of a sales contract?
3. What should the buyer do after taking delivery of the goods from the carrier?
4. When any dispute arises, what methods can be used to settle it?
5. In international sales, which transportation method of goods is used most frequently?

Part Ⅲ. Case Problem

An Austrian buyer and a Chinese seller made a contract for the purchase of scaffold fittings. The buyer conducted part of the negotiations in China, where the seller was located, and the buyer's liaison office in China has been involved in the negotiating process. The two parties did not agree upon the governing law in their sales contract.

Does the CISG apply?

Chapter 5
Introduction to International Sales Contracts

 导读

本章主要介绍国际货物销售合同的基本法律知识：合同的定义、合同的分类、合同的有效要件。本部分还介绍与国际货物销售合同相关的国际条约和国际贸易惯例，如:《联合国国际货物销售合同公约》《国际商事合同通则》《国际贸易术语解释通则》。在各国的国内法中与国际货物销售合同有关的内容也将在本章中予以介绍。

 Warm-up Questions

(1) Describe a situation in everyday life in which a contract exists.

(2) Contract may be made for different purposes. Name some of these purposes.

(3) Do you think a gambling contract will be enforced by the court in China? Why or why not?

5.1 Fundamentals of Contracts

A. Definition of Contract

The contract has been defined by scholars and legislators from various perspectives. The most classical definition may be the one found in ***Black's Law Dictionary***[1]. It states that a contract is an agreement between two or more parties which creates an obligation to do or not to do a particular thing, and which is enforceable in law[2].

Under common law, a contract tends to be regarded as a **promise or promises**. *Restatement (Second) of Contracts*[3] of the United States defines the contract as "A promise or a set of promises for

---

1. *Black's Law Dictionary*:《布莱克法律词典》。该书是一部权威性的美国法学词典，囊括了众多法律术语和法律警句（格言），并对这些术语和警句加以了定义。

2. 合同是双方或多方之间达成的协议，创设做某事或不做某事的义务，合同具有法律约束力。

3. *Restatement (Second) of Contracts*:《合同法重述（第二次）》。美国法学会从 20 世纪二三十年代开始，为解决美国司法中判例法的日益不确定性和过分复杂性，将已存在的大量判例法予以系统化、条理化、简单化，予以重新整编。一般认为，法律重述对司法并没有法定的拘束力，但具有很强的权威性和说服力。事实上，律师及各个法庭经常援用法律重述。

the breach of which the law gives a remedy, or the performance of which the law in some way recognizes as a duty"[1].

However, under civil law, the nature of a contract is a "meeting of minds" or "**mutual assent**"[2]. For instance, Article 464 of the *Civil Code of the People's Republic of China* states: "A contract is an agreement on the establishment, modification, or termination of a civil juristic relationship between persons of the civil law."[3]

One thing to note is that not all the business documents agreed upon the parties may be a contract. For example, a "**memorandum**"[4] is a proposed agreement in which two parties negotiate and reach a mutual assent on some terms, and also decide that they will subsequently put the entire agreement into a formal written document to be signed by them. Whether the memorandum may be deemed to be a contract will depend on if the parties, by actions or words, have clearly indicated their intention to be bound by the document. A similar problem can arise when the parties sign a so-called "**letter of intent**"[5]. Such a document memorializes the basic terms on which the parties have agreed but anticipates further negotiations on more minor issues. Usually, the letter of intent indicates that a fuller and more formal agreement will be prepared later. If the parties are unable to settle the supposedly minor issues, what happens if one party asserts that the letter of intent is binding, and the other disagrees? Usually, it depends on the test whether the parties have shown their intent to be bound by the document in the terms of the letter of intent.

There is an example helping you understand the question. The Seller plans to sell the assets of its company. After negotiation with the Buyer, the two sign a four-page document, which they entitle "Letter of Intent". The Letter summarizes the purchase price ($2 million) and says that the arrangement will be "subject to and incorporated into a formal Asset Purchase Agreement signed by both parties". The Letter also states that the purchase will be "subject to the satisfaction of certain conditions including approval by the shareholders and board of directors of the Buyer." The parties then fail to agree on what security the Seller will receive to ensure payment. After the Buyer learns that the Seller is now negotiating with a different potential purchaser, the Buyer claims that the Letter of Intent is enforceable. The decision should be held for the Seller. Here the text of the letter indicates that the parties do not indicate to be bound by the Letter and they need to further discuss some details (e.g., the Letter uses the phrase "subject to" repeatedly). Therefore, no contract shall be deemed to exist between the Seller and the Buyer. The seller is free to negotiate with any other potential purchaser under such a circumstance.

B. Classification of Contracts

Due to the different purposes a contract may serve, a variety of contracts are widely used in reality.

---

1. 美国《合同法重述（第二次）》第 1 条：合同指的是一个允诺或一组允诺，法律就其违反给予补偿，或某种意义上视其履行为义务。

2. mutual assent：合意，即双方意思表达一致。

3.《中华人民共和国民法典》第 464 条：合同是民事主体之间设立、变更、终止民事法律关系的协议。

4. memorandum：备忘录。当事人双方或多方之间对某项事务进行协商讨论，达成共识，然后用书面形式记载的谈判内容。

5. letter of intent：意向书。当事人双方或多方之间，在对某项事务正式签订协议之前，表达初步设想的意向性文书。

There are sales contracts, employment contracts, leasing contracts, construction contracts, agency contracts, warehousing contracts, licensing agreements for transfer of technology, contracts for carriage and contract for transportation of people and cargo, etc[1]. The list may be endless.

As for the form of contract, there are **written contracts and oral contracts**[2]. Article 469 of the *Civil Code of the People's Republic of China* provides the parties may conclude a contract in writing, orally, or in other forms. For example, you take a taxi and agree to pay a fee. Then the taxi driver drops you at your destination. An oral contract has been made and performed without signing a written document. For written contracts, Article 469 of the *Civil Code of the People's Republic of China* states that a writing refers to any form that renders the content contained therein capable of being represented in a tangible form, such as a written agreement, letter, telegram, telex, or facsimile. A data message in any form, such as electronic data interchange and e-mails, that renders the content contained therein capable of being represented in a tangible form and accessible for reference and use at any time shall be deemed as a writing.[3] However, there are a few kinds of contracts for which a written document is necessary according to the requirements of some laws. For example, Article 668 of the *Civil Code of the People's Republic of China* states: "A loan contract shall be made in writing, except for a loan between natural persons who agree otherwise."[4] And in accordance with the U.S. *Uniform Commercial Code*, contracts such as for the sale of land or the sale of goods of $500 or more must be in writing.

Considering the validity of the contract, there are valid, void and voidable contracts. **Valid contracts** are the usual contracts, which are enforced by either party. **Void contracts** are those agreements that have no legal effect. **Voidable contracts** are those contracts, which one party may at his option either enforce or not enforce.[5] In the *Civil Code of the People's Republic of China*, Article 143 states that "A civil juristic act is valid if the following conditions are satisfied: (1) the person performing the act has the required capacity for performing civil juristic acts; (2) the intent expressed by the person is true; and (3) the act does not violate any mandatory provisions of laws or administrative regulations, nor offend public order or good morals.[6]" Article 153 states that "A civil juristic act in violation of the mandatory provisions of laws or administrative regulations is void, unless such mandatory provisions do not lead to invalidity of such a civil juristic act. A civil juristic act that offends the public order or good morals is void.[7]" Article 147 states that "Where a civil juristic act is performed based on serious misunderstanding, the person who performs the act has the right to request the people's court or an

---

1. 买卖合同、劳动合同、租赁合同、建筑工程合同、委托合同、仓储合同、技术转让合同、客运合同、货运合同等。

2. written contract and oral contracts：书面合同和口头合同。

3.《中华人民共和国民法典》第 469 条：当事人订立合同，可以采用书面形式、口头形式或者其他形式。书面形式是合同书、信件、电报、电传、传真等可以有形地表现所载内容的形式。以电子数据交换、电子邮件等方式能够有形地表现所载内容，并可以随时调取查用的数据电文，视为书面形式。

4.《中华人民共和国民法典》第 668 条：借款合同应当采用书面形式，但是自然人之间借款另有约定的除外。

5. valid contract, void contract, voidable contract：有效合同；无效合同；可撤销合同。

6.《中华人民共和国民法典》第 143 条：具备下列条件的民事法律行为有效：（一）行为人具有相应的民事行为能力；（二）意思表示真实；（三）不违反法律、行政法规的强制性规定，不违背公序良俗。

7.《中华人民共和国民法典》第 153 条：违反法律、行政法规的强制性规定的民事法律行为无效。但是，该强制性规定不导致该民事法律行为无效的除外。违背公序良俗的民事法律行为无效。

arbitration institution to revoke the act.[1]" And according to Article 147-151, when a party induces the other party to perform a civil juristic act by fraud or duress, or by taking advantage of the other party's hardship, the damaged party is entitled to request the people's court or an arbitration institution to revoke the act.

C. Essential Elements of a Valid Contract

A valid contract is an enforceable agreement that contains all the essential elements of a contract. These elements can serve as a testing stone for the validity of a contract. Under the civil law system, including the law of China, these elements usually include: (1) Parties must have the legal capacity to contract; (2) The contract must be an agreement of mutual assent reached through offer and acceptance; and (3) The contract must not be illegal or contrary to public policy. Under the common law system, these elements for a valid contract are quite similar except for the requirement of legal and sufficient consideration.[2] In the following, these elements will be discussed one by one.

Element 1: Parties must have the legal capacity to contract.

Here parties mainly include natural persons and legal persons who enter into contracts. Legal persons are entities registered by the law of one country, which are deemed to have legal capacity commencing from the date of their registration and terminating on the date of their dissolution. For the natural persons, the circumstances are somewhat complex. Generally, minors and mental incompetents are regarded to be persons with limited legal capacity. According to the *Civil Code of the People's Republic of China*, minors refer to persons below the age of 18, and one exception is that a person, who is above the age of 16 but below the age of 18 and lives on his/her own labor income, will be deemed to have the full legal capacity to make a contract.[3]

Under the *Civil Code of the People's Republic of China*, the contracts, concluded by persons with limited capacity, may be valid in two situations. First, the contract will be valid upon its formation if the person with limited capacity accrues only benefits from it. Second, the conclusion of the contract is appropriate for his/her age, intelligence or mental health. In other situations, the contracts concluded by persons with limited capacity are valid upon ratification by the legal agent.[4]

Element 2: The contract must be an agreement of mutual assent reached through offer and acceptance.

First, for a contract to be formed, the parties must reach "mutual assent." That is, they must both intend to create legal relations. The intent to create legal relations shall be determined from the indications made by each of the parties, rather than by each party's subjective intention. Thus a party's

---

1.《中华人民共和国民法典》第 147 条：基于重大误解实施的民事法律行为，行为人有权请求人民法院或者仲裁机构予以撤销。

2. 合同的有效要件有以下 3 点。（1）合同当事人订立合同时具有相应的缔约行为能力。（2）合同当事人意思表示真实。一方在被欺诈、胁迫或者重大错误下订立的合同往往非其真实意思表示，属于可撤销的合同。（3）合同不违反法律或社会公共政策。在普通法下，合同的有效要件还包括合法的对价——一种等价有偿的允诺关系。

3.《中华人民共和国民法典》第 17 条：十八周岁以上的自然人为成年人。不满十八周岁的自然人为未成年人。第 18 条：成年人为完全民事行为能力人，可以独立实施民事法律行为。十六周岁以上的未成年人，以自己的劳动收入为主要生活来源的，视为完全民事行为能力人。

4.《中华人民共和国民法典》第 19 条：八周岁以上的未成年人为限制民事行为能力人，实施民事法律行为由其法定代理人代理或者经其法定代理人同意、追认；但是，可以独立实施纯获利益的民事法律行为或者与其年龄、智力相适应的民事法律行为。

intention must be decided objectively rather than subjectively. The reason underlying such a theory is not difficult to understand since neither contracting parties nor judges are mind readers.

Second, "mutual assent" means a party cannot be held to a contract if it is made where **fraud**, **duress**, or a **mistake** exists.[1] Fraud refers to intentional deceit. And duress is any wrongful act or threat, which overcomes the free will of a party. Here a person of ordinary firmness is usually used as a test for whether the act or threat done by one party to the other is strong enough to overcome the free will of the victim party. It may include "gun at head" type duress as well as economic duress. Generally, the party who enters into a contract by the fraud or duress committed by the other party is entitled to revoke the contract. Mistake denotes the situation in which a contract is made and a party attempts to rescind it because one or both parties acted on a mistaken belief about an existing fact. Like the contract made through fraud or duress, a contract concluded on the basis of mistake is generally permitted the revocation at the option of the victim party under the legal systems of civil law and common law. However, under the common law system, there is a distinction between mutual mistake and unilateral mistake. Mutual mistake is a situation where both parties have acted on the same mistaken belief. Generally, the contract of mutual mistake should be subject to either revocation or reformation (re-writing by the court) of the contract. Unilateral mistake refers to the circumstance under which only one party has acted on the mistaken belief. It is harder for the party to get a rescission than in a mutual-mistake situation. Revocation of the contract may be allowed if the following requirements are met. (1) the mistake is such that enforcement of the contract would be "unconscionable"; and (2) the other party had reason to know of the mistake, or his fault caused the mistake.

The following are two examples for your understanding of mistake. The first one as follow: Jack agrees to sell Giant a goose for $20. Both parties think the goose is a regular goose, which Giant wants for breeding. Before the goose transferred, the goose begins laying golden eggs, which makes her priceless. Jack refuses to uphold the agreement, and Giant sues to enforce the contract. The second one as follow: Jack is building himself a monument and needs a rock-cutting machine. He sees Giant's ad in the Bargain Trader Newspaper for a rock-cutting machine for $10,000. Jack goes to Giant's house and inspects the machine. Giant accurately answers all the questions Jack asked. Jack offers Giant $10,000 for the machine. Before the transaction takes place, Jack finds out the rock cutter will not be the type suitable for cutting his marble. For the above examples, the first one is a mutual mistake and the second one is a unilateral mistake.

Third, mutual assent is almost invariably reached through what is called "the offer" and "the acceptance". An offer is a party's manifestation of intention to enter into a contract with the other party. An acceptance is the offeree's manifestation of intention to assent to an offer.[2] An offer may be made in writing or oral form. An acceptance shall be manifested by notification, except where it may be manifested by conduct in accordance with the relevant usage or as indicated in the offer.[3] Specific rules about offer and acceptance will be discussed in detail in the next chapter.

Element 3: The contract must not be illegal or contrary to public policy.

---

1. fraud, duress, mistake：欺诈、胁迫、误解。合同合意不真实的 3 种情形。

2. 要约（又称发价或发盘）是希望和他人订立合同的意思表示，承诺（又称接受）是受要约人同意要约的意思表示。

3. 承诺应当以通知的方式做出，但根据交易习惯或者要约表明可以通过行为做出承诺的除外。

Illegal contracts are void because the activities carried out by these contracts are barred by relevant statutes in one party. For example, under the law of the United Kingdom, contracts for the commission of a criminal offence or civil wrong, usurious contracts, contracts with enemy aliens or nationals living in enemy territory, contracts illegal by the law of a friendly foreign party and contracts prejudicial to the administration of justice, contracts to defraud the revenue, both national and local, etc. are regarded to be void for their illegality.

The activities carried out by some contracts are not expressly prohibited by relevant laws, however, if they go against the public policy of a country where a party seeks to enforce the contract, the contract will be held void by the court. **Public policy**[1] is a widely used conception in the legislation of most countries. But its connotation seems not so obvious. Generally, public policy is interpreted to be the basic moral value, national security, and public interests of one nation. For instance, gambling contracts and contracts tending to corruption in public life are void ones in the United Kingdom. The core value of public policy is to defend the moral and ethical standards of a society.

Under the common law, a legal and sufficient consideration is traditionally required to enable a contract to be enforceable. A contract is deemed to be supported by consideration if two requirements are met: (1) The promisee (the party who is receiving the promise) gave up something of value, or circumscribed his liberty in some way ("Legal detriment" requirement); and (2) The promisor made his promise in exchange for the promisee's giving of value or circumscribing of liberty ("Bargain" requirement). Each party is required to furnish consideration to the other. So, if A's promise is not supported by consideration from B, then not only A is not bound, B is not bound either.

However, there are exceptions to the rule requiring consideration. That is under some circumstances, a contract (promise) can be enforceable even though there is no consideration for it: promises (in writing) to pay past debts, promise to pay for benefits/services received, modification of a contract for the sale of goods, option contract (i.e. a promise to hold an offer open for a set amount of time), guaranty contract, and **promissory estoppel**[2]. Under the doctrine of promissory estoppel, a promise will be enforceable without consideration if: (1) The promise acts or forbears in reliance on the promise and (2) this action or forbearance is reasonably foreseeable by the promisor. The doctrine is often applied in a situation where there has been a promise to make a gift.

5.2 Laws and Practices on International Sales Contracts

A. United Nations Convention on Contracts for the International Sale of Goods (CISG)[3]

Historically, the law governing the international sale of goods was first the province of merchants.

---

1. Public policy：公共政策。一般指一国的公共利益、基本价值和相关风俗。

2. promissory estoppel：允诺禁止反言。英美法系国家的一般契约理论，其基本内涵是言行一致，不得出尔反尔。

3. *United Nations Convention on Contracts for the International Sale of Goods (CISG)*：《联合国国际货物销售合同公约》。该公约是有关国际货物销售合同的国际公约，由联合国国际贸易法委员会起草，于 1988 年 1月 1 日生效。公约既是发展中国家和发达国家利益折中的产物，又是大陆法系和英美法系具体制度糅合的结果，具有广泛的国际性。

Indeed, businessmen are credited with developing one of the first bodies of law, via Lex Mercatoria, a necessary creation to manage trade with far-off individuals. Nevertheless, the domestic laws of various partyies often continued to develop along different lines. Thus, legal rules pertaining to the creation and completion of contracts differ from party to party. In more recent past decades, as international merchants have sought to take advantage of global sales opportunities, the differences have sometimes created problems. Consequently, countries, with the help of the international organization **United Nations Commission on International Trade Law (UNCITRAL)**[1], came together to create the *CISG* to standardize certain international contract principles.

As the principal international law regulating the sale of goods between parties in different countries, *CISG* has enjoyed wide acceptability. *CISG* came into force on 1 January 1988 with the original eleven States. By January 2023, the number of contracting parties has reached 95 including Australia, Canada, China, France, Germany, Italy, Russia, Singapore, Swiss, Switzerland, United States, and other major trading parties, covering parties from every geographical region, every stage of economic development and every major legal system.[2] Thus *CISG* is regarded to be one of the most successful instruments of international sales law harmonization. To provide a modern, uniform, and fair set of rules on contracts for the international sale of goods, *CISG* contributes significantly to introducing certainty in commercial exchanges and decreasing transaction costs.

The Convention is divided into **four parts**[3]. Part Ⅰ deals with the scope of application of the Convention and the general provisions. Part Ⅱ contains the rules governing the formation of contracts for the international sale of goods. Part Ⅲ deals with the substantive rights and obligations of the buyer and the seller arising from the contract. Part Ⅳ contains the final clauses. As the main body of *CISG*, Part Ⅱ and Part Ⅲ will be discussed in detail in the next chapter.

As to Part Ⅰ and Part Ⅳ, rules of the applicability of *CISG* and provisions for *CISG*'s ratification are included. Parrties may choose to be parties to this Convention (the Convention has to be ratified by the national congress or parliament to take legal effect in the party). Article 1 of *CISG* states: "This Convention applies to contracts of sale of goods between parties whose places of business are in different districts: (a) when the parties are Contracting parties; or (b) when the rules of private international law lead to the application of the law of a Contracting party."[4]

When the requirements are met and the *CISG* does apply, the parties to a contract, however, may **exclude** (i.e., they may "opt out") or **modify the application of *CISG*** by a "choice of law clause". Opting out of *CISG* is allowed in all legal regimes of contracting parties, but it requires the choice of law clause of clarity. A simple statement that a contract "shall be governed by the law of China" is somewhat ambiguous, because in a strict sense, *CISG* has become an integral part of the laws of China after China

---

1. United Nations Commission on International Trade Law (UNCITRAL)：联合国国际贸易法委员会。联合国系统在国际贸易法领域的核心法律机构，其主要职责是促进国际贸易法的协调和统一。

2. 截至 2024 年 1 月，《联合国国际货物销售合同公约》的成员方数目为 97 个，具体名单可参见联合国国际贸易法委员会网站。

3.《联合国国际货物销售合同公约》共分为 4 个部分：（1）适用范围和总则；（2）合同订立的规则；（3）买卖双方的权利和义务；（4）最后条款。

4.《联合国国际货物销售合同公约》第 1 条：（1）本公约适用于营业地在不同国家的当事人之间所订立的货物销售合同：（a）如果这些成员方是缔约方；或（b）如果国际私法规则导致适用某一缔约方的法律。

adopted *CISG*. "Opting out" of *CISG* would require at least: "This contract shall be governed by the laws of China applicable to domestic contracts of sale, and shall not be governed by the *United Nations Convention on Contracts for the International Sale of Goods, 1980*." Or in this way: "This contract shall be governed by the *Civil Code of the People's Republic of China* and other laws of China governing the domestic sale of goods."

When the parties can "opt out" of *CISG*, can they also "opt in"? In fact, whether the parties can "opt in" depends on the rules of the state where this question comes up. Usually, parties to an international sales contract are allowed to "opt in" *CISG* by choice of law clause. For example, parties can agree that "This contract shall be governed by the laws of France, including the *United Nations Convention on Contracts for the International Sale of Goods 1980*."

Although *CISG* is considered one of the core international trade law conventions whose universal adoption is desirable, it does not cover all the issues related to the contract for the international sale of goods. The Convention expressly includes two sets of issues, which arise under a sale contract, and expressly excludes two sets of contractual issues from its coverage. The issues covered by *CISG* are **the formation of the contract** and **the rights and obligations of the parties to the contract**. The excluded issues are the validity of the contract and property right (or title) to the goods.[1] These issues excluded from the coverage of *CISG* will be left to the governing of the law indicated by private international law rules or by choice of law clause. For the contractual issues to which both *CISG* and domestic law apply, *CISG* will preempt to domestic law.

B. National Laws

Despite the great influence of *CISG* on international sales contracts, national law is still an important source for rules governing the sale of goods, which is partly due to the incomplete coverage of contractual issues by *CISG*, and partly attributed to the legal and cultural traditions of different countries.

In common law countries, traditionally, the principles and rules governing the sale of goods are embodied in case law. However, in recent decades, to relieve the complexity of case law and facilitate the uniformity of sales law, statutes have been adopted. ***Uniform Commercial Code*** (**UCC**), proposed by the American Law Institute and the National Conference of Commissioners on Uniform State Laws, is the primary commercial law for domestic transactions in the United States. The *UCC* was drafted as a model law to be enacted by a particular state. However, now it has already been adopted by all states of the United states (only partially in Louisiana, which used to be a French colony, with the tradition of civil law system). Article 2 of the *UCC* applies to "sales and contracts of sales". Many early principles of the law merchant are still found in Article 2 in a modern, codified form such as trade terms. Contracts not covered by the *UCC* or other statutes are governed by the common law. That is where the *UCC* is silent, the case law of contracts applies to the transaction. Since the United States has been a contracting state to *CISG* since 1988, for many international sales involving U.S. companies, the *UCC* has been supplanted by *CISG*.

In England, ***Sale of Goods Act*** 1894 codified many rules from law merchants and was revised in 1979. New statutes related to the regulation of contracts such as ***Supply of Goods and Services Act*** have

---

1.《联合国国际货物销售合同公约》第 4 条：……本公约除非另有明文规定，与以下事项无关：（a）合同的效力，或其任何条款的效力，或任何惯例的效力；（b）合同对所售货物所有权可能产生的影响。

been passed to adapt to new social and technological changes.

In civil law countries, the principles and rules governing contracts for the sale of goods are usually found in codes, supplemented with some newly passed statutes. For example, in France, there are the *French Civil Code of 1804 (Napolenic Code)* and the *French Code of Commerce of 1807* (code de commerce) and in Germany, there was the *German Civil Code of 1896*.

In China, *Civil Code of the People's Republic of China* came into effect on January 1, 2021. In it, the Book One General Part provides some principles for a sales contract. Book Three Contracts provides detailed principles related to contracts. Chapter Nine in Book Three focuses on sales contracts.

C. Principles of International Commercial Contracts[1]

As we have known in Chapter 2, model law, a kind of soft law, also plays an undeniable role in international trade law. In the area of international sale of goods, *Principles of International Commercial Contracts* is such a good example.

The *Principles of International Commercial Contracts* was published in 1994 by the International Institute for the Unification of Private Law (UNDROIT) and was later updated three times in 2004, 2010, and 2016. The 2016 edition contains new Provisions, Comments, and Illustrations dealing with the special requirements of long-term contracts, in addition to some modifications and updating of existing Comments and Illustrations.

The *Principles of International Commercial Contracts* is applicable to all commercial contracts, not just sales of goods. The *Principles of International Commercial Contracts* has established several principles including **freedom to contract, good faith, fair dealing, and favor contractus**[2], which, like a thread, run through the *Principles of International Commercial Contract*. For example, freedom to contract is expressly stated in Article 1.1. It reads: "The parties are free to enter into a contract and to determine its content."[3] The comment of this article explains that "the rights of business people to decide freely to whom they will offer their goods or services and by whom they wish to be supplied, as well as the possibility for them freely to agree on terms of individual transactions, are the cornerstones of an open, market-oriented and competitive international economic order."[4] That is, under the principle of freedom to contract, the parties are free to conclude contracts with any other person, irrespective of their nationalities, and the parties are also free to agree on any terms and choose any law as the governing law in their contracts unless otherwise provided in the *Principles of International Commercial Contracts*. And the principle of favor contractus means endeavoring to facilitate the formation and existence of a contract. Michael Joachim Bonell has explained the rationale underlying

1. *Principles of International Commercial Contracts*：《国际商事合同通则》，又称《国际统一私法协会国际商事合同通则》。《国际商事合同通则》不是国际性条约或公约，不具备强制执行力，但可通过当事人选择适用的方式提高适用的灵活性。《国际商事合同通则》于 1994 年由国际统一私法协会理事会第 73 届会议通过，是国际统一私法协会为超越不同国家的法律传统和政治经济条件而制定的一套可以在世界范围内使用的均衡的国际商事交易一般规则体系，是继《联合国国际货物销售合同公约》之后，国际统一合同立法的又一里程碑。

2. freedom to contract, good faith, fair dealing, and favor contractus：缔约自由，善意，公平交易，支持合同。

3.《国际商事合同通则》第 1.1 条：（缔约自由）当事人可自由订立合同并确定合同的内容。

4.《国际商事合同通则》第 1.1 条的注释中指出：经营者有自由决定向谁供货或提供服务和希望由谁供货或提供服务的权利及自愿商定个人生意条件的可能性，这是开放的、适应市场规则的、竞争性的国际经济秩序的基石。

the principle: The reason behind this is the acknowledgement that despite shortcomings, which might arise in the course of the formation or performance of the contract, it is normally in the interest of both parties to do all possible to keep their original bargain alive than to renounce it and look for alternative goods or services elsewhere on the market.[1] Such principle has been embodied in Article 2.1.1 of the *Principles of International Commercial Contracts,* and it states that a contract may be concluded either by the acceptance of an offer or by conduct of the parties that is sufficient to show agreement.[2] And Paragraph 2 of Article 2.1.11 states: However, a reply to an offer which purports to be an acceptance but contains additional or different terms which do not materially alter the terms of the offer constitutes an acceptance, unless the offeror, without undue delay, objects to the discrepancy. If the offeror does not object, the terms of the contract are the terms of the offer with the modifications contained in the acceptance[3].

Unlike *CISG*, which is a binding convention on members, the *Principles of International Commercial Contracts* is drafted as a model law, not a binding legal document. However, the considerable functions of it cannot be denied. First, it can be used as a model for national and international legislators. Second, it is not only the subject of a substantial body of legal writings but is more and more frequently used in international contract practice and dispute resolution. That is, it can be chosen to be the governing law by the parties to an international commercial contract as an alternative to national law and *CISG*. And it can be used by international commercial arbitrators, even by judges, where local law is ambiguous. Third, compared with *CISG*, the *Principles of International Commercial Contracts* covers not only the international sale of goods but also the transactions in services and investment. And it covers almost all the contractual issues from the formation to the performance of the sales contract, while *CISG* keeps silent on some issues, for example, the requirements for the validity of the contract. Moreover, the substantive rules of the *Principles of International Commercial Contracts* are often different from those of *CISG*, because it was not drafted by official delegations of governments, and the individual drafters could adopt what they considered to be "best practices" in commerce.

D. International Customs and Usages: Incoterms[4]

Frequently, parties to a contract are unaware of the different trading practices in different parties.

---

1. Michael Joachim Bonell. *An International Restatement of Contract Law*, 2nd ed. Irvington-on-Hudson, New York, 1997, P118.

2.《国际商事合同通则》第 2.1.1 条：（订立方式）合同可通过对要约的承诺或通过能充分表明合意的当事人各方的行为而订立。

3.《国际商事合同通则》第 2.1.11 条（2）：对要约意在表示承诺但载有添加或不同条件的答复，如果所载的添加或不同条件没有实质性地改变要约的条件，则除非要约人毫不迟延地表示拒绝这类条件，此答复仍构成承诺。如果要约人不做出拒绝，则合同的条款应以该要约的条款以及承诺所载有的变更条件为准。

4. *Incoterms* (International Commercial Terms)：International Rules for the Interpretation of Trade Terms 《国际贸易术语解释通则》。国际商会为了统一各种国际贸易术语的解释而制定的一个国际通则，旨在对国际贸易合同中的主要术语作广泛适用的解释，力求最清楚、最准确地规定当事人的有关责任，避免因对术语作不同解释而引起的纷争和诉讼。1936 年，国际商会公布了第一个国际贸易术语解释通则。此后，为适应国际贸易的不断发展，国际商会分别于 1953 年、1967 年、1976 年、1980 年、1990 年、2000 年、2010 年和 2020 年对该通则进行了修订和补充。《国际贸易术语解释通则》无强制性，但在国际贸易中被广泛采用。

This can give rise to misunderstandings, disputes, and litigation, with all the waste of time and money that this entails. In order to remedy these problems, the International Chamber of Commerce (ICC) first published a set of international rules for the interpretation of trade terms in 1936. These rules were known as "*Incoterms 1936*". Amendments and additions were later made in 1953, 1967, 1976, 1980, 1990, 2000, 2010 and presently in 2020 (*Incoterms 2020* came into effect on 1 January 2020) in order to bring the rules in line with current international trade practices.

1. The purpose of *Incoterms*

The purpose of *Incoterms* is to provide a set of international rules for the interpretation of the most commonly used trade terms in foreign trade. Thus, the uncertainties of different interpretations of such terms in different countries can be avoided or at least reduced to a considerable degree.

2. The Scope of *Incoterms*

It should be stressed that the scope of *Incoterms* is *limited* to matters relating to the rights and obligations of the parties to the contract of sale with respect to the delivery of goods sold (here goods is in the sense of "tangibles", not including "intangibles" such as computer software). It appears that two particular misconceptions about *Incoterms* are very common. First, *Incoterms* are frequently misunderstood as applying to the contract of carriage rather than to the contract of sale. Second, they are sometimes wrongly assumed to provide for all the duties, which parties may wish to include in a contract of sale. Although *Incoterms* are extremely important for the implementation of the contract of sale, a great number of problems, which may occur in such a contract are not dealt with,such as transfer of ownership and other property rights, breaches of contract and the remedies for such breaches as well as exemptions from liability in certain situations. These problems must be resolved by other stipulations in the contract of sale and the applicable law.

3. The Classification of *Incoterms 2020* (See Exhibit 5-1, Exhibit 5-2)

Group 1. *Incoterms* that apply to any mode or modes of transport:

EXW   Ex Works （工厂交货）

FCA   Free Carrier（货交承运人）

CPT   Carriage Paid To（运费付至）

CIP   Carriage and Insurance Paid To（运费和保险费付至）

DAP   Delivered at Place（目的地交货）

DPU   Delivered at Place Unloaded（目的地卸货后交货）

DDP   Delivered Duty Paid（完税后交货）

Group 2. *Incoterms* that apply to sea and inland waterway transport only:

FAS   Free Alongside Ship（船边交货）

FOB   Free on Board（船上交货）

CFR   Cost and Freight（成本加运费）

CIF   Cost Insurance and Freight（成本、保险费加运费）

EXW-Ex Works (insert named place of delivery) means that the seller delivers the goods to the buyer when it places the goods at the disposal of the buyer at a named place (like a factory or warehouse), and that named place may or may not be the seller's premises. The seller does not need to load the goods on any collecting vehicle, nor does it need to clear the goods for export, where such clearance is applicable. The parties are well advised to specify as clearly as possible the precise point within the named place of delivery, as the costs and risks to that point are for the account of the seller. The buyer bears all costs and risks involved in taking the goods from the agreed point, if any, at the named place of delivery. EXW represents the minimum obligation for the seller.

Exhibit 5–1: Graphical Reference of *Incoterms 2020*

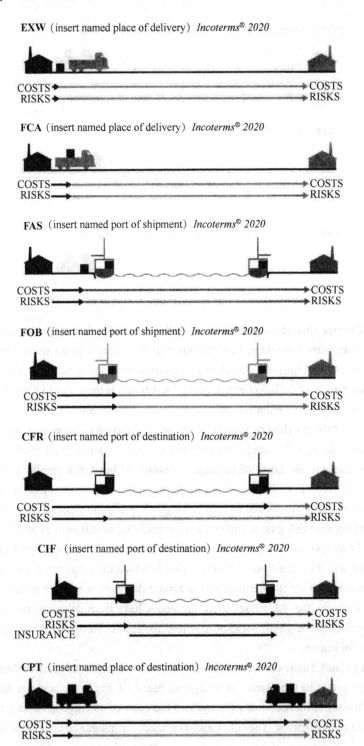

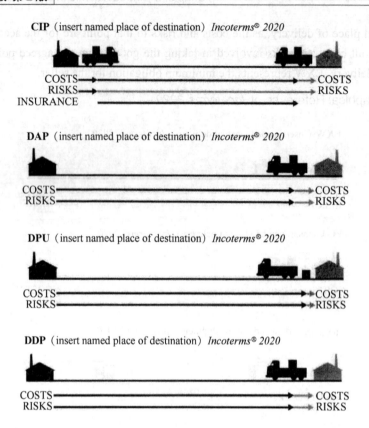

CIP（insert named place of destination）*Incoterms® 2020*

COSTS
RISKS
INSURANCE

DAP（insert named place of destination）*Incoterms® 2020*

COSTS
RISKS

DPU（insert named place of destination）*Incoterms® 2020*

COSTS
RISKS

DDP（insert named place of destination）*Incoterms® 2020*

COSTS
RISKS

FCA-Free Carrier (insert named place of delivery) means that the seller delivers the goods to the carrier or another person nominated by the buyer at the seller's premises or another named place. The parties are well advised to specify as clearly as possible the precise point within the named place of delivery, as the risk passes to the buyer at that point. FCA requires the seller to clear the goods for export, where applicable. However, the seller has no obligation to clear the goods for import.

CPT-Carriage Paid To (insert named place of destination) means that the seller delivers the goods to the carrier at an agreed place (if any such place is agreed between the parties) and that the seller must contract for and pay the costs of carriage necessary to bring the goods to the named place of destination. When CPT, CIP, CFR or CIF are used, the seller fulfils its obligation to deliver when it hands the goods over to the carrier and not when the goods reach the place of destination. CPT rule has two critical points because risk passes and costs are transferred at different places. The parties are well advised to identify as precisely as possible in the contract both the place of delivery, where the risk passes to the buyer, and the named place of destination to which the seller must contract for the carriage. If several carriers are used for the carriage to the agreed destination and the parties do not agree on a specific point of delivery, the risk passes when the goods have been delivered to the first carrier. CPT requires the seller to clear the goods for export, where applicable. However, the seller has no obligation to clear the goods for import.

CIP-Carriage and Insurance Paid To (insert named place of destination) means that the seller delivers the goods to the carrier at an agreed place (if any such place is agreed between the parties) and that the seller must contract for and pay the costs of carriage necessary to bring the goods to the named place of destination. The seller also contracts for insurance cover against the buyer's risk of loss of or damage to the goods during the carriage. The buyer should note that under the CIP *Incoterms 2020* rule, the seller is required to obtain extensive insurance cover complying with Institute Cargo Clauses (A) or similar clause, rather than with the more limited cover under Institute Cargo Clauses (C). It is, however, still open to the parties to agree on a lower level of cover. CIP requires the seller to clear the goods for export, where applicable. However, the seller has no obligation to clear the goods for import.

DAP-Delivered at Place (insert named place of destination) means that the seller delivers when the goods are placed at the disposal of the buyer on the arriving means of transport ready for unloading at the named place of destination or at the agreed point within that place if any such point is agreed. The seller bears all risks involved in bringing the goods to the named place of destination or to the agreed point within that place. DAP requires the seller to clear the goods for export, where applicable. However, the seller has no obligation to clear the goods for import. If the parties wish the seller to clear the goods for import, the DDP term should be used.

DPU-Delivered at Place Unloaded (insert named place of destination)   means that the seller delivers when the goods, once unloaded from the arriving means of transport, are placed at the disposal of the buyer at a named place of destination or at the agreed point within that place if any such point is agreed. The seller bears all risks involved in bringing the goods to and unloading them at the named place of destination. The seller is advised to procure a contract of carriage that matches this choice precisely. DPU requires the seller to clear the goods for export, where applicable. However, the seller has no obligation to clear the goods for import.

DDP-Delivered Duty Paid (insert named place of destination) means that the seller delivers the goods when the goods are placed at the disposal of the buyer, cleared for import on the arriving means of transport ready for unloading at the named place of destination or at the agreed point within that place, if any such point is agreed. The seller bears all the costs and risks involved in bringing the goods to the place of destination or to the agreed point within that place. And the seller has an obligation to clear the goods not only for export but also for import. The seller is advised to procure contracts of carriage that match this choice precisely. DDP represents the maximum obligation for the seller. The parties are well-advised not to use DDP if the seller is unable to obtain import clearance.

FAS-Free Alongside Ship (insert named port of shipment) means that the seller delivers when the goods are placed alongside the vessel (e.g., on a quay or a barge) nominated by the buyer at the named port of shipment or when the seller procures goods already so delivered. The risk of loss of or damage to the goods passes when the goods are alongside the ship, and the buyer bears all costs from that moment onwards. The parties are well advised to specify as clearly as possible the loading point at the named port of shipment. Where the goods are in containers, it is typical for the seller to hand the goods over to the carrier at a container terminal and not alongside the vessel. In such situations, the FAS rule would be inappropriate, and the FCA rule should be used. FAS requires the seller to clear the goods for export, where applicable. However, the seller has no obligation to clear the goods for import.

FOB-Free on Board (insert named port of shipment) means that the seller delivers the goods to the buyer on board the vessel nominated by the buyer at the named port of shipment or procures the goods already so delivered. The risk of loss of or damage to the goods passes when the goods are on board the vessel, and the buyer bears all costs from that moment onwards. The seller is required either to deliver the goods on board the vessel or to procure goods already so delivered for shipment. The reference to "procure" here caters for multiple sales down a chain (string sales), particularly common in the commodity trades.[1] FOB may not be appropriate where goods are handed over to the carrier before they are on board the vessel, for example, goods in containers, which are typically delivered at a container terminal. In such situations, the FCA rule should be used. FOB requires the seller to clear the goods for export, where applicable. However, the seller has no obligation to clear the goods for import.

CFR- Cost and Freight (insert named port of destination) means that the seller delivers the goods to the buyer on board the vessel or procures the goods already so delivered. The risk of loss of or damage to the goods passes when the goods are on board the vessel. The seller must contract for and pay the costs and freight necessary to bring the goods to the named port of destination. CFR may not be appropriate where goods are handed over to the carrier before they are on board the vessel, for example goods in containers, which are typically delivered at a container terminal. In such circumstances, the CPT rule should be used. CFR requires the seller to clear the goods for export, where applicable. However, the seller has no obligation to clear the goods for import.

CIF-Cost Insurance and Freight (insert named port of destination) means that the seller delivers the goods to the buyer on board the vessel or procures the goods already so delivered. The risk of loss of or damage to the goods passes when the goods are on board the vessel. The seller must contract for and pay the costs and freight necessary to bring the goods to the named port of destination. The seller also contracts for insurance cover against the buyer's risk of loss of or damage to the goods during the carriage. The buyer should note that under the CIP *Incoterms 2020* rule, the seller is required to obtain limited insurance cover complying with Institute Cargo Clauses (C) or similar clause, rather than with the more extensive cover under Institute Cargo Clauses (A). It is, however, still open to the parties to agree on a higher level of cover. CIF may not be appropriate where goods are handed over to the carrier before they are on board the vessel, for example, goods in containers, which are typically delivered at a container terminal. In such circumstances, the CIP rule should be used. CIF requires the seller to clear the goods for export, where applicable. However, the seller has no obligation to clear the goods for import.

4. Variations of *Incoterms*

In practice, it frequently happens that the parties themselves by adding words to an Incoterm to seek further precision than the term could offer. It should be underlined that *Incoterms* give no guidance whatsoever for such additions. Thus, if the parties cannot rely on a well-established custom of the trade for the interpretation of such additions, they may encounter serious problems when no consistent understanding of the additions could be proven. For instance, if the common expressions "FOB stowed" or "EXW loaded" are used, it is impossible to establish a worldwide understanding to the effect that the seller's obligations are extended not only with respect to the cost of actually loading the goods in the ship or on the vehicle respectively but also include the risk of fortuitous loss of or damage to the goods in the process of stowage and loading. For these reasons, the parties are strongly advised to clarify whether they only mean that the function or the cost of the stowage and loading operations should fall

---

1. 卖方应将货物在船上交付，或者取得已经如此交付运输的货物完成交货。此处的"取得"一词适用于交易链中的多层销售（链式销售），在大宗商品贸易中尤其常见。

upon the seller or whether the seller should also bear the risk until the stowage and loading have been completed. These are questions to which *Incoterms* do not provide an answer. Consequently, if the contract too fails to expressly describe the parties' intentions, the parties may be put to much unnecessary trouble and cost.

5. Practical guide for using the *Incoterms*

Each Incoterm specifies: First, the obligations of each party (e.g. who is responsible for services such as transport, import and export clearance, etc.); Second, the point in the journey where risk transfers from the seller to the buyer (this becomes important if the goods are lost or damaged in transit).

When the parties have agreed on an Incoterm rule to govern the transaction, it is incorporated into the commercial agreement by way of a reference such as the following:

CIP Hong Kong Terminal 4 *Incoterms 2020*

Note these three elements:

A three-letter abbreviation — CIP stands for "Carriage and Insurance Paid To"

A precisely-defined place. For the CIP *Incoterms* rule, this is a place of destination, to which the seller has contracted to transport the goods. For other *Incoterms* rules, the place may have a different meaning.

The applicable edition of the *Incoterms* rules—here, *Incoterms 2020*. (Parties who wish to use earlier editions of the rules such as *Incoterms* 2010 are free to do so, provided that they specify this.)

In general, the "transport by sea or inland waterway only" Incoterms should only be used for bulk cargos (e.g. oil, coal, etc.) and non-containerised goods, where the exporter can load the goods directly onto the vessel. Where the goods are containerised, the "all modes of transport" *Incoterms* are more appropriate.

A critical difference between the *Incoterms* in these two groups is the point at which risk transfers from seller to buyer. For example, the "Free on Board" (FOB) rule specifies that risk transfers when the goods have been loaded on board the vessel. However, the "Free Carrier" (FCA) rule specifies that risk transfers when the goods have been taken in charge by the carrier.

Another useful way of classifying the rules is by considering: Who is responsible for the main carriage—the buyer or the seller? If the seller is responsible for the main carriage, where does the risk pass from the seller to the buyer—before the main carriage, or after it? This gives us these four groups:

Buyer responsible for all carriage—EXW.

Buyer arranges the main carriage—FCA; FAS; FOB.

Seller arranges the main carriage, but the risk passes before the main carriage—CFR; CIF; CPT; CIP.

Seller arranges the main carriage,the risk passes after the main carriage—DAP; DPU; DDP.

The C group of rules often surprises newcomers, because although the seller pays for transport to the named place, the risk transfers at an earlier point in the journey. Consider, for example, goods that are taken in charge at Long Beach, California, for transport to Hong Kong Terminal 4, under the rule "*CIP Hong Kong Terminal 4 Incoterms 2020*". The seller will arrange and pay for freight to Hong Kong Terminal 4, but the risk will pass to the buyer upon delivery of the goods to the carrier at Long Beach, California, before the main carriage.

Exhibit 5-2: *Incoterms 2020*

Exhibit 5-2: *INCOTERMS 2020*

组别	术语	英文	中文	交货地点	风险转移界限	签订运输合同及支付运费	保险责任及费用	出口报关责任及费用	进口报关责任及费用	适用运输方式	详细概念
E组	EXW	Ex Works (insert named place of delivery)	工厂交货(填入指定交货地点)	卖方所在地或其地指定地点（如工厂或仓库等）	买方处置货物后		买方	买方	买方	任何运输方式或多式联运	指当卖方在其所在地或其他指定地点将货物交由买方处置时，即完成交货。代表卖方义务最低义务
F组	FCA	Free Carrier (insert named place of delivery)	货交承运人(填入指定交货地点)	卖方所在地或其他指定地点	买方指定的承运人或其他人处置货物后	买方	买方	卖方	买方	任何运输方式或多式联运	指当卖方在其所在地或其他指定地点将货物交给买方指定的承运人或其他人处置时，即完成交货
	FAS	Free Alongside Ship (insert named port of shipment)	船边交货（填入指定装运港）	指定的装运港	卖方将货物交到指定船边时（例如，置于码头或驳载船上）	买方	买方	卖方	买方	海运或内河水运	指当卖方在指定的装运港将货物放置于买方指定的船边（例如，置于码头或驳载船上）时，即完成交货
	FOB	Free on Board (insert named port of shipment)	船上交货(填入指定装运港)	指定的装运港	货物交到船上时	买方	买方	卖方	买方	海运或内河水运	指卖方以在指定的装运港将货物装上买方指定的船的方式交货
C组	CFR	Cost and Freight (insert named port of destination)	成本加运费(填入指定目的港)	指定的装运港	货物交到船上时	卖方	买方	卖方	买方	海运或内河水运	指卖方在船上交货。CFR价=FOB价+运费
	CIF	Cost Insurance and Freight (insert named port of destination)	成本、保险费加运费(填入指定目的港)	指定的装运港	货物交到船上时	卖方	卖方	卖方	买方	海运或内河水运	指卖方在船上交货。CIF价俗称"到岸价"=FOB价+运费+保险费，或=CFR价+保险费

续表

组别	术语	英文	中文	交货地点	风险转移界限	签订运输合同及支付运费	保险责任及费用	出口报关责任及费用	进口报关责任及费用	适用运输方式	详细概念
C组	CPT	Carriage Paid To (insert named place of destination)	运费付至(填入指定目的地)	双方约定地点(如,国内陆路口岸或港口)	在交货地点,卖方指定的承运人控制货物后	卖方	买方	卖方	买方	任何运输方式或多式联运	指卖方将货物在双方约定地点交给卖方指定的承运人时,即完成交货。CPT价=FCA价+运费
	CIP	Carriage and Insurance Paid To (insert named place of destination)	运费和保险费付至(填入指定目的地)	双方约定地点(如,国内陆路口岸或港口)	在交货地点,卖方指定的承运人控制货物后	卖方	卖方	卖方	买方	任何运输方式或多式联运	指卖方将货物在双方约定地点交给卖方指定的承运人时,即完成交货。CIP价=FCA价+运费+保险费,或=CPT价+保险费
D组	DAP	Delivered at Place (insert named place of destination)	目的地交货(填入指定目的地)	指定目的地	买方处置货物后	卖方	卖方	卖方	买方	任何运输方式或多式联运	指卖方在指定目的地将货物交由买方处置,卖方只需做好卸货前而无需卸货即完成交货。卖方应承担将货物运至指定的目的地的一切风险
	DPU	Delivered at Place Unloaded (insert named place of destination)	目的地卸货后交货(填入指定目的地)	指定目的地	买方处置货物后	卖方	卖方	卖方	买方	任何运输方式或多式联运	指当卖方在指定目的地的运输工具上卸载,交由买方处置,即完成交货。卖方应承担将货物运至指定目的地及卸载货物的一切风险
	DDP	Delivered Duty Paid (insert named place of destination)	完税后交货(填入指定目的地)	指定目的地	买方处置货物后	卖方	卖方	卖方	卖方	任何运输方式或多式联运	指当卖方在指定目的地,在处于抵达状态的运输工具上,将已完成进口清关,且已做好卸货准备的货物交由买方处置,即完成交货。代表卖方承担最大责任

6. Common mistake in using the *Incoterms*

A common mistake in using the *Incoterms* is the use of a traditional "sea and inland waterway only" Incoterm such as FOB or CIF (Under FOB or CIF, once the goods have been loaded on board, risk transfers to the buyer) for containerised goods, instead of the "all transport modes" *Incoterms*, e.g. FCA or CIP (Under FCA or CIP, risk transfers from seller to buyer at the point where the goods are taken in charge by a carrier). This exposes the exporter to unnecessary risks. A dramatic recent example was the Japanese tsunami in March 2011, which wrecked the container terminal. Many hundreds of goods awaiting dispatch were damaged. Exporters who were using FOB or CIF found themselves responsible for losses that could have been avoided.

 ## Chapter Summary

本章介绍的是国际货物销售合同的入门性内容，旨在为下一章的学习奠定基础。本章主要介绍了以下内容。

合同的定义：合同是双方或多方之间达成的协议，创设做某事或不做某事的义务，该协议具有约束力。

合同的种类：书面合同、口头合同、有效合同、无效合同、可撤销合同。

合同的有效要件有以下 3 点。（1）合同当事人订立合同时具有相应的缔约行为能力。（2）合同当事人意思表示真实。一方在被欺诈、胁迫或者重大错误下订立的合同往往非其真实意思表示，属于无效或可撤销的合同。（3）合同不违反法律或社会公共政策。在普通法下，合同的有效要件还包括合法的对价——一种等价有偿的允诺关系。

《联合国国际货物销售合同公约》为国际货物销售提供了现代、统一的法规，被视为国际贸易的核心公约之一，受到了大多数国家的重视，截至 2024 年 1 月已有 97 个成员。该公约适用于营业地位不同成员的当事方之间的货物销售合同。在这种情形下，《联合国国际货物销售合同公约》将直接适用。它还可因当事方的选择而适用。当事方也可以在合同中明确规定不适用该公约。

鉴于不同缔约方的法律和文化传统的不同，各方的境内法（如中国的《中华人民共和国民法典》和美国的《统一商法典》等）也是与国际货物销售合同相关的重要法律渊源之一。

作为示范法，《国际商事合同通则》可用于解释或补充国际统一法文件，可作为境内和国际立法的范本，为司法、仲裁所用，是起草合同、谈判的工具。

《国际贸易术语解释通则》作为惯例，只有在交易双方在合同中明确规定援用时才对当事人双方有约束力。在销售合同中，对这一最重要的国际贸易惯例的引用可帮助界定各方有关义务，并降低法律纠纷的风险。

 ## Exercises

Part Ⅰ. True or False Statements: Decide whether the following statements are True or False and explain why.

1. Contract is a written agreement between two or more parties, which is enforceable in the law.

2. Under the *Civil Code of the People's Republic of China*, a contract shall not be made through the exchange of e-mails.

3. Under the *Civil Code of the People's Republic of China*, contracts concluded by a person with limited legal capacity such as a minor are void.

4. If a party induces the other to enter into a contract by fraud, the contract will be deemed to be void under the *Civil Code of the People's Republic of China*.

5. The law of contract in different legal systems shares more similarities than differences. The elements for a valid contract required by common law are the same as those under civil law.

6. The UCC is a model law published by American Law Institute, thus it is not binding on any state of the U.S.

7. Private parties in contracting states of *CISG* cannot choose another law rather than *CISG* to govern their contract for the international sale of goods.

8. Principles of International Commercial Contracts published by UNIDROIT is a model law.

9. *Incoterms 2020* is a set of trade terms applying to the contract of carriage rather than the contract of sale.

10. *Incoterms 2020* covers all the matters, which parties wish to include in a contract of sale.

Part Ⅱ. Chapter Questions: Discuss and answer the following questions according to what you have learned in this chapter. You are encouraged to use your own words.

1. Give an example of a contract and illustrate why you think it is a contract.

2. What are the elements of a valid contract under the civil law system and common law system?

3. Under what circumstances will the contract be deemed to be void under the *Civil Code of the People's Republic of China*? Try to explain the reasons behind these provisions.

4. How do you understand voidable contracts? Give an example.

5. A contract must be an agreement of mutual assent. What's your understanding of "mutual assent"?

6. What are the main differences between *CISG* and *Principles of International Commercial Contracts*?

7. Find the full text of the *Civil Code of the People's Republic of China* and look through it.

8. What should you pay special attention to when using the trade term CIF?

9. In your opinion, what factors may determine the choice of a particular trade term used in an international sales contract?

10. What's the purpose and scope of *Incoterms 2020*?

11. There are different sources of rules governing the international sale of goods. What proposals will you make in order to avoid the uncertainty related to governing law on an international sales contract?

Part Ⅲ. Case Problem

1. After doing some spring cleaning in his wine cellar, Mr. Wang decides to sell several bottles of wine from the Magenta region of France. He enters into a contract with Ms. Lin to sell the wine for RMB 2, 500 Yuan. Both believe this to be the fair market value of the wine at the time. In fact, wines from the Magenta region have gone up in value recently and the collection is really worth RMB 50, 000 Yuan. Mr. Wang learns of this just before the sale is completed, and he seeks to cancel the sale.

Do you think Mr. Wang shall be permitted to do that? Why or why not?

2. Colorado Fuel sold some goods to a buyer in Mumbai under a CIF contract. The goods were fully loaded aboard the ship when a labor strike made it impossible for the vessel to sail. As a result, the goods arrived in Mumbai six months late. The buyer sued for the late shipment.

(1) Was Colorado Fuel liable for that?

(2) Did it matter that Colorado Fuel might have known that a strike was almost certain to happen very soon?

Chapter 6
Legal Issues on International Sales Contracts

 导读

本章以《联合国国际货物销售合同公约》为主要法律渊源，介绍有关国际货物销售合同的具体法律知识：合同的订立、买卖双方的义务、风险转移、违约免责事由、违约救济措施等。

 Warm-up Questions

(1) What are the rights and obligations of the seller and the buyer in an international sales contract?

(2) What kinds of disputes may arise from an international sales contract?

(3) In case of breach of an international sales contract, how many ways can you imagine to redress the victim party?

As the main parts of *CISG*, Part II has rules on the formation of contracts and Part III provides rules relating to the rights and obligations of buyers and sellers. In this chapter, these rules will be discussed in detail, and in the meantime, the corresponding rules under the *Civil Code of the People's Republic of China* and under the *UCC* will be mentioned from time to time.

6.1 Formation of International Sales Contracts

Part II (Articles 14-24) of *CISG* contains the contract formation provisions, with a focus on "offer" and "acceptance." Under the *CISG*, a contract is concluded (becomes binding) when an acceptance of an offer becomes effective.[1] There is no need for consideration (like the *UCC*), and no formal requirements.

A. The Offer

Under the *CISG*, an "offer" has four requirements. First, it must be "a proposal for concluding a contract". Second, it must indicate "an intention to be bound in case of acceptance". Third, the proposals

---

1.《联合国国际货物销售合同公约》第 23 条：合同于按照本公约规定对要约的承诺生效时订立。

must be addressed to a specific person or persons. The proposals addressed to the general public will be presumptively not offered "unless the contrary is clearly indicated." Fourth, an offer must be "sufficiently definite." This provision requires **the proposal must contain at least three contract terms: the description of the goods, their quantity and their price.**[1] Other terms can be left open, but not those three. The offer is definite enough if the goods are "indicated",which does not seem to require that they be described with any particularity. Similarly, an offer is definite if it "expressly or impliedly fixes or makes provision for determining the quantity and the price". The above requirements for an offer are based on the reason that the proposal has to describe the goods with sufficient clarity so that the parties know what is being offered for sale, and other elements of the proposal can be implied from the conduct of the parties or from similar contracts used in the trade.

Attention shall be paid to distinguish an offer and an **invitation to offer (invitation to deal)**[2]. The laws of some members hold that a public advertisement cannot create the power of acceptance. In Germany, for example, advertisements addressed to the public in general are mere invitations to offer. The United States, while treating most advertisements as mere invitation to offer, do recognize that specific advertisements that describe the goods, their quantity and price may be considered as an offer. In China, under its civil code, an invitation to offer is a manifestation that a person expects another person to make an offer to him. Auction announcements, bidding announcements, stock prospectuses, bond prospectuses, fund prospectuses, commercial advertisements and promotions, mailed price catalogs, and the like, are invitations to offer. A commercial advertisement and promotion constitute an offer if their content satisfies the conditions for an offer (Article 473)[3]. It seems the *CISG* takes a middle way by providing that an advertisement or circular is not an offer unless the contrary is clearly indicated by the person making the proposal. Thus, in international commercial practice, a seller may want to include a notice in all of its price catalogues and literatures that the material does not constitute an offer.

CISG Article 14 provides the requirements for an offer, and the three following articles concern the **withdrawal**, **revocation,** and **termination of an offer**. Many of these provisions are more similar to the civil law models in substance and language than to comparable common law models. Withdrawal of an offer is permissible only before or at the same time as the offer is received by the offeree. After such receipt, the only recourse of the offeror is to attempt to revoke the offer. Under *CISG*, any attempt to revoke an offer must be received by the offeree before the offeree has dispatched an acceptance. However, not all offers are revocable. There are two ways in which an offer can become irrevocable under Article 16. (a) through the offeror's statements. An offeror can indicate that an offer is irrevocable "by stating a fixed time for acceptance or otherwise." (b) through reasonable

1.《联合国国际货物销售合同公约》第14条：（1）向一个或一个以上特定的人提出的订立合同的建议，如果十分确定并且表明要约人在得到承诺时承受约束，即构成要约。一个建议如果写明货物并且明示或暗示地规定数量和价格或规定如何确定数量和价格，即为十分确定。（2）不是向一个或一个以上特定的人提出的建议，仅应视为邀请做出要约，除非提出建议的人明确地表示相反的意向。

2. invitation to offer (invitation to deal)：要约邀请。

3.《中华人民共和国民法典》第473条：要约邀请是希望他人向自己发出要约的表示。拍卖公告、招标公告、招股说明书、债券募集办法、基金招募说明书、商业广告和宣传、寄送的价目表等为要约邀请。商业广告和宣传的内容符合要约条件的，构成要约。

reliance by the offeree.[1] The first of these two approaches incorporates civil law norms, while the second applies common law norms. The criteria for irrevocability of an offer after reasonable reliance on the offer under Article 16(2)(b) seem to follow the United States case law and the *Second Restatement of Contracts*. Article 17 states that an offer, even if it is irrevocable, is terminated when a rejection reaches the offeror.[2]

B. The Acceptance

A contract comes into being at the time an offer is accepted. The *CISG* requires no particular form for acceptance; it only requires that the offeree communicates his assent (by statement or other conduct) to the offeror within the time period specified in the offer (if any). If no time period is given, then the offeree is given a "reasonable" time within which to accept. It is very common for a would-be buyer to place an order to purchase goods (an offer) but the seller responds simply by shipping the goods required, not by verbal or written confirmation. However, the general rule in most countries is that the offeree's silence should not be interpreted as an acceptance. That is, if you unexpectedly receive goods that you don't order, you should not have the duty to pay them. It would be unfair if a seller could force you to take goods simply by stating: "If I don't hear from you, I will assume you will take these goods and pay for them." Nevertheless, an exception will come up when the previous dealings between the parties entitle one party to interpret the other's silence as acceptance. For instance, during the past six years, Company A regularly purchased raw materials from Company B. At first, Company B confirmed all the orders. Soon, for cost-saving purpose, Company B stopped sending any confirmation and just shipped within one month. This time, Company A placed the order but Company B never shipped. Thus Company A suffered damages when unexpectedly running out the raw material. Company A can sue Company B for breach of contract on the basis of the established practice of the acceptance.

Under *CISG*, an acceptance is not effective until it reaches the offeror ("**Receipt Rule**"[3]). Thus, the offeree may withdraw the acceptance any time before or at the same time as the acceptance reaches the offeror. Here "reach" means the acceptance is made orally to the addressee or delivered by any other means to him personally, to his place of business or mailing address. In case that he does not have a place of business or mailing address, to his habitual residence (Article 24)[4]. Partly due to the undeveloped status of information technology in the 1980's, *CISG* does not define the meaning of "reach" where the electronic means such as e-mail is used to make an acceptance. For this point, the provision of Article 137 in the *Civil Code of the People's Republic of China* may furnish some help. The second paragraph of this article states: "An expression of intent made in a form other than a real-time

---

1.《联合国国际货物销售合同公约》第 16 条（2）：但在下列情况下，要约不得撤销：（a）要约写明接受要约的期限或以其他方式表示要约是不可撤销的；或（b）被要约人有理由信赖该项要约是不可撤销的，而且被要约人已本着对该项要约的信赖行事。

2.《联合国国际货物销售合同公约》第 17 条：一项要约，即使是不可撤销的，于拒绝通知送达要约人时终止。

3. "Receipt Rule"：到达生效原则。承诺应于到达要约人时才生效，合同于此时才成立。许多大陆法系国家及《联合国国际货物销售合同公约》都采用此原则。

4.《联合国国际货物销售合同公约》第 24 条：……"送达"对方，系指用口头通知对方或通过任何其他方法送交对方本人，或其营业地或通信地址，如无营业地或通信地址，则送交对方惯常居住地。

communication becomes effective from the time it reaches the person to whom the intent is expressed. Where such an expression of intent is made through an electronic data message and the person to whom the intent is expressed has designated a specific data-receiving system, it becomes effective from the time such a data message enters that system; where no data-receiving system is specifically designated, it becomes effective from the time the person to whom the intent is expressed knows or should have known that the data message has entered the system. Where the parties have agreed otherwise on the effective time of the expression of intent made in the form of an electronic data message, such an agreement shall prevail."[1]

The Receipt Rule under *CISG* allows the offeree to speculate for a day or two while the offeror is bound when an acceptance is sent by a slow transmission method. However, on the other hand, the offeror's power to revoke the offer under *CISG* is terminated upon dispatch of the acceptance [Article 16 (1)].

Under *CISG*, the rules for the effectiveness of acceptance follow the basic rules in effect in China[2] and the civil law countries. They are different from those rules established by the common law. Under the common law, the acceptance becomes effective when the acceptance is dispatched by the offeree ("**Mailbox Rule**"[3]). In case of an acceptance made by letter, the time of dispatch is the time the letter is put into the hands of the postal authority. This rule makes some sense. A seller of fresh flowers may expect the contract to be formed upon the dispatch of the acceptance rather than wait until the arrival of acceptance. However, it also means the offeree may not have any opportunity to regret by withdrawing the acceptance once the acceptance is dispatched.

For the late acceptance, it is effective if without delay the offeror orally informs the offeree or dispatches a notice to that effect. In simple words, when the offeror receives a late acceptance, it is at his option to make the late acceptance effective or not. If the offeror does not, without delay, orally informs or dispatches a notice to the offeree to show that he would like to accept the late acceptance, the late acceptance will be ineffective. Under the circumstances in which an acceptance would have reached the offeror in due time if its transmission had been normal, the late acceptance will be presumed to be effective unless, without delay, the offeror orally informs the offeree that he considers his offer as having lapsed or dispatches a notice to that effect.[4]

1.《中华人民共和国民法典》第137条：以对话方式作出的意思表示，相对人知道其内容时生效。以非对话方式作出的意思表示，到达相对人时生效。以非对话方式作出的采用数据电文形式的意思表示，相对人指定特定系统接收数据电文的，该数据电文进入该特定系统时生效；未指定特定系统的，相对人知道或者应当知道该数据电文进入其系统时生效。当事人对采用数据电文形式的意思表示的生效时间另有约定的，按照其约定。

2.《中华人民共和国民法典》第484条：以通知方式作出的承诺，生效的时间适用本法第一百三十七条的规定。承诺不需要通知的，根据交易习惯或者要约的要求作出承诺的行为时生效。

3. Mailbox Rule：投邮生效原则。英美法系国家对合同的承诺何时生效所采用的原则，即凡是以信件、电报等作出承诺的，承诺的函电一经投邮、派发，立即生效。

4.《联合国国际货物销售合同公约》第21条：（1）逾期承诺仍有承诺的效力，如果要约人毫不迟延地口头或书面将此种意见通知被要约人。（2）如果载有逾期承诺的信件或其他书面文件表明，它是在传递正常，本可及时送达要约人的情况下寄发的，则该项逾期承诺具有承诺的效力，除非要约人毫不迟延地用口头或书面通知被要约人：他认为他的要约已经失效。

C. Battle of Forms[1]

In the commercial reality, a contract is often formed after several rounds of negotiation. The chains of correspondence or exchange of documents between the seller and the buyer often make it difficult to tell which one is the offer and which one is the acceptance. Most countries follow the **mirror image rule**[2]. The rule requires that the terms in an acceptance shall match the terms of the offer exactly and unequivocally. Under this rule, a purported acceptance that contains different or additional terms is considered a counteroffer and thus a new offer. The requirements under the mirror image rule present special problems when both parties negotiate back and forth via standard business forms such as purchase order or order confirmation. According to the mirror image rule, if the buyer's purchase order form and the seller's order confirmation form differ in any term, there will be no acceptance. Instead, there is a counteroffer and a rejection of the original offer. Thus, theoretically, the parties cannot "conclude" a contract by exchanging conflicting forms; and if one party reneges on its obligations, before the performance, it probably is not bound to perform. However, a vast majority of transactions involving exchanges of such conflicting forms are performed by the parties. Once the goods have been shipped, accepted and paid for, there has been a transaction, and a contract underlying that transaction has been formed by the parties. Then what are its terms? To put the same question in a different way, is the seller's shipment of the goods "conduct" which accepts the terms in the buyer's purchase order? Or, is the buyer's acceptance and payment for the goods "conduct" which accepts the terms in the seller's confirmation form? When such a problem occurs, lawyers in common law countries often call it in a vivid way: "battle of forms".

The common law analysis would make the terms of the form last sent to another party controlling since that last form (usually the seller's) would be a counteroffer and a rejection and termination of all prior unaccepted offers. It may be worth noting that both the United States and civil law countries have developed more sophisticated methods of dealing with the "battle of the forms" than the "mirror-image" rule followed by the **"last shot" principle**[3], but they each use different mechanisms. *CISG* drafters seemed to agree that the mirror-image and last-shot doctrines should not be resurrected, and thus there are more sophisticated tools to resolve the "battle of forms" under *CISG*.

Article 19(1) of the *CISG* establishes the mirror image rule as a general doctrine. However, as an express exception to the mirror image rule, Article 19(2) provides that a non-mirror image response can be an acceptance if it contains additional or different terms, which do not materially alter the terms of the offer. Here **"materially alter"** is defined in the last paragraph of Article 19, and would include **any term, which relates to "the price, payment, quality and quantity of the goods, place and time of delivery, extent of one party's liability to the other or the settlement of disputes."**[4] This list is so

---

1. Battle of Forms：格式之争。在销售合同订立的过程中，买卖双方交换的表单中附带的条款不一致，形成可能的纠纷，有时僵持不下。

2. mirror image rule：镜像原则。买卖双方条件必须完全吻合（双方达成共识）才能构成合同的法律原则。

3. "last shot" principle：最后一枪原则。据此，在格式之争中适用最后一方的表单。第一份表单为要约，而第二份表单为反要约，则送货、收货行为视为对反要约的承诺。

4.《联合国国际货物销售合同公约》第 19 条：（1）对要约表示接受但载有添加、限制或其他更改的答复，即为拒绝该项要约，并构成反要约。（2）然而，对要约表示接受但载有额外或不同条件的答复，如所载的额外或不同条件在实质上并不变更该项要约的条件，则除要约人在不过分迟延的期间内以口头或书面通知反对其间的差异外，仍构成承诺。如果要约人不做出这种反对，合同的条件就以该项要约的条件以及承诺中所载的更改为准。（3）有关货物价格、付款、货物质量和数量、交货地点和时间、一方当事人对另一方当事人的赔偿责任范围或对争端的解决等的额外或不同条件，均视为在实质上变更要约的条件。

broad that almost any term could conceivably be interpreted as "material". A purported acceptance that contains additional or different terms that do materially alter the terms of the offer would constitute a rejection of the offer and a counteroffer. However, under *CISG*, an acceptance containing new terms that do not materially alter the terms of the offer becomes a part of the contract unless the offeror promptly objects to the change. Suppose that a German Company, Pillow International Inc. sends a purchase order to Fort, a U.S. supplier of feathers. Fort replies with a confirmation adding a clause that a charge of 1 percent per month will be applied to the outstanding balances if the account is not paid within thirty days. Pillow International Inc. said nothing more. If the seller (Fort) ships, it might not have recourse against Pillow for refusing the goods. Because under *CISG*, the new term has materially altered the terms in the offer, and the confirmation made by Fort constitutes a counteroffer to Pillow's purchase order, thus no contract is formed to protect the seller.

6.2　Seller's Obligations

A seller is required to deliver the goods, hand over any documents relating to them, and transfer the property in the goods.[1] In fact, *CISG* just provides basic rules for these obligations and leaves most of the things to be determined by the contractual terms.

A. Obligations of Delivery

"Delivery" under *CISG* is a limited concept, relating to transfer of possession or control of the goods. The *CISG* draftsmen do not attempt to consolidate all the aspects of the sale - physical delivery, passing of risk of loss, passing of title, etc. into a single concept or make them turn on a single event, as has been done in many sales statutes. Instead, they provide separate provisions for each of these concepts.

As to **the place of delivery**, *CISG* recognizes four distinct types of delivery: (1) Destination contracts or delivery contracts in which the seller must deliver to the place specified in the contract; (2) shipment contracts, in which the contract "involves carriage of the goods," but does not require delivery to any particular place; (3) sales of goods at a known location which are not expected to be transported; and (4) sales of goods whose location is not known or specified, and which are not expected to be transported.[2]

In "destination" or delivery contracts, the seller may be obligated to deliver the goods to the buyer's place, or to any location specified in the contract. However, it should be noted that *CISG* has no provisions directly describing the seller's duties in such contracts, and all interpretation is left to contract

---

1.《联合国国际货物销售合同公约》第 30 条：卖方必须按照合同和本公约的规定，交付货物，移交一切与货物有关的单据并转移货物所有权。

2.《联合国国际货物销售合同公约》第 31 条和第 32 条。第 31 条：如果卖方没有义务在任何其他特定地点交付货物，他的交货义务如下：（a）如果销售合同涉及货物的运输，卖方应把货物移交给第一承运人，以运交给买方；（b）在不属于上一款规定的情况下，如果合同指的是特定货物或从特定存货中提取的或尚待制造或生产的未经特定化的货物，而双方当事人在订立合同时已知道这些货物是在某一特定地点，或将在某一特定地点制造或生产，卖方应在该地点把货物交给买方处置；（c）在其他情况下，卖方应在他于订立合同时的营业地把货物交给买方处置。第 32 条（2）：如果卖方有义务安排货物的运输，他必须订立必要的合同，以按照通常运输条件，用适合的运输工具，把货物运到指定地点。

terms only. The goods must be conforming when delivered not merely when shipped, unless performance is excused by force majeure.

In a shipment contract, the seller has no obligation to accomplish delivery of goods to their destination, or to any particular place, but it is clear that transportation of the goods by an independent third-party carrier is involved. The usual reference for such a contract is through trade terms like "FOB" or "CIF". Since the goods are to be "handed over" to the carrier and not to the buyer, transactions involving carriage by the buyer seem to be excluded. The shipment contract may require the seller to take more than one action to accomplish its obligation of "delivery".First, the seller must transfer ("hand over") the goods to a carrier—the first carrier. There is no duty under *CISG* for the seller to arrange for the carriage of the goods. It is trade terms that may impose such a duty. Second, depending upon the sale contract terms, the seller must either "effect insurance" coverage of the goods during transit or, at the buyer's request, provide the buyer with all available information necessary to effect insurance. Third, if the goods are not "clearly identified to the contract" by the shipping documents or by their own markings, the seller must notify the buyer of the consignment specifying the goods. Finally, the contract may require the seller to arrange for the transportation of the goods, in which case the seller must contract for "appropriate" carriage under "usual terms".

Where carriage of the goods is not "involved," the buyer may or may not be told where the goods are or will be. Absent a contrary provision in the contract, in such a transaction, if the buyer is told the location of the goods, he is expected to pick them up at that location; otherwise at the seller's place of business. The seller's obligation under *CISG* is to put the goods "at the buyer's disposal" at the appropriate place.

As to **the time of delivery**, as stated in *CISG*, it all relates to the contract terms: The goods must be delivered on or before a stated or determinable date set in the contract, or within a stated or determinable span of time specified in the contract, or, if no date or span of time is set, within a "reasonable time" after the conclusion of the contract.[1] "Reasonable time" is not defined, and will depend on trade usage, but at least it precludes demands for immediate delivery.

If the seller is bound to **hand over documents relating to the goods**, *CISG* requires the seller to hand over the documents at the time and place and in the form required by the contract. If the seller has handed over documents before that time, he may, up to that time, cure any lack of conformity in the documents, if the exercise of this right does not cause the buyer unreasonable inconvenience or unreasonable expense. However, the buyer retains any right to claim damages as provided for in *CISG*.[2]

CISG has no provisions concerning the seller's duties in regard to export and import licenses and taxes but leaves the determination of these incidents of delivery to the contract terms or usage. Where

---

1.《联合国国际货物销售合同公约》第 33 条：卖方必须按以下规定的日期交付货物：(a) 如果合同规定有日期，或从合同可以确定日期，应在该日期交货；(b) 如果合同规定有一段时间，或从合同可以确定一段时间，除非情况表明应由买方选定一个日期外，应在该段时间内任何时候交货；或者(c) 在其他情况下，应在订立合同后一段合理时间内交货。

2.《联合国国际货物销售合同公约》第 34 条：如果卖方有义务移交与货物有关的单据，他必须按照合同所规定的时间、地点和方式移交这些单据。如果卖方在那个时间以前已移交这些单据，他可以在那个时间到达前纠正单据中任何不符合同规定的情形。但是，此一权利的行使不得使买方遭受不合理的不便或承担不合理的开支。而且，买方保留本公约所规定的要求损害赔偿的任何权利。

these issues are not covered by the contract terms or usage, the concepts are to be interpreted according to the general principles of *CISG*.

B. Obligations of Quality of the Goods

Under *CISG*, **the seller has the obligation to deliver goods of the quantity, quality, description and packaging required by the contract.**[1] In determining whether the quality of the goods conforms to the contract, *CISG* neither draws on the concept of "warranty" from the common law analysis, nor the concepts of "fault" or "negligence" from civil law. Instead, *CISG* focuses on the simpler concept that the seller is obligated to deliver the goods as described in the contract and then elaborates on the connotations of that contractual description.

The basic requirements that the goods conform to the contract description are: That the goods are fit for ordinary use, that they are fit for any particular use made known to the seller, that the goods are properly packaged, and that they conform to any goods which seller has held out as a sample or model. Each of these obligations, however, arises out of the contract, so that the parties may "agree otherwise" and limit the seller's obligations concerning quality. [2]

There are no conditions on the imposition on the seller of the obligation of fitness for ordinary use. For example, in a contract for wine purchase, the wine delivered by the seller become chaptalized (it turned to vinegar). Because the chaptalized wine is obviously not fit for the ordinary use of it—be sold as drinking wine. Thus, the seller has breached the contract.

The obligation of fitness for a particular purpose arises only if (1) the buyer makes the particular purpose known to the seller (expressly or impliedly) at or before the "conclusion of the contract"; (2) the buyer also relies on seller's skill and judgment; and (3) such reliance is reasonable. There is no express requirement that the buyer inform the seller of the buyer's reliance, but only that the buyer informs the seller of the particular purpose. More importantly, there is no requirement that the buyer inform the seller of any of the difficulties, which the buyer may know are involved in designating or designing goods to accomplish this particular use. However, it is likely that courts can avoid any abuse of these gaps in the statute by the "reasonable reliance" criterion.

Seller is relieved of any of the obligations under Article 35(2) against defects in quality whenever buyer is aware or "could not have been unaware" of a defect at the time the contract is "concluded".[3] However, knowledge gained at the time of delivery or inspection of the goods will not affect seller's obligation, as the "could not have been unaware" language is the subject of much dispute among common law and civil law authorities. Most common law authorities consider it to be "subjective" and relate to buyer's actual state of mind, rather than to impose "constructive knowledge" on the buyer for

---

1.《联合国国际货物销售合同公约》第 35 条（1）：卖方交付的货物必须与合同所规定的数量、质量和规格相符，并须按照合同所规定的方式装箱或包装。

2.《联合国国际货物销售合同公约》第 35 条（2）：除双方当事人业已另有协议外，货物除非符合以下规定，否则即为与合同不符：（a）货物适用于同一规格货物通常使用的目的；（b）货物适用于订立合同时曾明示或默示地通知卖方的任何特定目的，除非情况表明买方并不依赖卖方的技能和判断力，或者这种依赖对他是不合理的；（c）货物的质量与卖方向买方提供的货物样品或样式相同；（d）货物按照同类货物通用的方式装箱或包装，如果没有此种通用方式，则按照足以保全和保护货物的方式装箱或包装。

3.《联合国国际货物销售合同公约》第 35 条（3）：如果买方在订立合同时知道或者不可能不知道货物不符合同，卖方就无须按上一款（a）项至（d）项负有此种不符合同的责任。

items he should have learned. In practice, the usual dispute seems to arise out of the sale of used goods, where the courts refuse to allow claims for defects, which are not notified to the buyer, but which seem to be predictable for such goods.

Under *CISG*, a seller is generally not obligated to supply goods that conform to the public laws and regulations in the buyer's state. However, there are at least three exceptions to this general rule. First, if those laws and regulations are identical to those in the seller's state, the goods must conform to them. Second, if the buyer informs the seller about the laws and regulations in its state, the goods must conform to them. Third, if the seller know or should have known of the laws and regulations in the buyer's state due to special circumstances, such as having a branch office in the buyer's state, then the goods must conform to them.

How long do these obligations of delivering conforming goods continue? Under *CISG*, even after the risk of loss has passed to the buyer, the seller is still liable for the nonconformity of goods, which exists at the time the risk of loss passes, even if such nonconformity is discovered later.[1] Thus, the buyer is still able to recover for any nonconformity, which becomes apparent long after delivery, but the buyer may have to prove that the defect is present at delivery and is not caused by the buyer's use, maintenance or protection of the goods.

If the goods are defective, the seller may have **a disclosure obligation**. Under Article 40 there is an obligation to notify the buyer of any nonconformity not only if known to the seller, but also if "he could not have been unaware. " If the seller does know of a defect and does not notify, then the seller may not be able to rely on the buyer's failure to inspect the goods quickly or to notify seller of any discovered defects. Thus, even though the buyer may lose its right to rely on a nonconformity because the buyer did not inspect the goods "within as short a time as is practicable or did not notify the seller of any defects, specifying the nature of the defects, within a reasonable time after it discovered or "ought to have discovered" them, the buyer's right to rely on the nonconformity revives if the seller, in turn, knew of the nonconformity and did not notify the buyer of it. However, in any event, the buyer loses the right to rely on a lack of conformity of the goods if he does not give the seller notice within a period of two years from the date on which the goods were actually handed over to the buyer.

Can the seller exclude these obligations concerning the quality of the goods by terms in the contract? *CISG* Article 6 states that the parties may, by agreement, derogate from any provision of the Convention, and Article 35(2) supports that ability to limit obligations concerning the quality of the goods.

C. Obligations of Property Issues

Even though *CISG* Art. 4(b) states that the *CISG* is not concerned with property or title to the goods sold, *CISG* does impose obligations on sellers that **the goods should be sold free from any right or claim of a third party, unless the buyer agreed to take the goods subject to that right or claim.**[2] Seller's obligation concerning title to the goods under *CISG* is to deliver the goods not only free from any encumbrances on their title but also free from any claim of a third party. The legal issue

---

1.《联合国国际货物销售合同公约》第 36 条（1）：卖方应按照合同和本公约的规定，对风险转移到买方时所存在的任何不符合同情形，负有责任，即使这种不符合同情形在该时间后方始明显。

2.《联合国国际货物销售合同公约》第 41 条：卖方所交付的货物，必须是第三方不能提出任何权利或要求的货物，除非买方同意在这种权利或要求的条件下，收取货物。但是，如果这种权利或要求是以工业产权或其他知识产权为基础的，卖方的义务应依照第 42 条的规定。

is whether *CISG* language should be interpreted to require that seller convey title that is free from all claims, or only title that is free from valid claims. The language in the English version is not clear and, the debates and legislative history suggest conflicting interpretations, but the language in the French and Spanish versions suggest that the goods are to be free from all claims. There are no *CISG* cases yet which analyze the issue. The parties may derogate from the terms of these provisions of *CISG* by agreement, but the buyer's knowledge that the goods are subject to a bailee's lien does not necessarily imply such an agreement. Instead, the buyer may expect the seller to discharge the lien before delivery.

In addition to good title, the **seller is obligated to deliver the goods free from patent, trademark and copyright claims under the law of the buyer's "place of business" or the place where both parties expect the goods to be used or resold.** This obligation is, however, subject to multiple qualifications. First, the seller's obligations arise only with respect to claims of which "seller knew or could not have been unaware." Second, the seller has no obligation with respect to intellectual property rights or claims of which buyer had knowledge when the contract was formed, Third, the seller is not liable for claims which arise out of its use of technical drawings, designs or other specifications furnished by the buyer, if the seller's action is in "compliance with" buyer's specifications. Fourth, seller is excused from these obligations if the buyer does not give notice to the seller specifying the claim of the third party within a reasonable time unless the seller knows of the claim, which knowledge may be required in order to create liability initially. With all these qualifications on the seller's obligation, does the mere assertion of an intellectual property infringement claim create a violation of seller's title obligations? In order to have a violation, the buyer must show that "seller knew or could not have been unaware" the third party claims.[1] One survey of the legislative history concludes that it does not require the seller to research the trademark and copyright registries of the buyer's country, but only requires seller to use due care.

6.3   Buyer's Obligations

Buyer has two primary obligations in a sale contract under *CISG*: To pay the price, and to take delivery of the goods (Article 53)[2]. The former duty is more important than the latter.

1.《联合国国际货物销售合同公约》第 42 条。(1) 卖方所交付的货物, 必须是第三方不能根据工业产权或其他知识产权主张任何权利或要求的货物, 但以卖方在订立合同时已知道或不可能不知道的权利或要求为限, 而且这种权利或要求根据以下国家的法律规定是以工业产权或其他知识产权为基础的:(a) 如果双方当事人在订立合同时预期货物将在某一国境内转售或做其他使用, 则根据货物将在其境内转售或做其他使用的国家的法律; 或者(b) 在任何其他情况下, 根据买方营业地所在国家的法律。(2) 卖方在上一款中的义务不适用于以下情况:(a) 买方在订立合同时已知道或不可能不知道此项权利或要求; 或者(b) 此项权利或要求的发生, 是由于卖方要遵照买方所提供的技术图样、图案、程式或其他规格。《联合国国际货物销售合同公约》第 43 条内容如下。(1) 买方如果不在已知道或理应知道第三方的权利或要求后一段合理时间内, 将此一权利或要求的性质通知卖方, 就丧失援引第 41 条或第 42 条规定的权利。(2) 卖方如果知道第三方的权利或要求以及此一权利或要求的性质, 就无权援引上一款的规定。

2.《联合国国际货物销售合同公约》第 53 条: 买方必须按照合同和本公约规定支付货物价款和收取货物。

A. Obligations of Payment

Unless the sales contract expressly grants credit to the buyer, the sale is a cash sale, and payment and delivery are concurrent conditions. Payment is due when the seller places the goods, or their documents of title, "at buyer's disposal according to the contract". If the sales contract involves carriage of the goods, the seller may ship the goods under negotiable documents of title and demand payment against those documents, even though no particular method of payment was actually agreed upon by the parties. In such circumstances, the buyer still has a right of inspection before payment. If, however, the buyer has expressly agreed to "pay against documents" (such as using CFR or CIF term), the buyer has agreed to pay upon handing over of the documents, regardless of whether the goods have yet arrived, and without inspection of the goods.

If the buyer is to pay against "handing over" of the documents or handing over the goods, the place of "handing over" is the place of payment. Otherwise, **the place of the seller's business is the place of payment unless the contract provides otherwise**.[1] Such a provision requires the buyer to "export" the funds to the seller, which is a critical issue when the buyer is from a country with a "soft" currency, or with other restrictions on the international transfer of funds. In addition, the buyer has an obligation to cooperate and take all necessary steps to enable payment, including whatever formalities are imposed by the buyer's country to obtain administrative authorization to make a payment abroad.[2] Failure to take such steps may create a breach by the buyer even before payment is due.

The buyer's second obligation, to take delivery, also imposes duties of cooperation. The buyer must not only take over the goods but also do everything that could reasonably be expected in order to enable the seller to make delivery.[3] This includes a duty to make the expected preparations to permit the seller to make delivery and may include such acts as providing for containers, transportation, unloading and import licenses.

B. Obligations of Inspection and Notice of Defects[4]

The buyer has a right to inspect the goods before taking delivery and a duty to notify the seller of any nonconformity of the goods. Where the contract involves the carriage of goods, the buyer may defer the inspection until the goods have arrived at their destination.[5] Timeliness of inspection is important, and several decisions hold that the buyer is not permitted to pass the goods on to sub-purchasers and await their complaints, but has a duty to inspect the goods immediately when

---

1.《联合国国际货物销售合同公约》第 57 条（1）：如果买方没有义务在任何其他特定地点支付价款，他必须在以下地点向卖方支付价款，（a）卖方的营业地；或者（b）如凭移交货物或单据支付价款，则为移交货物或单据的地点。

2.《联合国国际货物销售合同公约》第 54 条：买方支付价款的义务包括根据合同或任何有关法律和规章规定的步骤和手续，以便支付价款。

3.《联合国国际货物销售合同公约》第 60 条：买方收取货物的义务如下，（a）采取一切理应采取的行动，以期卖方能交付货物；和（b）接收货物。

4. Notice of Defects：缺陷通知。就产品等存在的不符合合同约定或法律规定的缺陷，向销售者发出的通知，通常为提起索赔程序的前提。

5.《联合国国际货物销售合同公约》第 38 条（1）和第 38 条（2）。（1）买方必须在按情况实际可行的最短时间内检验货物或由他人检验货物。（2）如果合同涉及货物的运输，检验可推迟到货物到达目的地后进行。

they arrive.

The buyer may also have a natural incentive to inspect at the place of delivery because the goods must be conforming at the time the risk passes, which will be at the place or port of shipment in the usual FCA, FOB or CIF contract. There are numerous specialized inspection companies that will, for a fee, inspect goods for a distant buyer.

The buyer must notify the seller within a reasonable time after the buyer discovers any nonconformity. The notice must specify the nature of the lack of conformity. If, without a reasonable excuse, it fails to duly notify the seller, the buyer may not rely on the lack of conformity in any remedy proceeding.[1]

The contract may include such terms as a provision on how many days the buyer will have to inspect, where the inspection will take place, how many days the buyer will have to notify the seller of the defects, how and where the notice is to be sent, and a statement as to when the specification of a defect is sufficient.

If the seller delivers nonconforming goods, it will often wish to cure any defects in the goods delivered. It is for that reason that *CISG* requires early notice by the buyer to the seller of any defects in the goods. *CISG* has different rules for cure, which depend upon whether the defects are discovered before or after the contract date for delivery.

Where non-conforming goods are delivered before the contract date for delivery, the seller has the right to remedy any lack of conformity, "provided that the exercise of this right does not cause the buyer unreasonable inconvenience or unreasonable expense". The cure may be repair, replacement or making up a shortage in quantity. Even if the seller cures the nonconformity, it is still liable to the buyer for any damages caused by the defects.[2] If the buyer prohibits the seller from attempting a cure, that is a breach of the buyer's obligations, so the buyer will be responsible for any damages, which arise from not permitting the cure.

Even **after the date for delivery has passed**, the seller may remedy the non-conformity but its right to do so is subject to more conditions. In addition to not causing the buyer unreasonable inconvenience or unreasonable expense, the seller must cure without unreasonable delay. Unlike the specific references in *CISG* Article 37 to various ways in which a nonconformity delivery might be remedied, *CISG* Article 48[3] says only that the seller may remedy any failure. If asked whether it will accept the cure, the buyer apparently has the option to say "No". If the buyer does so and the seller proceeds nevertheless to make a conforming delivery, the buyer would not be obligated to accept the

---

1.《联合国国际货物销售合同公约》第 39 条（1）：买方对货物不符合同，必须在发现或理应发现不符情形后一段合理时间内通知卖方，说明不符合同情形的性质，否则就丧失声称货物不符合同的权利。

2.《联合国国际货物销售合同公约》第 37 条：如果卖方在交货日期前交付货物，他可以在那个日期到达前，交付任何缺漏部分或补足所交付货物的不足数量，或交付用以替换所交付不符合同规定的货物，或对所交付货物中任何不符合同规定的情形做出补救，但是，此一权利的行使不得使买方遭受不合理的不便或承担不合理的开支。而且，买方保留本公约所规定的要求损害赔偿的任何权利。

3.《联合国国际货物销售合同公约》第 48 条（1）：在第 49 条的条件下，卖方即使在交货日期之后，仍可自付费用，对任何未履行义务做出补救，但这种补救不得造成不合理的迟延，也不得使买方遭受不合理的不便，或使买方无法确定卖方是否将偿付买方预付的费用。但是，买方保留本公约所规定的要求损害赔偿的任何权利。

delivery. One arbitral award has stated that the seller's right to cure after the delivery date is dependent on the consent of the buyer. If the buyer does agree to the seller's offer of cure, it may not seek a remedy, which is inconsistent with the seller's offered performance, such as avoidance of the contract.

6.4   Risk of Loss

CISG contains provisions that allocate the risk of loss in Article 66-70. **These provisions apply only if the parties don't specify by agreement when the risk of loss passes from seller to buyer.** In business practice, the contract will often contain a term, which expressly allocates the risk of loss, such as "FOB" or "CIF", and such terms supersede the *CISG* provision. If there is no such trade term, under *CISG*, the risk in **a shipment contract** passes to the buyer when the seller completes its delivery obligations, which is **when the goods are "handed over" by the seller to the first carrier**.[1] For example, suppose that a company located in Guangzhou, China enters into a contract for the export of its products to a foreign customer located in New York. The contract simply reads "Seller will handle all transportation charges and arrangements". The seller arranges for a trucking company to pick up the goods and deliver them to Baiyun International Airport, 25 kilometers away from his company. The risk of loss will pass from seller to buyer when the goods are first handed over to the trucking company. If the goods are damaged after that point, on land or in the air, the buyer will bear the loss. However, if the seller uses his or her own vehicle to transport the goods, the seller bears the risk of loss until the goods are handed over to an independent carrier, arranged by the buyer.

In a destination contract, where the contract requires that the seller deliver the goods to the buyer's location, or that seller provide part of the transportation and then "hand the goods over to a carrier at a particular place", **the seller bears the risk of loss to that location or particular place**.[2] Thus, in a contract between a seller in Buffalo, N.Y.US, and a buyer in Beijing, China: (1) in a shipment contract, the risk would pass to the buyer when the goods were delivered to the first carrier in Buffalo; (2) in a destination contract, the seller would bear the risk during transit, and risk would not pass to the buyer until the goods were delivered in Beijing.

If the goods are not to be transported by a carrier (e.g., when the buyer or an agent are close to the seller and will pick up the goods), the risk passes to the buyer when the buyer or an agent picks them up or, if the buyer or an agent is late in doing so, when the goods are "at his disposal" and the delay in picking them up causes a breach of contract.

If the **goods are already in transit when sold, the risk passes when the contract is concluded**.[3] This rule reflects the use of "title" concepts in risk allocation. However, in most situations, title and risk are treated separately. Thus, manipulation of title through the use of title retention clauses or documents

---

1.《联合国国际货物销售合同公约》第 67 条（1）：如果销售合同涉及货物的运输，但卖方没有义务在某一特定地点交付货物，自货物按照销售合同交付给第一承运人以转交给买方时起，风险就移转到买方承担。

2.《联合国国际货物销售合同公约》第 67 条（1）：……如果卖方有义务在某一特定地点把货物交付给承运人，在货物于该地点交付给承运人以前，风险不移转到买方承担。

3.《联合国国际货物销售合同公约》第 68 条：对于在运输途中销售的货物，从订立合同时起，风险就移转到买方承担。

of title, such as negotiable bills of lading, is irrelevant and has no effect on the point of transfer of risk of loss.

6.5 Excused Performance

Under *CISG*, a party's failure to perform an obligation is excused when the following conditions are met. (1) The party's failure to perform the obligation was due to an "impediment" which was **beyond his control**, and which he **could not reasonably foresee** when the contract was made. (2) The party seeking excuse must prove that he could **neither avoid nor overcome** the "impediment" or its consequences.[1] (3) The excuse is available only so long as the impediment continues, and the party seeking excuse must **notify** the other party to the contract both of the "impediment" and of its effect on performance. [2]

Even if the party seeking excuse proves all these elements, it is protected only from damages claims.[3] It is not protected from other remedial actions by the other party, such as avoidance of the contract or restitution of benefits received from the other party or derived from goods received.

This brief summary of the provisions of Article 79 should demonstrate that great weight is placed on the concept of "impediment." In part, that word was chosen by the drafters of *CISG* because it was believed to reflect a requirement of an outside force, which arose to prevent performances, rather than a change in the general economic climate. Thus, economic recessions or increases in inflation rates were not expected to qualify as impediments, and relief has been denied where the price of goods increased by 30%.[4] A buyer is not excused from payment because the funds were stolen from a foreign bank through allegedly criminal conduct. Transferring the funds to the seller is a part of the buyer's obligation and should be at the buyer's risk.[5] Most of the cases involve defaults by the seller's suppliers. The *CISG* provisions establish a high standard for obtaining an excuse when a third party such as the seller's supplier has defaulted. The party to the sales contract (seller) is excused by a default of a third party (supplier) only if both the seller and the supplier can prove they failed due to an impediment, which was beyond their control, unforeseeable, unavoidable and could not overcome.

The language in Article 79 does not, however, resolve the issue of whether it can excuse only a complete failure to perform (deliver or pay for goods), or whether it can also be used to excuse defective performance (late delivery or delivery of non-conforming goods). The debates indicate that it is intended to excuse only the obligation to deliver or pay, and not to include the obligation to deliver conforming goods.

1.《联合国国际货物销售合同公约》第 79 条（1）：当事人要对不履行义务、不负责任免责，必须能证明此种不履行义务，是由于某种非他所能控制的障碍，而且对于这种障碍，没有理由预期他在订立合同时能考虑到或能避免或克服它或它的后果。

2.《联合国国际货物销售合同公约》第 79 条（3）和第 79 条（4）。第 79 条（3）：本条所规定的免责对障碍存在的期间有效。（4）：不履行义务的一方必须将障碍及其对他履行义务能力的影响通知另一方。

3.《联合国国际货物销售合同公约》第 79 条（5）：本条规定不妨碍任一方行使本公约规定的要求损害赔偿以外的任何权利。

4. CLOUT Case No. 54 (1994).

5. UNILEX Case D. 1998-5.2.

Parties that prefer to establish their excuses for performance may incorporate a **force majeure**[1] clause into a contract. The term force majeure means "superior force". A force majeure clause in a contract is an exculpatory clause. It excuses a party from failing to perform on the occurrence of an event specified in the clause. The events included in the clause are determined by the negotiation of the parties. These clauses usually list such events as war, fire, acts of government, acts of Gods, failure to transport, quarantine restrictions, strikes and others. It is advised that force majeure clauses should not just provide for the events as those listed above, but should be tailored to the special nature of the contract and the type of business involved. For example, Force majeure clauses for the steel industry would not be the same as those for the textile industry.

6.6   Remedies for Breach of Contract

Remedies for breach of contract are provided by the laws of almost every country, which are intended to give the parties the benefit they expected to obtain from the contract and to put the parties into the economic position they would have been in, had the breach not occurred. The remedies available to a buyer or seller under *CISG* are drawn from both common law and civil law systems. These remedies include (1) suspension of performance, (2) avoidance of the contract, (3) damages, (4) specific performance, (5) seller's right to cure, (6) seller's additional time to perform and (7) price reduction. The remedies of (1), (2), (5), (6) and (7) may be undertaken without judicial intervention, the other two involve proceedings in court or before an arbitral tribunal. The remedies which do not require judicial intervention are usually preferred by merchants because of their low cost; and merchants, who have traded with each other in the past and hope to do so in the future, are much more likely to use these remedies than to go to court. We organize the discussion of these remedies by following the order in the above list. However, it by no means indicates the varying importance of them in international sales practice.

A. Suspension of Performance[2]

Suspension of Performance is a kind of remedy for the anticipatory breach. **Anticipatory breach** occurs when, before the date for the performance of the contract comes, it becomes apparent that one party to the contract will not perform his obligations or a substantial part of his obligations.

Either party may stop performing (suspend performance) under a contract once it becomes clear that the other party will fail to perform a "substantial part" of his obligations because of a lack of ability, a lack of creditworthiness, or inadequate preparation such as a failure to open a letter of credit or to provide specifications for the goods.[3] If a seller has shipped goods with a carrier and learns that the buyer is insolvent or that there is a serious deficiency in his creditworthiness, the seller may order the carrier not to hand over the goods to the buyer. The provision is neutral between the

---

1. force majeure：不可抗力。指当事人在订立合同时不可预见、无法避免和无法预防的使合同无法履行的事件，包括自然原因所致的，如水灾、旱灾、地震等和社会原因所致的，如战争、罢工、政府禁运等。根据一些国家的法律，当不可抗力存在时，当事人可以被免除履行合同的责任或有权迟延履行合同义务。

2. Suspension of Performance：（合同）履行中止。

3.《联合国国际货物销售合同公约》第 71 条（1）：如果订立合同后，另一方当事人由于下列原因显然将不履行其大部分重要义务，一方当事人可以中止履行义务。（a）他履行义务的能力或他的信用有严重缺陷；或（b）他在准备履行合同或履行合同中的行为显示他将不履行其主要义务。

buyers and the sellers. Thus, a buyer who has agreed to pay, or to prepay, for the goods may suspend that performance if it learns that there is a "serious deficiency" in the seller's ability to perform, or that necessary preparations for performance, including making shipping insurance arrangements or obtaining the proper documents, have not been made.

A party who suspends performance must give reasonable notice to the other party of that suspension in order to permit him to provide adequate assurance. If sufficient adequate assurance has been provided by the other party, the party who suspends performance must continue to perform, otherwise, a breach will be deemed to be committed by the party.[1] Failure to notify triggers the other party's rights to a remedy in accordance with the remedies provisions of *CISG*. None of these remedies authorizes the other party to treat the suspension as ineffective because no notice has been given. However, the non-notified party may have an immediate cause of action for damages.

The *CISG* permits a seller to suspend performance, if possible, after shipment of the goods but before delivery of them—stoppage in transit. The *CISG* provision, however, only deals with rights and duties between the parties to the contract.[2] There is a question concerning whether a carrier will comply with the seller's direction to stop delivery. *CISG* does not require the carrier to do so, and the carrier's obligations are left to other laws (It will be discussed in the next chapter of this book). After the carrier has delivered the goods to the buyer, then it is no longer possible to stop delivery under *CISG*. What the seller would do is to seek other remedies for breach of contract such as damages.

Instead, if, **prior to the date for the performance of the contract, it is clear that one party will not perform his obligations, the other party may avoid (rescind) the contract.**[3] In contrast to the right to suspend, as just discussed, avoiding the contract is allowed where one party will be unable to perform the contract. For example, the seller or the buyer has declared that he will not perform his obligation, or the seller's plant has been burnt down, or an embargo in the seller's country makes it legally impossible to ship the contracted goods. However, the party avoiding the contract also must give a reasonable notice to the other party, unless the other party has declared that he will not perform his obligation.

Similar remedies for anticipatory breach are also provided by *Civil Code of the People's Republic of China*. Article 578 states: "Where one party explicitly expresses or indicates by his act that he will not perform his contractual obligation, the other party may request the former party to bear default liability before the expiration of the time of performance."[4]

B. Avoidance of the Contract

"Avoidance of the contract[5]", a terminology used in *CISG*, is the equivalent of "cancellation of

---

1.《联合国国际货物销售合同公约》第 71 条（3）：中止履行义务的一方当事人不论是在货物发运前还是发运后，都必须立即通知另一方当事人，如经另一方当事人对履行义务提供充分保证，则他必须继续履行义务。

2.《联合国国际货物销售合同公约》第 71 条（2）：如果卖方在上一款所述的理由明显化以前已将货物发运，他可以阻止将货物交付给买方，即使买方持有其有权获得货物的单据。本款规定只与买方和卖方间对货物的权利有关。

3.《联合国国际货物销售合同公约》第 72 条（1）：如果在履行合同日期之前，明显看出一方当事人将违反合同，另一方当事人可以宣告合同无效。

4.《中华人民共和国民法典》第 578 条：当事人一方明确表示或者以自己的行为表明不履行合同义务的，对方可以在履行期限届满之前请求其承担违约责任。

5. Avoidance of the contract：解除合同。

contract". Either buyer or seller can avoid a contract under the conditions that there has been a fundamental breach committed by the other party, and the party avoiding the contract has given notice to the other party within a reasonable time.

What constitutes a "fundamental breach"? Article 25 of *CISG* defines a fundamental breach as one that will "**substantially deprive him of what he is entitled to expect under the contract**".[1] The focus is on the contract and what the non-breaching party is entitled to expect. According to the cases decided under *CISG*, t**he seller's shipment of seriously defective goods that cannot be repaired, or that have no value to the buyer under the contract, is probably a fundamental breach. So too would be the seller's failure and refusal to ship at all or the buyer's failure and refusal to pay. A partial shipment may also constitute a fundamental breach if it presents a serious problem for the buyer, which cannot quickly be solved.** Of course, the further interpretation of fundamental breach will have to be left up to the courts.

In one case, compressors for air conditioning units were delivered which did not have either the cooling capacity or the power consumption contained in the contract specifications. The United States court held that cooling capacity was an important factor in determining the value of air conditioner compressors, so the buyer did not in fact receive the goods that it was entitled to expect.[2]

In another case, the buyer stated that "it was unable to work with" the substandard steel wire delivered by the seller. The German court held that since the buyer was unable to use the goods, the defect was a fundamental breach.[3] However, where the buyer alleged only that the material used in the goods was different from the contract specifications, but did not allege that the goods could not be used or resold, the breach was not considered fundamental.[4]

Where the **installment contract** is involved, there are separate criteria for the avoidance with respect to an individual installment and with respect to the whole contract. For example, a fundamental breach with respect to the first installment might not be a fundamental breach for the whole contract. To declare avoidance with respect to the whole contract, the buyer would have to give "good grounds to conclude" that a fundamental breach will reoccur with respect to future installments.[5]

Given the uncertainty of the "fundamental breach" test, sometimes it will be difficult for the buyer, or the buyer's attorney, to know whether "avoidance of the contract" is permissible or not. *CISG* Article 47[6] and Article 49[7] attempt to cure this uncertainty. If the seller fails to deliver the goods on the agreed

---

1.《联合国国际货物销售合同公约》第 25 条：一方当事人违反合同的结果，如使另一方当事人蒙受损害，以至于实际上剥夺了他根据合同规定有权期待得到的东西，即为根本违反合同……

2. Delchi Carrier V. Rotorex Corp., 71 F. 3d 1024 (2d Cir. 1995).

3. CLOUT Case 235 (Ger.1997).

4. UNILEX Case 1994-2.

5.《联合国国际货物销售合同公约》第 73 条。（1）对于分批交付货物的合同，如果一方当事人不履行对任何一批货物的义务，便对该批货物构成根本违反合同，则另一方当事人可以宣告合同对该批货物无效。（2）如果一方当事人不履行对任何一批货物的义务，使另一方当事人有充分理由断定对今后各批货物将会发生根本违反合同，该另一方当事人可以在一段合理时间内宣告合同今后无效。

6.《联合国国际货物销售合同公约》第 47 条：（1）买方可以规定一段合理时限的额外时间，让卖方履行其义务。

7.《联合国国际货物销售合同公约》第 49 条：（1）买方在以下情况下可以宣告合同无效：（a）卖方不履行其在合同或本公约中的任何义务，等于根本违反合同；或（b）如果发生不交货的情况，卖方不在买方按照第 47 条第（1）款规定的额外时间内交付货物，或卖方声明他将不在所规定的时间内交付货物。

delivery date, the buyer may notify the seller that performance is due by a stated new date (after the contract date for performance), and the seller's failure to perform by the new date permits the buyer to declare the contract avoided. There are similar rules in *CISG* Articles 63[1] and Article 64[2] to protect the seller against the buyer's breach of contract.

C. Damages[3]

CISG Articles 74-78 provide that the aggrieved party (seller or buyer) is entitled to damages for the other party's breach of obligations, and damages can be available when the contract has been "avoided" (cancelled) and even when the defects have been successfully cured. There is no requirement that the aggrieved party should prove that the breaching party was "at fault" as a prerequisite to damage recovery. As long as the aggrieved party can prove that the other party has committed a breach of contract and suffers economic loss from such a breach, courts will grant damages under *CISG*.

The *CISG* provides that a breaching party shall be liable for damages in an amount sufficient to make the aggrieved party whole in the event of a breach. *CISG* Article 74 states that **damages to an aggrieved party shall consist of a sum equal to the loss**. Damages under the *CISG* may also include an amount for lost profits. The **damages for lost profits[4] are limited under *CISG* Article 74 to those losses that "the party in breach foresaw or ought to have foreseen at the time of the conclusion of the contract".[5] (foreseeability rule[6])**

There are some reasons underlying such a rule. In the ordinary breach of contract circumstances, the court will attempt to protect the plaintiff's (the non-breaching party's) expected interests, that is, the court will try to put the plaintiff in the position he would have been in, had the contract been performed. In some circumstances, however, the plaintiff may sustain unusual and great losses as a result of breach of contract. For example, the sender of a telegram may lose a million-dollar deal if the postal office mis-transmits his bid. For a long time, the courts have realized that awarding the plaintiff full compensation for all of his losses due to the breach, no matter how strange or unforeseeable these losses are, would be unfair for the defendant, and would possibly affect the commerce as well. Therefore the courts have developed certain limits on damages that the plaintiff may recover.

The so-called "**foreseeability rule[1]**" originated from the principles established by the famous English case of *Hadley v. Baxendale* (See **Case 6-1**).

1.《联合国国际货物销售合同公约》第 63 条:(1)卖方可以规定一段合理时限的额外时间,让买方履行义务。

2.《联合国国际货物销售合同公约》第 64 条:(1)卖方在以下情况下可以宣告合同无效:(a)买方不履行其在合同或本公约中的任何义务,等于根本违反合同;或(b)买方不在卖方按照第 63 条第(1)款规定的额外时间内履行支付价款的义务或收取货物,或买方声明他将不在所规定的时间内这样做。

3. damages: 损害赔偿,损害赔偿金。意指一方当事人的行为致另一方当事人的人身、财产或权益受损害,从而由前者向后者支付的用以作为赔偿或补偿的金钱。该词可用于指因侵权行为或违约行为而支付的损害赔偿金。

4. damages for lost profits:对违约导致的利润损失的损害赔偿。在普通法和《统一商法典》中常被称为间接损害赔偿或结果损害赔偿(consequential damages)。

5.《联合国国际货物销售合同公约》第 74 条:一方当事人违反合同应负的损害赔偿额,应与另一方当事人因他违反合同而遭受的包括利润在内的损失额相等。这种损害赔偿不得超过违反合同一方在订立合同时,依照他当时已知道或理应知道的事实和情况,对违反合同预料到或理应预料到的可能损失。

6. foreseeability rule: 可预见性原则。合理确定损害赔偿范围的原则,在英美法系又称哈德雷案原则。

【Case 6-1】

Hadley v. Baxendale
9 Exch. 341, 156 Eng. Rep 145 (1854)

BACKGROUNDS AND FACTS

Hadley (Plaintiff) operated a mill which was forced to suspend operations because of a broken shaft. Hadley hired Baxendale (Defendant) to transport the broken mill shaft to another city for an engineer there to make a duplicate. Baxendale knew that the item to be carried was a shaft for Hadley's mill, but was not told that the mill would remain shut down until the new shaft arrived. Baxendale negligently delayed delivery of the shaft. As a result, Hadley's mill was closed for several more days than it would have been. Hadley sued for the profits he lost during these extra days.

DECISION

The court held that Hadley could not recover for the lost profits. In deciding this case, the court established two rules for recovering lost profits: The damages must either (1) arise "naturally, i.e. according to the usual course of things, from the breach of contract itself" or (2) arise from "the special circumstances under which the contract was actually made" if and only if these circumstances "were communicated by the plaintiff to the defendant and thus known to both parties".[1] Another way to express the rules is the court will impute foreseeability to the defendant as to those damages, which any reasonable person should have foreseen, whether or not the defendant actually foresaw them. In this case, an enterprise of a mill might be shut down for lack of a shaft would not normally be foreseen by one in the position of Baxendale. Therefore, the damages did not fall in the first class of "natural" damages. Nor did Hadley give Baxendale notice of the possibility of the continuous shutdown of the mill. Therefore, the damages did not fall in the second class of "special" damages.

The above rules of *Hadley v. Baxendale* were followed and refined in other similar American cases such as *Victoria Laundry Ltd. v. Newman Industries* (1949), *Koufus v. Czarnikow Ltd.* (*The heron II*) (1969), *Parsons v. Uttley Ingham* (1978), etc. And similar foreseeability rule was also developed in civil law countries and incorporated into their civil codes.

Under *Civil Code of the People's Republic of China*, the foreseeability rule is embodied in Article 584. This Article states: "Where a party fails to perform its obligations under the contract or its performance fails to conform to the agreement, thereby causing loss to the other party, the amount of damages payable shall be equal to the other party's loss resulting from the breach, including any benefit that may be accrued from performance of the contract, provided that the amount shall not exceed the likely loss which the breaching party foresaw or should have foreseen at the time of the conclusion of the contract."[2]

---

1. Hadley v. Baxendale, supra note 116, 358 at 359.
2.《中华人民共和国民法典》第 584 条：当事人一方不履行合同义务或者履行合同义务不符合约定，造成对方损失的，损失赔偿额应当相当于因违约所造成的损失，包括合同履行后可以获得的利益，但是，不得超过违约一方订立合同时预见到或者应当预见到的因违约可能造成的损失。

Of course, the parties to contracts for international sale of goods are free to allocate the risks by express agreement in a way different from the foreseeability rule. The parties may agree that the breaching party will not be liable for certain reasonably foreseeable consequences, which would otherwise be deemed foreseeable under the foreseeability rule.

According to *CISG*, a party who relies on a breach of contract (non-breaching party) must take "reasonable measures" to **mitigate its damages**, including loss of profit. For example, when the seller's breach of contract occurs, if similar goods may be purchased in the market, the most usual reasonable measure of the buyer is to buy substitute goods, as a way to mitigate or reduce the losses arising from a breach of contract. To some degree, mitigation of damages is a duty imposed on the non-breaching party by law. This rule is justified by the purpose to encourage the efficient use of economic resources and to avoid the avoidable losses. Since mitigation of damages is a kind of legal duty, liability will be incurred if such a duty is not fulfilled. Article 77 of *CISG* requires that if the non-breaching party fails to take such reasonable measures, the breaching party may claim a reduction in the damages in the amount by which the loss should have been mitigated.[1]

D. Specific Performance

Specific performance[2] is used when a court requires a breaching party to a contract to perform. This remedy is available to both seller and buyer. In case of nonperformance, the seller may petition the court to require the buyer to pay the price, while the buyer may petition the court to require the seller to deliver the goods as required in the contract, rather than claim damages.

In the establishment of the scheme of specific performance, the difficulty facing the drafters of the *CISG* is the fact that specific performance is the preferred remedy in the civil law system, while the action for damages is preferred in the common law system. Under the common law system, specific performance is considered a harsh remedy to be used only when damages cannot be calculated or are inadequate, which may occur when the subject matter of the contract is unique. For instance, in a dispute over the sale of a prized racehorse, a common law court may require the seller to deliver it to the buyer because of the unique nature of the goods. In contrast, the civil law courts prefer the use of specific performance under much more circumstances, without regard to whether monetary damages are inadequate. This reflects the basic civil law theory that legal compulsion of performance is the best relief to the aggrieved buyer and that the seller's actual performance is preferable to substitution relief (such as a monetary award).

CISG draws strongly on the civil law's preference of specific performance as a remedy for breach of contract. Under Article 46 of this Convention, a court may grant specific performance if the following conditions are met: (1) The buyer has not resorted to any "inconsistent" remedy such as avoidance of contract; (2) the seller has failed to deliver or in the case of nonconforming goods, the nonconformity is so serious that it constitutes a fundamental breach; (3) the buyer has given timely notice to the seller that

---

1.《联合国国际货物销售合同公约》第77条：声称另一方违反合同的一方，必须按情况采取合理措施，减轻由于该另一方违反合同而引发的损失，包括利润方面的损失。如果他不采取这种措施，违反合同一方可以要求从损害赔偿中扣除原本可以减轻的损失数额。

2. specific performance：特定履行、强制履行、实际履行。对合同违约的判决救济方法之一，即命令违约方履行合同义务。

the goods are nonconforming; (4) the buyer has made a timely request that the seller should provide substitute goods.[1] However, the above provisions of *CISG* may not have much effect on the use of specific performance in common law countries, because *CISG* has provided a limitation on the party's right to seek specific performance. Article 28 of *CISG* provides that a court needn't grant specific performance unless it would do so under its own law.[2] This article has a negligible effect on civil law courts because they are authorized to order the seller's performance in many more cases. Thus, if specific performance is sought in a civil law court, it will usually apply *CISG* Article 46 and order the seller to perform its obligations.

The *CISG* provision gives the buyer the right to seek specific performance, rather than damages, but does not require it to do so. Thus, any preference for this remedy must arise from the buyer's perspective, not from the court's perspective. In actual fact, even in civil law jurisdictions, buyers may often prefer to recover damages and purchase substitute goods.

There is also a *CISG* provision, which permits a court to issue a specific performance order against a buyer, requiring the buyer to perform its obligations. The preferred remedy for an aggrieved seller, if the buyer breaches, is a cause of action for the price, which is the seller's functional equivalent of action for specific performance. In addition, the seller may wish to reclaim the goods if they are delivered or obtain some protection for them if they are refused. As to the seller's recovery of the price, *CISG* Article 62 gives the seller a right to require the buyer to pay the price unless the seller has resorted to an "inconsistent remedy".[3] Of course, there are implicit conditions on this right, first, that seller has himself performed to the extent required by the terms of the contract and, second, that payment of the price is due.

Under *Civil Code of the People's Republic of China*, Article 579 and Article 580 provide the remedy of specific performance for breach of contract. It states that where a party fails to pay the price, remuneration, rent, or interests, or fails to perform another pecuniary obligation, the other party may request for such payment. Where a party fails to perform a non-pecuniary obligation or his performance does not conform to the agreement, the other party may request for such performance unless: (1) the performance is impossible either *de jure* or *de facto*; (2) the object of the obligation is not suitable for a compulsory performance or the expenses for the performance are too high; or (3) the creditor fails to request for performance within a reasonable period of time. [4]

1.《联合国国际货物销售合同公约》第 46 条（1）和第 46 条（2）。（1）买方可以要求卖方履行义务，除非买方已采取与此一要求相抵触的某种补救办法。（2）如果货物不符合同，买方只有在此种不符合同情形构成根本违反合同时，才可以要求交付替代货物，而且关于替代货物的要求，必须与依照第 39 条发出的通知同时提出，或者在该项通知发出后一段合理时间内提出。

2.《联合国国际货物销售合同公约》第 28 条：如果按照本公约的规定，一方当事人有权要求另一方当事人履行某一义务，法院没有义务做出判决，要求具体履行此一义务，除非法院依照其本身的法律对不属本公约范围的类似销售合同愿意这样做。

3.《联合国国际货物销售合同公约》第 62 条：卖方可以要求买方支付价款、收取货物或履行他的其他义务，除非卖方已采取与此一要求相抵触的某种补救办法。

4.《中华人民共和国民法典》第 579 条和第 580 条。第 579 条，当事人一方未支付价款、报酬、租金、利息，或者不履行其他金钱债务的，对方可以请求其支付。第 580 条，当事人一方不履行非金钱债务或者履行非金钱债务不符合约定的，对方可以请求履行，但是有下列情形之一的除外：（一）法律上或者事实上不能履行；（二）债务的标的不适于强制履行或者履行费用过高；（三）债权人在合理期限内未请求履行。

E. Other Remedies Available under CISG

In addition to refusing to accept goods, which do not conform to the contract, through avoidance of the contract, the aggrieved buyer has another informal remedy, which appears to give it the power of self-help. Under *CISG*, the buyer who receives nonconforming goods "may reduce the price" it pays to the seller. This remedy of price reduction is available whether the buyer has already paid or not. But if the buyer has actually paid, the remedy is likely to require an action in court, rather than self-help.

CISG Article 50[1] spells out a mathematical formula for calculating the permissible amount of the price reduction. The reduction requires a comparison of the value that the goods actually delivered have at the time of that delivery to the value that conforming goods would have had at the time of that actual delivery. There is little guidance in the provision on how to determine the value of the actual goods delivered at the time of delivery, or as to what evidence of value should be sent to the seller. The provision for **price production, therefore, seems better suited to deliveries, which are defective as to quantity, rather than as to quality.** One United States court decision has indicated that, if the buyer resells the defective goods, the resale price is evidence of their value at the time of delivery.

Article 582 of *Civil Code of the People's Republic of China* provides "in circumstances of improper performance of contract, the nonbreaching party may, in light of the nature of the subject matter and the degree of loss, require the other party to assume liabilities for breach by way of repair, replacement, remaking, restitution, or reduction in price or remuneration, etc".[2]

As we have discussed in the part of buyer's obligations, a **seller**, who has delivered some goods to the buyer prior to the delivery date, even if the goods are nonconforming or the shipment is incomplete, **has the right to cure or correct the problem** by sending substitute or replacement goods, if it can be done **before the date for delivery**. The seller maintains this right to cure, and the buyer may not avoid the contract until the time for performance expires. However, Article 37 of *CISG* states that the seller may exercise this right only if it does not cause unreasonable inconvenience or expense to the buyer.

In the event that the seller has failed to deliver the goods, and the time for delivery under the contract has passed, the buyer may grant the seller extra time (a **grace period**[3]) to do so. During this time, the buyer may not avoid the contract. If the seller does not perform within the grace period, the buyer may avoid the contract whether the breach is fundamental or not. Article 48 of *CISG* contains a provision entitling the seller to invoke such a grace period, which allows a seller, who fails to perform on time, or who delivers nonconforming goods, to cure performance if it does not cause the buyer "unreasonable delay" or "unreasonable inconvenience." If a seller asks for a grace period for delivery and the buyer fails to respond within a reasonable time, the seller may perform within the time indicated

---

1.《联合国国际货物销售合同公约》第 50 条：如果货物不符合同，不论价款是否已付，买方都可以减价，减价按实际交付的货物在交货时的价值与符合合同的货物在当时的价值两者之间的比例计算。

2.《中华人民共和国民法典》第 582 条：履行不符合约定的，应当按照当事人的约定承担违约责任。对违约责任没有约定或者约定不明确，依照本法第 510 条的规定仍不能确定的，受损害方根据标的的性质以及损失的大小，可以合理选择请求对方承担修理、重作、更换、退货、减少价款或者报酬等违约责任。

3. grace period：（履行合同的）宽限期。

in his request for grace period.[1] These provisions of *CISG* intend to encourage the parties to stay in their contract rather than to repudiate it in the event of a dispute.

 ## Chapter Summary

本章以《联合国国际货物销售合同公约》为主要法律渊源，具体介绍了有关国际货物销售合同的主要法律知识：

合同的订立。合同于对要约的承诺生效时订立。（1）要约，向一个或一个以上特定的人提出的订立合同的建议，如果十分确定并且表明要约人在得到承诺时承受约束的意旨，即构成要约。一个建议如果写明货物并且明示或暗示地规定数量和价格或规定如何确定数量和价格，即为十分确定。在订立合同之前，要约得予撤销，如果撤销通知于被要约人发出承诺通知之前送达被要约人。一项要约，即使是不可撤销的，得予撤回，如果撤回通知于要约送达被要约人之前或同时，送达被要约人。一项要约，即使是不可撤销的，于拒绝通知送达要约人时终止。（2）承诺，承诺是受要约人同意要约的意思表示。关于承诺的生效，有以下2种不同的原则。（a）到达生效原则：承诺应于到达要约人时才生效，合同于此时才成立。许多大陆法系国家以及《联合国国际货物销售合同公约》都采用此原则。根据此原则，承诺得予撤回，如果撤回通知于承诺原应生效之前或同时，送达要约人；（b）投邮生效原则：英美法系国家对合同的承诺何时生效所采用的原则，即凡是以信件、电报等做出承诺时，承诺的函电一经投邮、拍发，立即生效。（3）表单战争，在销售合同订立的过程中，买卖双方交换的表单中附带的条款不一致，形成可能的纠纷，有时僵持不下。为应对表单战争，形成了镜像原则和最后一枪原则。而《联合国国际货物销售合同公约》则对此另有规定：对要约表示接受但载有额外或不同条件的答复，如所载的额外或不同条件在实质上并不变更该项要约的条件，则仍构成承诺。有关货物价格、付款、货物质量和数量、交货地点和时间、一方当事人对另一方当事人的赔偿责任范围或对争端的解决等的额外或不同条件，均视为在实质上变更要约的条件。

卖方义务。卖方必须交付货物，移交一切与货物有关的单据并转移货物所有权。（1）交付义务：卖方必须按照合同约定或法律规定的时间、地点和方式交付货物，移交一切与货物有关的单据。（2）货物相符义务：卖方交付的货物必须与合同所规定的数量、质量和规格相符，并须按照合同所规定的方式装箱或包装。卖方应按照合同和法律的规定，对风险转移到买方时所存在的任何不符合同情形，负有责任，即使这种不符合同情形在该时间后方始明显。（3）与第三方要求相关的义务：卖方所交付的货物，必须是第三方不能提出任何权利或要求的货物，除非买方同意在这种权利或要求的条件下，收取货物。

买方义务：买方必须支付货物价款和收取货物。（1）付款义务：买方支付价款的义务包括遵从合同或任何有关法律和规章规定的步骤和手续，以便支付价款。（2）检验货物、通知缺陷的义务：买方必须在按情况实际可行的最短时间内检验货物或由他人检验货物。若货物不符合同，买方必须在发现或理应发现不符情形后一段合理时间内通知卖方，说明不符合同情形的性质，否则就丧失声称货物不符合同的权利。

风险转移：《联合国国际货物销售合同公约》中关于风险转移的规定仅在合同双方未就此在合同中具体约定的情况下适用。如国际货物销售合同中采用了"FOB"或"CIF"等《国际贸易术语

1.《联合国国际货物销售合同公约》第 48 条（2）：如果卖方要求买方表明他是否接受卖方履行义务，而买方不在一段合理时间内对此一要求作出答复，则卖方可以按其要求中所指明的时间履行义务。买方不得在该段时间内采取与卖方履行义务相抵触的任何补救办法。

解释通则》中的术语，则以该术语中所包含的风险转移规定为准。

违约免责事由：关于当事人的不履行义务，不负责任，如果他能证明此种不履行义务，是由于某种非他所能控制的障碍，而且对于这种障碍，没有理由预期他在订立合同时能考虑到或能避免或克服它或它的后果。这种免责对障碍存在的期间有效。不履行义务的一方必须将障碍及其对他履行义务能力的影响通知另一方。合同双方可就违约免责事由在合同的不可抗力条款中进行具体约定。

违约救济措施。（1）（合同）履行中止。如果订立合同后，由于下列原因显然可知另一方当事人将不履行其大部分重要义务，则一方当事人可以中止履行义务：（a）他履行义务的能力或他的信用有严重缺陷；或（b）他在准备履行合同或履行合同中的行为显示他将不履行主要义务。中止履行义务的一方当事人不论是在货物发运前还是发运后，都必须立即通知另一方当事人，如经另一方当事人对履行义务提供充分保证，则他必须继续履行义务。（2）废止合同。如果在履行合同日期之前，明显看出一方当事人将根本违反合同，另一方当事人可以宣告合同无效。一方当事人违反合同的结果，如使另一方当事人蒙受损害，以至于实际上剥夺了他根据合同规定有权期待得到的东西，即为根本违反合同。（3）损害赔偿。一方当事人违反合同应负的损害赔偿额，应与另一方当事人因他违反合同而遭受的包括利润在内的损失额相等。这种损害赔偿不得超过违反合同一方在订立合同时，依照他当时已知道或理应知道的事实和情况，对违反合同预料到或理应预料到的可能损失。声称另一方违反合同的一方，必须按情况采取合理措施，减轻由于该另一方违反合同而引发的损失，包括利润方面的损失。如果他不采取这种措施，违反合同一方可以要求从损害赔偿中扣除原本可以减轻的损失数额。（4）实际履行。买方可以要求卖方履行义务，除非买方已采取与此一要求相抵触的某种补救办法。卖方可以要求买方支付价款、收取货物或履行他的其他义务，除非卖方已采取与此一要求相抵触的某种补救办法。（5）其他救济措施。（a）减少价款；（b）卖方交付用以替换所交付不符合同规定的货物；（c）（履行合同的）宽限期。

Exercises

Part Ⅰ. True or False Statements: Decide whether the following statements are True or False and explain why.

1. The parties to a contract may decide when the risk of loss passes, but if the parties do not specifically agree on such time, the *CISG* provides rules for them.

2. The contract contains trade terms, such as "FOB" or "CIF", these terms supersede the CISG provision as to risk of loss.

3. Under *CISG*, a contract of sale needn't be concluded in writing. The contract may be proved by any means including witnesses.

4. Offers can be revoked if the notice to revoke reached the offeree before the acceptance becomes effective under *CISG*.

5. Dramatic increase of inflation can constitute an impediment under the *CISG*, and thus may be invoked by the party as an excuse for nonperformance.

6. To recover the damages for breach of contract, the aggrieved party must prove that the breaching party was at fault if *CISG* applies to the contract.

7. After duly avoiding the contract, the aggrieved party may still seek damages if he can prove that damages have arisen from the fundamental breach committed by the other party.

8. Under the *UN Convention on Contracts for the International Sale of Goods* (CISG), if a party seeking to claim damages fails to mitigate the losses suffered by the other party, the former will not be entitled to any damages at all.

9. A party may suspend performance under a contract once it becomes clear that the other party will fail to perform a substantial part of his obligations because of a lack of ability, or a lack of creditworthiness.

10. Under *Civil Code of the People's Republic of China,* the court will grant specific performance only where the subject matter of the contract is unique goods.

Part Ⅱ. Multiple Choices: Choose the best answer from the multiple choices.

1. A party is excused for a failure to perform a contract if he proves that the failure

A. was due to an event beyond his control.

B. can not be reasonably foreseen by him when concluding the contract.

C. can not be avoided.

D. all of the above.

E. only A and B.

2. Buyer and seller contract for the sale of certain goods, currently in the seller's possession. The contract requires that the goods be delivered by the seller to the buyer's place of business. The risk of these goods passes to the buyer when:

A. The buyer picks up the goods.

B. The seller tenders for delivery of these goods at the buyer's place.

C. The buyer receives a document of title.

D. The seller places the goods in the possession of a common carrier and makes a proper contract for delivery.

E. The contract is concluded.

3. X agrees to ship 1,000 widgets from the United States for delivery to Y in Italy. X actually ships 1,500. According to the UN *Convention on Contracts for the International Sale of Goods* (CISG), Y may

A. accept the 1,500 widgets.

B. accept only 1,000 widgets.

C. reject all of the widgets.

D. All of the above.

E. Either a. or b.

4. X and Y entered into a contract for X to ship from Country A 1,000 widgets for delivery to Y in Country B. X failed to make delivery, and Y now sues for damages. The damages will be calculated by subtracting the contract price from

A. the price for the goods prevailing in Country A at the time the contract was avoided.

B. the price for the goods prevailing in Country A at the time the contract was made.

C. the price for the goods prevailing in Country B at the time the contract was avoided.

D. the price for the goods prevailing in Country B at the time the contract was made.

E. None of the above.

5. *CISG* states the following are key terms that will materially alter the offer, except

A. price.

B. time of delivery.

C. quantity of goods.

D. specifications of goods.

E. settlement of disputes.

Part Ⅲ. Chapter Questions: Discuss and answer the following questions according to what you have learned in this chapter. You are encouraged to use your own words.

1. Seller contracted to sell lumber to the buyer. The contract was a shipment contract and the goods were to be shipped by a common carrier. The lumber was destroyed by fire before the common carrier delivered the lumber to the buyer. Did the seller have to compensate for the loss?

2. Seller contracted to sell goods to the buyer. The goods were to be held by the seller until the buyer could pick them up. The seller informed the buyer that the goods were ready to be picked up. Several days later, before the buyer could pick up the goods, the goods were destroyed by fire. Who should bear the loss?

3. Under what circumstances will an offer be deemed to be irrevocable?

4. In China, if a real estate developer does not intend their advertisements to be treated as an offer in law, what suggestions will you put forward?

5. What are the rules for passing the risk of loss under *CISG*? When the risk has passed from the seller to the buyer, will the seller be excused from damages for delivering nonconforming goods?

6. The seller must deliver conforming goods as required by the contract. How would you understand the concept of "conforming goods"?

7. If the seller knew the buyer was a middleman in international trade at the time of concluding the contract, could the damages for the buyer's lost profits be recoverable if later the seller failed to perform the obligation of delivery? Explain.

8. How do you understand the force majeure clauses in a contract?

9. Where no force majeure clauses have been incorporated into a contract, is there any other excuse for nonperformance the party may resort to?

10. Suppose the seller delivered 900 widgets to you rather than 1,000 widgets, which is the quantity required by the contract. There are similar widgets available in the local market, however, the price is somewhat higher than the contract price and you are in urgent need of the widgets. What remedies would you prefer to seek if *CISG* applies to the contract? Explain.

Part Ⅳ. Case Problem

1. Miss Li passed Hindmoor's shop on the Friday before the start of the sale, saw a fur coat in the window, and determined it would be hers. She ran home and packed some food and with a sleeping bag rushed back to the store and relieved to see she was the only person wanting to queue at that time. She settled down at the front entrance for the weekend. Other people joined the queue on Sunday evening and as the opening time approached, Miss Li, knowing she was the first, began to get very excited. Just fifteen minutes before the shop was due to open, she noticed that the employee entered the window and removed the fur coat and the notice. She thought no more about this and rushed into the shop to claim her prized fur coat, however, she was told that it was no longer for sale. Miss Li sued Hindmoor's shop

for breach of contract.

Decide whether a contract has formed between Miss Li and Hindmoor's shop under *Civil Code of the People's Republic of China*.

2. Fort Fabricators, Paris France entered into a contract with ABS Computer Inc. in Texas U.S.A. The contract provided that Fort Fabricators delivered 1,000 personal housings by November 1 to ABS Computer Inc. for a total price of $ 50,000. On July 1, Fort Fabricators e-mailed ABS Computer Inc. that due to a rise in raw material, they could not deliver the computer housings for less than $ 60,000. ABS Computer Inc. replied it would insist on the original price in the contract. Fort Fabricators did not reply further. From July 1 to October 1, ABS Computer Inc. could have purchased the substitute housings from other suppliers for $55,000. On November 1, ABS Computer Inc. bought the housings for 64,000 for delivery on January 5. Because of the delay until January 5, ABS Computer Inc. suffered additional damages of $2,000.

What is the amount of damages ABS Computer Inc. was entitled to? And explain in detail.

Chapter 7
International Transportation of Goods

 导读

本章主要按照运输方式的不同，分别介绍各类国际货物运输法：国际货物海上运输法、国际货物航空运输法、国际货物铁路运输法、国际货物公路运输法、国际货物多式联运法以及国际货物海上运输保险法。

 Warm-up Questions

(1) What are the advantages and disadvantages of the different modes of transportation used in the international sale of goods?

(2) Suppose you deliver a parcel worth $ 500 by air to a friend in Paris, can you get the recovery of its full value if the parcel is lost?

(3) How much do you know about the bill of lading?

7.1 Transportation of Goods by Sea

Compared to most other options, transportation of goods by sea is cheap but slow, and transshipment (i.e., having to unload and reload goods between different modes of transport) may be necessary. Most transportation of goods by sea is done by common carriers, that is, a carrier holding itself to carry goods for more than one party, and an important document of a bill of lading is often used by common carriers. However, sometimes a few shipments that are large enough to require the shipper to hire an entire vessel are generally carried by means of a charter party, i.e., the contract to employ an entire vessel. We will talk about charter parties after discussing common transportation.

A. Bills of Lading

1. Fundamentals of Bills of Lading

A **bill of lading**[1] is a document that is issued by a carrier to a shipper upon receipt of goods from

---

1. bill of lading：提单。承运人或其代理人签发给托运人确认已收到货物的凭证。持有人可在货运目的地凭提单提货。

the shipper. A bill of lading serves three purposes: (1) It is a carrier's receipt for goods; (2) it is evidence of a contract of transportation; (3) it is a document of title.[1] First, a bill of lading signed by or on behalf of a carrier usually describes the goods put on board, states the quantity and conditions of the goods, and sets forth the terms on which those goods have been carried. The form of a bill of lading is normally preprinted. Before issuing a bill of lading, the carrier's tally clerk will check to see that the goods loaded comply with the goods listed. However, the carrier is responsible only to check for the outward appearance of the goods—the labels comply and the packages are not damaged. Second, the bill of lading is evidence of the contract of transportation between the shipper and the carrier. In the international sale, when the bill of lading is negotiated to a third party (**consignee**[2]), it may be deemed to be an evidence of the contract of transportation between the carrier and the consignee. The terms in the bill of lading may be rebutted by other terms between the shipper and the carrier. However, the bill of lading becomes conclusive evidence of the terms of the contract of transportation, once it is negotiated to a good-faith third party. Because the third party's knowledge of the terms of the contract of transportation is limited to what appears on the bill of lading. Third, a bill of lading is described as the key that permits the holder to unlock the door of the place where the goods are held. The bill of lading evidences the ownership of or title to the goods described in it. In other words, the holder of the bill of lading is the owner of the goods described in it. In an international sale of goods, only when the buyer produces the bill of lading, will the ship's crew release the goods to him, if the goods are transported by sea.

Different types of bills of lading are used in the international transportation of goods to serve diverse purposes.

(1) Straight (non-negotiable) bills of lading[3] and order (negotiable) bills of lading[4]. These two types of bills of lading are also known in the trade as "white" and "yellow" for the different colors of paper on which they are often printed. Straight bills of lading are also called "air waybills", "sea waybills" and "freight receipts", depending upon the intended method of main transportation for the goods. Straight bills of lading are nonnegotiable and are not documents of title. A non-negotiable, or "straight", bill of lading is just a receipt for the goods, and serves as a contract with the carrier stating the terms and conditions of transportation. Such a document is used by the ocean carrier only if the seller intends that the goods be delivered directly to a consignee, a specific person named in the document. The consignee may be the buyer or the buyer's bank or agent. Straight bills of lading are also used when the seller is shipping to its own agents, such as its subsidiary company in a foreign country.

An "order", or negotiable, bill of lading serves all purposes of a bill of lading as a contract with the carrier, a receipt for the goods, and a document of title for the goods. A negotiable bill of lading is issued

---

1. 提单有 3 个作用（1）提单是承运人签发给托运人的货物收据；（2）提单是承运人与托运人订有货物海上运输合同的证明；（3）提单是代表货物所有权的凭证。

2. consignee：收货人。收货人是有权提取货物的人，可能是合法持有提单的人，也可能是运单上记载的有权提取货物的人。

3. straight (non-negotiable) bills of lading：记名提单（不可转让提单）。记名提单载有发货人的姓名，承运人只能依据提单的此项记载向该收货人交付货物。

4. order (negotiable) bills of lading：指示提单（可转让提单）。指示提单是指示将货物交付给提单上载明的人或依其背书指示的其他人的可转让提单。

to a named person "or order". This allows the named person (the consignee) to **endorse**[1] the bill of lading to "order" delivery of the goods to others. If possession of the bill of lading is transferred to a third party by endorsement, then the third party becomes a "holder" of the bill of lading. The original consignee may endorse the negotiable bill of lading either "in blank"[2] by a bare signature of the endorser (e.g., "Richard Folsom") or by a **"special endorsement"**[3], which specifies the name of the intended holder (e.g., "Deliver the goods to Michael George, or order, Richard Folsom"). Under a blank endorsement, any person in possession becomes a holder, and is entitled to demand delivery from the carrier. Under a special endorsement, only the named endorsee can become a holder, and only that person can demand delivery from the carrier or endorse the bill of lading to another party so as to make it a holder. Thus, **the special endorsement better protects the interests of the parties from thieves and forgers than a blank endorsement.**

A carrier under a negotiable bill of lading is required to obtain the **original bill of lading**[4] prior to releasing the goods. If the carrier does not obtain the original bill of lading, it will be held liable to the shipper for misdelivery.[5] The negotiable bill of lading is used in the documentary sale described in the next chapter and is required for CIF and CFR contracts, as well as the letter of credit transaction.

(2) On board (loaded) bills of lading and received-for-shipment bills of lading.[6] Shippers and carriers often refer to an "on board" bill of lading. An "on board" or "loaded" bill of lading is issued once the goods have been loaded on board the vessel. The document gives some assurance that the goods described in the bill of lading are underway to the buyer. A received-for-shipment bill of lading, on the other hand, is issued by a carrier only upon having received goods for transport. There is usually a time delay between the delivery of goods to the carrier and their being loaded on board the ship. Suppose a buyer is required to pay for a received-for-shipment bill of lading for bananas being shipped from Thailand to the United States. The buyer has no guarantee that the bananas won't be sitting on the sun-parched dock for several weeks waiting to be loaded. Thus most sales contracts will require the seller to tender an on board bill of lading.

(3) Clean bills of lading[7] and **foul bills of lading**[8]. A "clean" bill of lading is one that has no

---

1. endorse：背书。流通票据持有人为转让其票据权利并承担由此产生的法律责任而在票据背面签名记载的行为或事实。

2. in blank or blank endorsement：空白背书，不记名背书。

3. special endorsement：特定背书，记名背书。特定背书是指写明向某人或其指定人付款的背书。如果是单据，则为写明向某人或其指定人交付货物的背书。任何经特别背书之票据只能依指定之被背书人的指示付款。经过被背书人的再背书，该票据可继续流通。

4. original bill of lading：提单正本。

5. 对于指示提单（可转让提单），承运人的责任是把提单项下的货物交给提单持有人，而不问提单持有人的权利来源是否正当。假如承运人把货物交给不是持有提单的人，他就得自行承担风险。

6. on board (loaded) bill of lading and received-for-shipment bills of lading：已装船提单和待装船提单（备运提单）。

7. clean bills of lading：清洁提单。承运人对已装船货物的表面状况未做任何不良批注的提单，记载"表面状况良好"或不做任何批注的提单均为清洁提单。清洁提单表明该提单项下的货物已以适当的方式装船，而且货物表面状况良好。

8. foul bills of lading：不清洁提单，不洁提单。承运人对所装载承运的货物的表面状况加以不良批注的提单，如批注"破损""包装不固"或"油污"等。此种提单表明，货物是在表面状况不良的情况下装船的。如果在交付货物时发现货物受损或灭失，而致损原因可归于批注事项，则承运人对此损失不负责任。在国际贸易中，货物的买方和银行一般都不愿意接受不清洁提单。

clause or notation on the face of the bill indicating visible or possible defects in the packaging or condition of the goods. Otherwise, the bill is "foul" and will detail the shortfalls or damage to the goods observed. In most sales contracts, the buyer will require the seller to tender a clean bill of lading.

(4) Multimodal bills of lading[1]. Multimodal bills of lading, also named combined transport bills of lading or through bills of lading, are used when the carrier agrees to transport and deliver the goods to their final destination using connecting carriers such as railroads, trucks, and air carriers so that the bill of lading governs all of the links of transportation.

(5) Electronic bills of lading. This area of law, like many others, is entering into the electronic age. Electronic substitutes for non-negotiable bills of lading have been in use for about two decades and have proved to be successful. However, electronic substitutes for negotiable bills of lading have been less successful and are still in the developmental stage. The difficulties mainly lie in how to guarantee the authenticity and confidentiality of negotiable electronic bills of lading.

2. International Conventions Governing Bills of Lading

Regulation of the terms of a bill of lading or the relationship between the carrier and its customers is the subject of three international conventions: **the *Hague Rules*, the *Hague-Visby Rules* and the *Hamburg Rules*.**[2] All cover contracts of transportation and bills of lading, but have different approaches and are progressively more customer-oriented.

The *Hague Rules*[3] were adopted in 1924 and set forth uniform rules governing carrier liability to shippers for cargo loss and damage. These rules represent an international effort to achieve uniformity of bills of lading and thus were intended to reduce the uncertainties concerning the liabilities of ocean carriers. The *Hague Rules* preclude contractual exculpatory clauses in bills of lading, providing that the carrier is liable for its failure to use due diligence in providing a seaworthy ship before or at the beginning of the voyage, and the carrier is also responsible for properly loading, storing and carrying the goods. The *Hague Rules* provide considerable protection to the carrier by setting forth 17 defenses against carrier and carrier liability and limit liability to a maximum of £100 per package or unit. A detailed discussion will be made below on the part of the carrier's liability and immunities. Virtually every trading nation of the world today has incorporated them into its national law.

---

1. multimodal bills of lading：多式联运提单。

2. 2008 年 12 月 11 日，联合国大会通过了《联合国全程或者部分海上国际货物运输合同公约》(《鹿特丹规则》)，其中确立了管辖托运人、承运人和发货人在含有国际海上运程的门到门运输合同下所享权利和所承担义务的统一现代法律制度。《鹿特丹规则》借鉴了《海牙规则》《海牙-维斯比规则》以及《汉堡规则》并旨在成为其现代替代文书，但目前由于缔约方太少，尚未生效。

3. *Hague Rules*：《海牙规则》。《海牙规则》是《统一有关提单的若干法律规则的国际公约》(*International Convention for the Unification of Certain Rules of Law Relating to Bills of Lading*) 的简称，在 1924 年于布鲁塞尔被正式签订前，该公约的草案曾由国际法协会在 1921 年的海牙会议上批准，故得其名。《海牙规则》是有关提单的第一个国际性公约，规定了提单项下承运人与托运人之间的权利义务关系，遏制了从事国际海上货物运输的船东（承运人）滥用契约自由原则，随意扩大免责范围的现象。自 1931 年 6 月 2 日正式生效以来，《海牙规则》已为包括英、美在内的众多国家和地区参加和使用，并为许多非缔约方所参照。

The ***Hague-Visby Rules***[1] were adopted in 1968 and amended the *Hague Rules*. *The Hague-Visby Rules* addressed certain issues that had arisen under the *Hague Rules*, such as the broadness of the carrier defenses and the inadequacy of the provision on maximum liability per package in light of multimodal transportation and containerized packaging. The *Hague-Visby Rules* defines the term "package" to include containerized cargo, increase the liability limit to 666.67 **SDR**[2] per package or unit (or 2 SDR per kilogram of gross weight of the goods lost or damaged, whichever is the higher), and restrict a carrier's limitations of liability for damage caused by its own intentional or reckless actions.

The ***Hamburg Rules***[3] of 1978 is a major departure from the *Hague Rules* and *Hague-Visby Rules* by substantially decreasing carrier and carrier defenses and increasing potential liability. It eliminates many defenses, leaving three from the 17 defenses provided in the previous conventions, increases the liability limit to 835 SDR per package or other shipping units (or 2.5 SDR per kilogramme of the gross weight of the goods lost or damaged, whichever is the higher) and provides the shipper an opportunity to recover based on the weight of the cargo instead, and includes liability for on deck cargo and shipments without a bill of lading for the first time (these items are specifically excluded by the prior conventions). The *Hamburg Rules* was drafted by the United Nations to serve the interests of cargo owners and shippers in developing countries. However, the rules are strongly opposed by developed countries, which have large carrier fleets.

Some countries have chosen one set of these rules to apply as their national law. Although China is not a contracting state to any of the above Conventions, the *Maritime Law of the People's Republic of China*, which took effect as of 1 July 1993, does incorporate some rules (e.g., rules on carrier liability and immunities) of the *Hague Rules* and also draws on the other conventions. English law is based on the *Hague-Visby Rules*. The United States not only enacted the *Hague Rules* into its domestic law as the ***Carriage of Goods by Sea Act*** (**COGSA**)[4] in 1936 but also has non-conforming pre-COGSA legislation (the ***Harter Act***[5]) in force. The *Harter Act* governs liability for cargo between

---

1. *Hague-Visby Rules*：《海牙-维斯比规则》。1968 年在布鲁塞尔通过了对《海牙规则》进行修订的议定书，即《修改统一有关提单的若干法律规则的国际公约的议定书》（Protocol to Amend the International Convention for the Unification of Certain Rules of Law Relating to Bills of Lading），该议定书对《海牙规则》做了一些非根本性的修订和补充。由于在讨论制定该议定书的会议期间，会议代表曾对中世纪《维斯比海法》的发源地维斯比城进行了访问，因此就以《维斯比规则》（Visby Rules）来命名该议定书。经《维斯比规则》修订和补充后的《海牙规则》，被称为《海牙-维斯比规则》。

2. SDR（Special drawing rights）：特别提款权。国际货币基金组织成员方间用于国际收支结算的国际储备记账单位。因为这一记账单位和国际货币基金组织原有的基金份额及会员提款权有关联，但又是其另外的补充，故称特别提款权。特别提款权体系由国际货币基金组织创设，特别提款权根据成员方在基金组织中摊付的基金份额按比例分配，以增加成员方的国际清偿手段总额。特别提款权是黄金与主要国际货币的补充，因此又被称为"纸黄金"。

3. *Hamburg Rules*：《汉堡规则》，全称《联合国海上货物运输公约》（United Nations Convention on the Carrier of Goods by Sea），由联合国国际贸易法委员会受联合国贸易和发展会议的委托，对《海牙规则》和《维斯比规则》做了全面的实质性修改，于 1978 年在汉堡通过，1992 年 11 月 1 日生效。《汉堡规则》对于原明显偏袒承运人利益的《海牙规则》在涉及船货双方的权益和责任方面做了比较合理的修改和调整。

4. *Carriage of Goods by Sea Act* (COGSA)：（美国）《海上货物运输法》是一部规定承运货物损失或丢失时提单签发人和持有人的权利、义务、责任及免责情形的法律。

5. *Harter Act*：（美国）《哈特法》。（美国）《哈特法》是一部关于规定在海上运输中船主（承运人）应负责任的联邦海商法规。

the vessel owner or carrier and the shipper in the domestic trade. *COGSA*, derived from the *Hague Rules*, applies to every bill of lading or document of title that evidences a contract for the transportation of goods by sea to or from a U.S. port but does not automatically apply to solely domestic bills of lading. *COGSA* governs the liability of a carrier from the time goods are loaded onto the ship until the time the cargo is unloaded. *COGSA* does not apply to losses that occur prior to loading or after discharge from the vessel, during which the *Harter Act* applies. Thus, it is commonly said that *COGSA* applies from "**tackle to tackle**"[1]. However, *COGSA* does permit the shipper and the carrier to extend the application of it beyond such period of "tackle to tackle". In international transportation of goods by sea, virtually all bills of lading issued in the United States provide that they are controlled by *COGSA*. But *UCC* Article 7 governs the intrastate transfer of the bill of lading. Because of this multiplicity of statutes governing the terms of bills of lading and their use, conflicting concepts and rules can often be expected.

3. Carrier's Duties and Immunities under a Bill of Lading

Article 3 of the *Hague Rules* provides the carrier's duties or liabilities under a bill of lading. It requires a carrier to exercise due diligence before or at the beginning of the voyage in:

(a)Make the ship seaworthy.

(b)Properly man, equip and supply the ship.

(c)Make the holds, refrigerating and cool chambers, and all other parts of the ship in which goods are carried, fit and safe for their reception, carriage and preservation.

(d)Properly and carefully load, handle, stow, carry, keep, care for, and discharge the goods carried.[2]

The carrier is liable for damage to cargo resulting from its failure to use due diligence before or at the beginning of the voyage to make the ship seaworthy. This duty has been called assurance of **seaworthiness**[3]. A vessel is seaworthy if it is reasonably fit to carry the cargo it has undertaken to carry on the intended voyage. The standard of seaworthiness includes a number of factors: The type of ship, the condition and suitability of the ship's equipment, the competence of its crew, the type of cargo being carried and the manner in which it is stowed, the weather (i.e., is the ship prepared for the types of weather expected?), and the nature of the voyage. The carrier must also properly load, store and carry

---

1. tackle to tackle：钩至钩。吊钩到吊钩，用于确定承运人责任期间的一个原则，即承运人对货物在装货港挂上船舶吊杆或吊车的吊钩时起至货物在卸货港脱离吊钩时止的期间内发生的货物的灭失或损害负赔偿责任。

2.《海牙规则》第3条（1）：承运人须在开航前和开航时恪尽职守，（a）使船舶适于航行；（b）适当地配备船员、装备船舶和供应船舶；（c）使货舱、冷藏舱和该船其他载货处所能适宜和安全地收受、运送和保管货物。（2）：除遵照第4条规定外，承运人应适当和谨慎地装载、搬运、配载、运送、保管、照料和卸载所运货物。

3. seaworthiness：适航。承运人用于货物运输的船舶应该处于适于航行的正常状态，能够安全收受、载运和保管货物。它的内容主要包括3方面。其一是针对船体本身的，即船舶应该坚固、水密，各种航行设备处于良好状态，简称"适船"。其二是针对船上人员的：船长、船员应该数量充足，经过良好训练，取得适当资格证书并有必需的技能，简称"适船员"。其三是针对船上的载货处所的，船舱应该清洁安全，适于装载特定的货物，简称"适货"。适航义务3方面的内容都是针对特定航次的，航次不同、装载的货物不同、运输中的风险不同，这3方面的要求标准也就不同。船舶适航义务并不是绝对的，在班轮运输中，只要承运人尽到适当谨慎的义务，使船舶在开航前和开航时适航，即认为承运人已经尽到了船舶适航的义务。但是需要注意的是，承运人是否已经"适当谨慎"是一个事实问题，实践中必须结合具体案情予以确认。

the goods. For example, the ship's holds must not be in such a condition that causes moisture damage to the goods through condensation. Cargo should not be stowed in a manner that causes it to shift and be crushed. Cargo shall not be exposed to rain and seas, etc.

The above provisions under the *Hague Rules* have been widely incorporated into national laws. For example, much similar provisions can be found in Article 46-48 of *Maritime Law of the People's Republic of China*[1] and *COSGA* in the United States.

Most courts strictly enforce this obligation. For example, in *Riverstone Meat Co. Pty., Ltd. V. Lancashire Shipping Co. Ltd.*, goods were damaged by water due to the negligent work of a shipfitter employed by a ship repair company. The court held that the carrier had failed to use due diligence in making the ship seaworthy.[2]

However, on the other hand, a carrier is exempt, under the *Hague Rules*, from liability for damages that arise out of a variety of perils:

(a) Act, neglect, or default of the master, mariner, pilot, or the servants of the carrier in the navigation or in the management of the ship;

(b) Fire, unless caused by the actual fault or privity of the carrier;

(c) Perils, dangers, and accidents of the sea or other navigable waters;

(d) Act of God;

(e) Act of war;

(f) Act of public enemies;

(g) Arrest or restraint or princes, rulers or people, or seizure under legal process;

(h) Quarantine restrictions;

(i) Act or omission of the shipper or owner of the goods, his agent or representative;

(j) Strikes or lockouts or stoppage or restraint of labour from whatever cause, whether partial or general;

(k) Riots and civil commotions;

(l) Saving or attempting to save life or property at sea;

(m) Wastage in bulk or weight or any other loss or damage arising from inherent defect, quality or vice of the goods;

(n) Insufficiency of packing;

(o) Insufficiency or inadequacy of marks;

(p) Latent defects not discoverable by due diligence.

1.《中华人民共和国海商法》第 46 条：承运人对集装箱装运的货物的责任期间，是指从装货港接收货物时起至卸货港交付货物时止，货物处于承运人掌管之下的全部期间。承运人对非集装箱装运的货物的责任期间，是指从货物装上船时起至卸下船时止，货物处于承运人掌管之下的全部期间。在承运人的责任期间，货物发生灭失或者损坏，除本节另有规定外，承运人应当负赔偿责任。前款规定，不影响承运人就非集装箱装运的货物，在装船前和卸船后所承担的责任，达成任何协议。第 47 条：承运人在船舶开航前和开航当时，应当谨慎处理，使船舶处于适航状态，妥善配备船员、装备船舶和配备供应品，并使货舱、冷藏舱、冷气舱和其他载货处所适于并能安全收受、载运和保管货物。第 48 条：承运人应当妥善地、谨慎地装载、搬移、积载、运输、保管、照料和卸载所运货物。

2. Ray August. *International Business Law-Text, Cases, and Readings.4th ed.* New York：Person Education Ltd. 2004. P651.

(q) Any other cause arising without the actual fault of the carrier and without the fault or negligence of the agents or servants of the carrier, but the burden of proof shall be on the person claiming the benefit of this exception to show that neither the actual fault or privity of the carrier nor the fault or neglect of the agents or servants of the carrier contributed to the loss or damage.[1]

These immunities are narrowly construed. If cargo is damaged and the damage falls within one of the immunities, the carrier will nonetheless be responsible if the underlying cause was the result of the carrier's failure to exercise due diligence in carrying out its fundamental duties provided in Article 3 of the *Hague Rules*. For example, among the above listed situations in which a carrier is not liable for damage of cargo, one of the most important is that the carrier is not liable for errors in navigation or mismanagement of the ship caused by the master, mariner, pilot, or the servants of the carrier. That is, even when the error in navigation or mismanagement of the ship is caused by the actual fault of the carrier or carrier's crew, the carrier will not be liable for any loss or damage to the goods arising from such an error. This immunity shows great partiality to the carrier, thus often be criticized by shippers or cargo owners. Thus, in practice, some courts have held carriers liable for their crew's negligence by reasoning that a crew errs in navigating or managing a ship is not competent, and a ship is not seaworthy without a competent crew. As a result, carriers can be held liable despite the protection they receive from the defense. The (q) clause of the immunities serves as a catch-all clause covering any other cause arising without the actual fault of the carrier or its agents and crew. However, the carrier must prove that neither the actual fault of the carrier itself nor the actual fault or neglect of its agents and crew contributed to the loss of or damage to the cargo.

4. Other Questions

Liability Limits. Carriers have long attempted to set monetary limits on their liability in the event that they are found liable for loss of or damage to a cargo. The *Hague Rules* limit the carrier's liability to a maximum of UK £ 100 per package or unit. The limits were dramatically raised in the *Hague-visby Rules* and *Hamburg Rules* (see the part of "International Conventions Governing Bills of Lading"). One thing to note is that the limits don't apply if the parties agree to higher amounts. They also don't apply if the carrier acted either "within the intent to cause damage" or "recklessly and with the knowledge that damage would probably result".[2]

Time Limitations. Claims for loss or damages have to be lodged within **a year** after the goods were or should have been delivered. The claim may be initiated by filing suit or by commencing

---

1. 《海牙规则》第4条（2）：承运人或船舶，对下列原因引起或造成的灭失或损坏不负责，（a）船长、船员、引水员或承运人的雇佣人员，在航行或管理船舶中疏忽或不履行义务。（b）火灾，但由于承运人的实际过失或私谋所引起的除外。（c）海上或其他能航水域的灾难、危险和意外事故。（d）天灾。（e）战争行为。（f）公敌行为。（g）君主、当权者或人民的扣留或管制，或依法扣押。（h）检疫限制。（i）托运人或货主、其代理人或代表的行为或不作为。（j）任何原因引起的局部或全面罢工、关厂停止或限制工作。（k）暴动和骚乱。（l）救助或企图救助海上人命或财产。（m）由于货物的固有缺点、性质或缺陷引起的体积或重量亏损，或任何其他灭失或损坏。（n）包装不善。（o）唛头不清或不当。（p）虽恪尽职守亦不能发现的潜在缺陷。（q）非由于承运人的实际过失或私谋，或者承运人的代理人，或雇佣人员的过失或疏忽所引起的其他任何原因；但是要求引用这条免责利益的人应负责举证，证明有关的灭失或损坏既非由于承运人的实际过失或私谋，亦非承运人的代理人或雇佣人员的过失或疏忽所造成。

2.《海牙-维斯比规则》第4条（5）（e）：如经证明，损害系承运人故意造成，或明知可能造成损害而轻率地采取的行为或不行为所引起，则无论是承运人或船舶，都无权享有本款规定的责任限制的利益。

arbitration proceedings.

Third Party Rights (Himalaya Clauses[1]). The *Hague Rules* apply only to the carrier and the party shipping goods under a bill of lading. Third parties, including officers, crew members, agents, and stevedores, who help in the transport of the goods but are not parties to the transportation-of-goods contract contained in the bill of lading, normally have no contractual right to claim the liability limits established by the *Hague Rules*. To extend the liability limits of the conventions to these individuals, many carriers add a clause to their bills of lading known as a **"Himalaya Clause"**, which takes its name from a decision of the English Court of Appeal in the case of *Adler v. Dickson* (See Case 7-1). **This clause purports to extend to third parties the carrier's immunities established by the** *Hague Rules.*

【Case 7-1】

Adler v. Dickson
[1954] 2 Lloyd's Rep 267, [1955] 1 QB 158

BACKGROUNDS AND FACTS

In June, 1952, Mrs. Adler, who keeps a shop, decided to go for a cruise upon the P. & O. Steamship "Himalaya". She booked her passage through the travel agents Thomas Cook & Son. She travelled first-class and paid £188 for the trip. In return, the Steamship Company issued her with a first-class passage ticket by virtue of which she joined the ship at Southampton and sailed on the cruise. On the 16th July, 1952, the ship reached Trieste and Mrs. Adler went ashore. A gangway was placed horizontally from the ship to a gantry on the quay. She went ashore across that gangway. When she returned to the ship, she was walking along the gangway and had got about half way across when suddenly the gangway came adrift from the gantry at the shore end, and it fell down against the side of the ship. She was thrown onto the wharf below, a distance of 16 feet, and suffered severe injuries, including a broken leg, broken pelvis, and broken ribs. The passage ticket contained a non-responsibility clause exempting the carrier, so the claimant sued the master of the ship and the boatswain. The defendant argued that under the normal rules of **privity of contract[2]**, the defendants could not rely on the terms of a contract that they were not party to.

DECISION

The Court of Appeal declared that in the carriage of passengers as well as in the carriage of

---

1. Himalaya Clauses：喜马拉雅条款。提单和租船合同中经常援引的有关承运人的代理人或者雇佣人员甚至独立合同人（包括装卸工人、港站经营人甚至干坞公司）对货损免责的条款。该条款源于 1953 年英国法院审理的 *Alder v. Dickson* 案。在该案中，英国半岛及东方公司的客轮 "Himalaya"（喜马拉雅）号，在一次靠码头时，由于没有系好缆绳，使一名女乘客摔倒。事后，该女乘客控告该轮水手长疏忽职守。水手长认为自己作为船公司的雇员，同样可以享受船票上印明的船公司许多过失都可以免责的权利。但是法庭认为船票上的免责条款并没有明示或默示地将承运人之外的第三人包括在内，因此水手长不能援引船票上的免责条款，水手长必须负女乘客损害赔偿之责。由于有了上述判例，船东们为了保护自己，纷纷在提单或者船票加上一条 "喜马拉雅" 条款。条款内容是：由于承运人的代理人或者雇佣人员的疏忽或者过失直接或间接地引起货物的灭失、损害或者延误，在提单中适用于承运人的有关免责、责任限制、豁免、抗辩等权利也扩大到承运人的代理人及其雇佣人员。

2. privity of contract：合同相对性原则。此规则阻止把合同责任加诸任何非合同当事人的身上。

goods the law permitted a carrier to stipulate not only for himself, but also for those whom he engaged to carry out the contract. It was held as well that the stipulation might be expressed or implied. Ironically, on the facts before the court, it was held that the passenger ticket did not expressly or by implication benefit servants or agents and thus the defendants could not take advantage of the exception clause.

After the decision, specially drafted Himalaya clauses benefiting stevedores and others began to be included in bills of lading.

B. Charterparties

Shippers who need to hire entire ships to carry their goods would choose "charter parties". A **"charter party" (CP)** [1] is a contract for the hire of an entire ship for a particular voyage or a set period of time. Oil, sugar, ores, coal and other bulk commodities are almost always shipped under such contracts.

The *Hague Rules*, *Hague-Visby Rules* and *Hamburg Rules* do not apply to charter parties, unless a bill of lading issued by the ship owner comes into the hands of a third party. The shipper (or charterer) and the ship owner are free to set the terms governing the transportation of goods in their contract. Commonly they use standardized contracts drafted by various conferences and nongovernmental organizations. These standard contracts include the **Uniform General Charter (Gencon)** [2] drafted by the **Baltic and International Maritime Conference (BIMCO)** [3] and the **Chamber of Shipping Australian Grain Charter (Austral)** [4].

Voyage Charter parties [5]. A voyage charterparty involves the employment of a ship and its crew for the transportation of goods from one place to another. Under this contract, the owner provides the ship at a named port at a specified time to carry the goods to an agreed destination. The charterer provides a full cargo and arranges for its loading at an agreed time. If the charterer provides less than a full load, the ship owner will charge **"dead freight"** [6] for the amount of the deficiency. If the ship owner fails to arrive at the named port for loading at the specified time, the charterer will commonly be able to terminate the contract by citing a cancellation clause in the contract. If the charterer keeps the ship lying idle too long for loading or unloading, the ship owner will charge **"demurrage"** [7]. The obligation to pay

---

1. charter party (CP)：租船合约。租船人为一次航行或一连串航行或在一段时间内使用或利用整艘船舶或其若干主要部分而签订的一种合约。租船合约的缔约方是船东和租船人。

2. Uniform General Charter (Gencon)：统一杂货租船合同（金康合同）。统一杂货租船合同是有关普通货物运输的航次租船合同的标准格式，该格式不分货种和航线，适用范围较广。

3. Baltic and International Maritime Conference (BIMCO)：波罗的海国际航运公会。该公会成立于 1905 年，总部设在哥本哈根，最初旨在结束驶往波罗的海和白海的船东间异常激烈的竞争，后发展为世界上最大的代表船舶所有人利益的国际航运民间组织之一。

4. Chamber of Shipping Australian Grain Charter (Austral)：澳大利亚谷物运输租船合同（奥斯特拉尔合同）。波罗的海国际航运公会采用的租船合同格式之一，专门用于澳大利亚至英国、爱尔兰和欧洲大陆港口的小麦或面粉运输。

5. voyage charter parties：航次租船合约。于一次规定的航行或一连串的航行运送特定货物的合约，船东以运费方式获取酬金。

6. dead freight：空舱费。空舱费是指租船人对其已经租用但未能装满的船舶载运吨位所付的费用。其实质是对空余吨位的运输损失支付的赔偿金。

7. demurrage：滞期费。因船舶滞留的时间超过租船合同或提单中规定的载货、卸货或航行的天数，由承租人或托运人向船东或承运人支付费用作为补偿，此项规定旨在加速载货、卸货，便于商业流通。

the demurrage will be secured by a **lien**[1] on the cargo, which any holder of the corresponding bill of lading will have to pay off before taking delivery.

Time Charter parties[2]. A time charter party involves the employment of a vessel for a stated period of time. Problems of dead freight and demurrage do not arise because the charterer must pay for the use of the ship for a certain period of time, whether or not the ship is carrying a cargo. The charterer has the right to direct the ship to proceed wherever it is needed. Usually, the only limitation on this right is the charterer's promise to engage only in lawful trades, to carry only lawful goods, and to only direct the ship to safe ports. If the ship owner attempts to interfere with the charterer's legal right of using the ship, he will commit a breach of the charter party.

Charter parties and Bills of Lading. The ship owner will commonly issue the charterer a bill of lading when goods are loaded on board. Between the two parties, the bill will only be a receipt for goods and a document of title. However, where the bill is transferred by the charterer to a third party by endorsement, the *Hague Rules* will apply, and the contract between the ship owner and the third party will be governed by the bill of lading.

7.2   Transportation of Goods by Air

The liability of air carriers for loss of or damage to cargo and baggage as well as the bodily injury or death of passengers is governed by a host of international conventions and national laws. The governing international conventions are collectively called "Warsaw Regime". This regime consists of the *Warsaw Convention 1929*, its subsequent Protocols, and the *Montreal Convention 1999*, which enters into force since 2003. The focus of the *Warsaw Convention 1929* was on the protection of air carriers, while the newer *Montreal Convention 1999* generally modernized the law, including issuing tickets and air waybills electronically, and eliminated many of the criticisms of the older treaty.

A. The Warsaw Convention 1929[3]

The *Warsaw Convention 1929* sets uniform rules governing the transportation of international cargo, baggage as well as passengers. It governs the form of **air waybill**[4], passenger tickets, and baggage claim receipts, defining the liability of airlines for injuries to passengers and damage to or loss of their

---

1. lien：留置权。债权人在债务人特定财产上设定的一种担保权益，一般至债务清偿时止。债务人如逾期未清偿，债权人可通过变卖留置物等法定程序优先受偿。留置权可表现为债权人合法占有留置物，如，承运人占有所承运的货物，在托运人未付清运费前可留置货物不给予提取。

2. time charter parties：定期租船合约。定期租船合约是指在某特定时期内执行服务的合约，以租金为代价，以租船人有权使用该船舶的期间计算。

3. *Warsaw Convention 1929*：《华沙公约》(1929)。1929年在波兰首都华沙签订的国际航空货物运输方面的国际公约，其全称是《关于统一国际航空运输某些规则的公约》(Convention for the Unification of Certain Rules Relating to International Transportation by Air)。于1933年2月13日起正式生效。其主要内容为：对国际航空运输的条件、运输凭证及航空承运人的责任等作了规定。

4. air waybill：航空货运单。航空货物运输中的运输合同。它是由承运人或其代理人所出具的重要的货运单据。但性质上它不同于海运提单，不是代表货物所有权的物权凭证，是不可议付的单据。

baggage or cargo. It also provides a uniform limitation on the liability of an air carrier to both shippers and passengers. The limitation on air carrier's liability is set at 250 francs (gold value) per kilogram of cargo or baggage. The limitation applies where the shipper has not declared a higher value for the goods on the air waybill. And such a limitation does not apply if the shipper has declared the goods to be of higher value on the air waybill and has paid an additional fee.

The application of the liability limits is illustrated in the following case.

Williams Dental Company (Plaintiff) shipped 50 ounces of dental gold and equipment to Sweden aboard Air Express International (Defendant), an air carrier. Plaintiff's employee checked, packaged and sealed the gold in a pail. When the shipment was delivered to the buyer in Sweden, it was found that the seals on the pail were broken and the gold was missing. On the air waybill, Plaintiff declared a special value for the entire shipment of $ 23,474, and declared separately a value of $21,680 for the gold. Plaintiff sued to recover the $ 23,474, while Defendant claimed that its liability would be limited to $ 1,262 under the Warsaw Convention. In this case, the court finally decided that since the shipper (Plaintiff) has declared a higher value for the missing gold, the liability limits provided in the *Warsaw Convention* would not apply and Plaintiff was entitled to get the recovery of $ 21,680, neither the amount of $ 1,262 nor $ 23,474.

B. The Montreal Convention 1999[1]

Under the *Montreal Convention 1999*, the air carrier is liable for damage to or loss of the cargo upon condition that the event, which caused the damage or loss, took place during the transportation by air. However, the carrier is not liable if it proves that the **damage to or loss of the cargo** resulted from one or more of the following reasons:

(a) inherent defect, quality or vice of that cargo;

(b) defective packing of that cargo performed by a person other than the carrier or its servants or agents;

(c) an act of war or an armed conflict;

(d) an act of public authority carried out in connection with the entry, exit or transit of the cargo.[2]

The carrier is also liable for **damage to or loss of the luggage** upon condition that the event, which caused the damage or loss, took place during the transportation by air. However, the air carrier is not liable if it proves that the damage to or loss of the luggage resulted from the inherent defect, quality or

---

1. *Montreal Convention 1999*:《蒙特尔尔公约》(1999)。1999 年 5 月 28 日订于蒙特尔尔的《统一国际航空运输某些规则的公约》(Convention for the Unification of Certain Rules for International Transportation by Air)。随着历史的发展,华沙公约中的某些规定已显陈旧,而且相关修订文件数量较多。为了使华沙公约及其相关文件现代化和一体化,国际民用航空组织起草定稿了《蒙特尔尔公约》。于 2003 年 11 月 4 日生效。根据其规定,国际航空承运人应当对旅客的人身伤亡、行李和货物损失,以及由于延误造成旅客、行李或货物的损失承担责任并予以赔偿。

2.《蒙特尔尔公约》(1999)第 18 条货物损失(1),对于因货物毁灭、遗失或者损坏而产生的损失,只要造成损失的事件是在航空运输期间发生的,承运人就应当承担责任。(2),但是,承运人证明货物的毁灭、遗失或者损坏是由于下列一个或者几个原因造成的,在此范围内承运人不承担责任:(a)货物的固有缺陷、质量或者瑕疵;(b)承运人或者其受雇人、代理人以外的人包装货物的,货物包装不良;(c)战争行为或者武装冲突;(d)公共当局实施的与货物入境、出境或者过境有关的行为。

vice of that luggage.[1] The *Montreal Convention 1999* dramatically increased **the limitation on air carrier's liability**. For damage, loss or delay to cargo, the limit is 17 SDR per kilogram. For damage, loss or delay to luggage, 1000 SDR per passenger.[2] And an airline is liable for **death or injury to a passenger** ticked for international travel, including a passenger who is injured or killed in an accident in his own country, provided that his ticket includes travel to or from another country. For death or bodily injuries of passengers, the *Montreal Convention 1999* provides a unique two-layer scheme: The carrier is strictly liable for damages not exceeding 100,000 SDR, and the carrier is liable for damages above 100,000 SDR unless it can show either (1) the damages are not due to the negligence or other wrongful act or omission of the carrier or its servants or agents; or (2) the damages are solely due to the negligence or wrongful acts or omission of third parties.[3]

On 28 February 2005, the Standing Committee of the National People's Congress ratified the *Montreal Convention 1999* and this convention has been binding on China as of 31 July 2005. However, this Convention only applies to **international transportation** of cargo, luggage and passenger by air. For **domestic transportation**, the *Civil Aviation Law of the People's Republic of China* and relevant regulations will apply. *Regulations on Liability Limits of Air Carriers in Domestic Transportation by Air* was published by the Civil Aviation Administration of China on 28 March 2006. These Regulations increase the air carrier's liability limit from RMB 70,000 yuan to RMB 400,000 yuan for the death and bodily injury of passengers. For the damage to or loss of the luggage or the cargo, the limit is 100 yuan RMB per kilogram.[4]

1.《蒙特利尔公约》(1999) 第 17 条旅客死亡和伤害——行李损失。(1) 对于因旅客死亡或者身体伤害而产生的损失，只要造成死亡或者伤害的事故是在航空器上或者在上、下航空器的任何操作过程中发生的，承运人就应当承担责任。(2) 对于因托运行李毁灭、遗失或者损坏而产生的损失，只要造成毁灭、遗失或者损坏的事件是在航空器上或者在托运行李处于承运人掌管之下的任何期间内发生的，承运人就应当承担责任。但是，行李损失是由于行李的固有缺陷、质量或者瑕疵造成的，在此范围内承运人不承担责任。

2.《蒙特利尔公约》(1999) 第 22 条延误、行李和货物的责任限额 (2) 在行李运输中造成毁灭、遗失、损坏或者延误的，承运人的责任以每名旅客 1,000 特别提款权为限，除非旅客在向承运人交付托运行李时，特别声明在目的地点交付时的利益，并在必要时支付附加费。在此种情况下，除承运人证明旅客声明的金额高于在目的地点交付时旅客的实际利益外，承运人在声明金额范围内承担责任。(3) 在货物运输中造成毁灭、遗失、损坏或者延误的，承运人的责任以每千克 17 特别提款权为限，除非托运人在向承运人交运包件时，特别声明在目的地点交付时的利益，并在必要时支付附加费。在此种情况下，除承运人证明托运人声明的金额高于在目的地点交付时托运人的实际利益外，承运人在声明金额范围内承担责任。(注：2019 年，国际民航组织对第 24 条规定的责任限额进行了修改，自 2019 年 12 月 28 日起生效。据此，本条中的 1,000 特别提款权被修改为 1288 特别提款权，17 特别提款权被修改为 22 特别提款权。)

3.《蒙特利尔公约》(1999) 第 21 条，旅客死亡或者伤害的赔偿 (1)，对于根据第 17 条第一款所产生的每名旅客不超过 100,000 特别提款权的损害赔偿，承运人不得免除或者限制其责任。(2)，对于根据第 17 条第一款所产生的损害赔偿每名旅客超过 100,000 特别提款权的部分，承运人证明有下列情形的，不应当承担责任：(a) 损失不是由于承运人或者其受雇人、代理人的过失或者其他不当作为、不作为造成的；或者 (b) 损失完全是由第三人的过失或者其他不当作为、不作为造成的。[注：2019 年，国际民航组织根据 1999 年 5 月 28 日于蒙特利尔签订的《统一国际航空运输某些规则的公约》(Doc 9740 号文件)(《1999 年蒙特利尔公约》) 第 24 条规定对责任限额进行了修改，自 2019 年 12 月 28 日起生效。据此，本条中的 100,000 特别提款权被修改为 128,821 特别提款权。]

4.《国内航空运输承运人赔偿责任限额规定》第 3 条：国内航空运输承运人（以下简称承运人）应当在下列规定的赔偿责任限额内按照实际损害承担赔偿责任，但是《民用航空法》另有规定的除外：(1) 对每名旅客的赔偿责任限额为人民币 40 万元；(2) 对每名旅客随身携带物品的赔偿责任限额为人民币 3000 元；(3) 对旅客托运的行李和对运输的货物的赔偿责任限额，为每公斤人民币 100 元。

Up to now, 139 members[1], including Canada, China, Japan, Mexico, New Zealand, and the United States, etc. have ratified the *Montreal Convention 1999* and more members are expected to be contracting members to this convention. For those members not ratifying this convention, but a contracting member to the *Warsaw Convention 1929*, they will still be bound by the *Warsaw Convention 1929* in regulating the international transportation of goods, luggage and passengers.

7.3 Transportation of Goods by Rail and Road

Transportation of goods by rail is suitable for bulky goods sent over long distances. The cost-effectiveness of this method increases when the journey is longer, especially in Continental Europe where there are many high-speed railway services. A problem with the transportation of goods by rail is the need for transshipment, although this can sometimes be avoided for consignments large enough to use **"swap body"**[2] trailers, i.e., self-contained trailers on their own wheels that can be exchanged between vehicle cabs, as opposed to **"flat" trailers**[3] onto which containers have to be loaded. The entire swap body can be uncoupled from a cab, rolled on to a train for long haul rail transport, and rolled off and attached to another cab at its final destination.

China has a developed rail transportation network. The longest route of international transportation of goods by rail runs across China starting from the city of Lian Yungang, Jiangsu Province to Xinjiang Autonomous Region, which is directly to the city of Rotterdam. The international transportation of goods by rail can play a more important role in China.

Transportation of goods by road offers door-to-door collection and delivery of goods. There is no need for transshipment, thus reducing handling costs and pilferage losses. In international sales, transportation of goods by road is often an integral part of transportation by sea or by air. Problems with road transportation are its vulnerability to bad weather; limited load sizes; and the fact that lorries often return empty.

Several regional inland transportation conventions regulate transport by rail and road. In Europe, these include the ***Convention on the Contract for the International Carriage of Goods by Road* (CMR)**[4] and the ***Convention Concerning International Carriage by Rail* (COTIF)**[5]. China is a contracting state to

---

1. 具体名单可参见国际民用航空组织网站。

2. swap body：可卸式箱式车身。可卸式箱式车身为一独立的货箱或集装箱，可装放在专用的底盘上载运。

3. flat trailers：平板挂车。

4. *Convention on the Contract for the International Carriage of Goods by Road* (CMR)：《国际公路货物运输合同公约》，简称"公路货运公约"（以下简称《公约》）。为了统一公路运输所使用的单证和承运人的责任，联合国所属欧洲经济委员会负责草拟了该公约，并于 1956 年 5 月 19 日在日内瓦由欧洲 17 个国家参加的会议上一致通过并签订。公约于 1961 年 7 月 2 日生效。该公约共有 12 章，就公约的适用范围、承运人责任/合同的签订与履行、索赔与诉讼，以及连续承运人履行合同等作了较详细的规定。根据《公约》的规定，关于通过公路运输方式运送货物的合同，不管其缔约方住地和国籍，只要该合同规定接管和交付货物的地点位于两个不同成员方，并且其中至少有一个是缔约方时，就适用《公约》。《公约》也适用于属《公约》范围内而由国家或政府机构或组织所从事的运输。《公约》主要适用于欧洲国家，但它仍不失为当前国际公路运输的一项重要的国际公约。

5. *Convention Concerning International Carriage by Rail* (COTIF)：《国际铁路货物运输公约》。该公约是 1980 年签订、1985 年生效的关于铁路运输的国际公约，替代 1975 年《国际铁路货物运送公约》。

another international agreement regulating transport by rail: *Agreement on International Goods Transport by Rail* (**SMGS**)[1], to which Russia, Mongolia, North Korea, Vietnam and several Eastern European countries are also signatories. Because those Eastern European countries are also the contracting states to *COTIF*, thus the goods to or from *SMGS* contracting states may be transshipped to the contracting states of *COTIF*. Similar agreements exist in most other regions of the world.

The *CMR* is typical of the conventions governing road transport. It applies whenever goods are shipped between two members, at least one of which is a signatory of the convention. The *CMR* requires a carrier to issue a **consignment note**[2] that serves as **prima facie evidence**[3] of the making of a transport contract, and of the receipt and the condition of the goods. It also gives the consignee the right to take delivery of the goods in exchange for a receipt, and to sue the carrier in his own name for any loss, damage or delay for which the carrier is responsible. In exchange for the benefits given to the consignee, the carrier is allowed to limit its liability for loss or damage to consigned goods to 8.33 SDR per kilogram, unless the consignor declares a higher value and pays a surcharge.

Governing rail transport, the *COTIF* was enacted on 9 May 1980 and applies in Europe, North Africa and the Middle East. *COTIF* includes the **CIV** (*Uniform Rules concerning the Contract for International Carriage of Passengers and Luggage by Rail*)[4] and **CIM** (*Uniform Rules concerning the Contract for International Carriage of Goods by Rail*)[5] as appendices and an integral part of it. Regulations of the *CIM* are similar to the *CMR*, except that it sets the carrier's liability at 17 SDR per kilogram. The document under which goods are carried by rail is the International Consignment Note which lays down internationally agreed standard conditions of transportation. Such a document serves the purposes of a receipt of goods and an evidence of the transportation contract. However, it is not a document of tile and cannot be negotiated.

For the liability limits, Article 44 of *SMGS* provides that in cases where the Agreement requires

---

1. *Agreement on International Goods Transport by Rail* (SMGS):《国际铁路货物联运协定》。简称《国际货协》，自 1951 年 11 月 1 日起施行，后由铁路合作组织（铁组）进行了多次修改与补充。协定对涉及运输双方当事人权利和义务的运送契约的缔结、发货人和收货人的权利和责任、承运人的责任、索赔和诉讼等都作了详细而且具体的规定。协定规定，凡《国际货协》有规定，而缔约方内部规章也有规定时，不论两者是否相同，应适用《国际货协》的规定。《国际货协》中没有规定的事项，适用缔约方内部铁路规章。

2. consignment note: 托运通知书。一种由托运人准备的文件，该文件特别记载了将货物从某地运送到另一个地方的细节，比如运费的支付方式和目的地。它是被承运人认可的作为货物移转其控制的凭证。货物托运通知单与提单相似，但它不是所有权凭证。

3. prima facie evidence: 表面证据；初步证据，指表面上充分有效的证据，在法律上足以证明当事人的请求或答辩所依据的事实，但对方当事人可以提出反证加以反驳。在此情况下，审判人员应对各种证据进行综合比较与权衡。

4. CIV (*Uniform Rules concerning the Contract for International Carriage of Passengers and Luggage by Rail*):《国际铁路客运和行李托运协定》。为统一国际铁路运输中旅客及行李运输的合同、法律责任、诉讼等内容而订立。

5. CIM (*Uniform Rules concerning the Contract for International* Carriage of Goods by Rail):《国际铁路货物运送公约》（以下简称《公约》）。简称《国际货约》，是调整国际铁路货物运输当事人之间权利义务关系的公约。国际铁路货物运输始于 19 世纪后半期。欧洲各国曾于 1890 年在瑞士首都伯尔尼举行会议，制定了《国际铁路货物运送规则》，后于 1934 年经修订后改称为《国际铁路货物运送公约》，后又经多次修改，最后一次修订是 1975 年。《国际货约》分 6 个部分：《公约》的目的和适用范围、运输合同、责任与法律诉讼、各种规定、特殊规定和最终规定。《国际货约》已为 1980 年《国际铁路运输公约》所取代，适用于欧洲、北非和西亚各国。

the carrier to compensate the consignor or the consignee for damage to (spoilage of) goods, the amount of compensation payable shall be equivalent to the amount by which the value of the goods has decreased.[1] In case of delayed delivery, the carrier will be held liable for the payment of fines, the amount of which depends on the delayed period. For example, if the delayed period is not more than 1/10 of the total delivery period, 6 percent of the transportation charge will be paid as fines. And if the delayed period is more than 3/10 of the total delivery period, fines will be 30 percent of the transportation charge.[2]

7.4   Multimodal Transportation of Goods

When the transport of goods is accomplished by using more than one mode of transportation, it is multimodal transportation of goods. In multimodal transportation of goods, the multimodal transport operator represents a shipper whose cargo will be sent via several different carriers (truck, rail, air or ship) in one journey. The multimodal bill of lading or the combined transport document is a single contract between the shipper and the operator, who in turn contracts with each of the carriers involved. Thus, the multimodal transport operator becomes responsible for the transport of goods throughout the time of their transport. *United Nations Convention on International Multimodal Transport of Goods* was concluded at Geneva on 24 May 1980, but has not yet and may never enter into force, because of not enough signatories.

7.5   Marine Cargo Insurance

As for the transportation of goods, the insuring of goods is also an essential element of international trade. The risks of damage to or loss of goods possibly occur at every time of transportation, particularly during ocean shipments, which are lengthier and more dangerous. Sometimes, the damage to or loss of goods arising from these risks is tremendous enough to weep out all the profits from the business. In the previous chapter, we have discussed the allocation of risks between the seller and the buyer in international sales. If damage or loss does occur, the party bearing the risk (perhaps the holder of the bill of lading) will surely seek to shift its financial burden to an insurer. Sellers, buyers, and even banks that finance international sales may want to be certain that their interests in the goods can be fully protected by insurance.

A. Types of Losses

As is shown in **Exhibit 7-1**, marine insurance policies usually cover two main types of loss: (1) total loss, (2) partial loss.

1.《国际铁路货物联运协定》第44条货物毁损（腐坏）的赔偿额（1）在本协定规定承运人应向发货人或收货人赔偿货物毁损（腐坏）损失的情况下，损失赔偿额应相当于货物价格降低部分的款额。

2.《国际铁路货物联运协定》第45条货物运到逾期的赔偿额（2）货物运到逾期的违约金额度根据造成运到逾期承运人的运费和逾期（期限）的长短，即逾期（天数）占总运到期限的比例确定。即：逾期不超过总运到期限1/10时，为运费的6%；逾期超过总运到期限1/10但不超过3/10时，为运费的18%；逾期超过总运到期限3/10时，为运费的30%。

Exhibit 7-1: Types of Losses

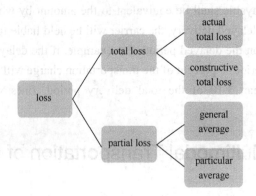

Total loss[1] includes **actual total loss**[2] and **constructive total loss**[3]. The former refers to the situations in which the goods are totally lost or, due to the damage to them, fail to serve their intended purpose. The latter refers to the circumstances under which the repairing costs for the damaged goods plus extra freights will possibly exceed the value of the goods themselves. For the total loss, the insurer will compensate. For the constructive total loss, the insured has options: (1) claiming for total loss; or (2) claiming for partial loss. If the insured chooses the first option, he must dispatch **Notice of Abandonment**[4] to the insurer. Otherwise, he is deemed to claim for partial loss.

Partial loss[5] includes **general average**[6] and **partial / particular average**[7]. The general average is an important concept in maritime transport. The world of "average" in maritime law means loss. General average is a loss that results when extraordinary expenses or losses are incurred in **saving the vessel or its cargo** from danger at sea. Everyone with an interest in the ship and the cargo benefits from the general average. Each must then contribute, in proportion to the value of their interests, to restoring the party who suffered the loss or damage, or who incurred the expense. This is called a "**general average**

---

1. total loss：全损。在海上保险中，全损指投保船舶遭到彻底的、实质性的损坏，无法通过修理得以恢复。

2. actual total loss：实际全损。实际全损是指保险标的物全部毁灭，或标的物受损以致失去原有的用途，或被保险人已无可挽回地丧失了保险标的物。在这种情况下，不需发出委付通知。

3. constructive total loss：推定全损。推定全损是指被保险财产虽未完全灭失毁损，但已不能修复，完全丧失使用价值，被保险人已不能从中获益，应推定为财产全损并获得全部赔偿。

4. notice of abandonment：委付通知；委弃通知。委付通知是指受保人向承保人或指定代理人就受保人放弃受保财产及将其交由承保人处置提交的资料。受保人可申索推定全损，但以该放弃具有正当理由为限。为了追讨全损，受保人须作出委付通知。

5. partial loss：部分损失，简称"分损"。部分损失是指保险标的遭受的损失程度尚未达到实际全损或推定全损，只是一部分遭受损失，又称局部损失。对于部分损失，保险人只能按照保险单条款的规定对其损失部分负责赔偿。海损的部分损失，在保险单中包括单独海损和共同海损。

6. general average：共同海损。如在发生危险时，一方为了保存共同冒险中陷于危险中的财产而自愿和合理地做出或招致任何特殊牺牲或费用，则已获得保存财产的另一方须在海商法施加的条件的规限下，按比率分担蒙受损失一方的损失。

7. partial / particular average：单独海损。共同海损的对称。在海上运输中，船舶或货物因遭遇海难及其他意外事故而发生的只涉及受损财产所有人单独利益的局部损失。如货物被盗、焚毁等损失。单独海损由受损的一方或造成损失有责任的一方单独负担。但如果保险契约上有"单独海损赔偿"的条款时，其损失由保险人偿付。

contribution"[1], an ancient principle of maritime law. Under this rule, if A's cargo is damaged or sacrificed in the process of saving the ship, and B's cargo is saved as a result, B and the ship owner must contribute to A for the loss. A's claim is a general average. Similarly, the owners of cargo that is thrown overboard to save a sinking ship may have a general average claim against those whose cargo was thereby saved. The principle of general average contribution also applies when a carrier incurs extraordinary expenses in rescuing, saving or repairing an endangered ship.

In order to prove a general average claim, the claimant must show that: (1) The ship, cargo and crew were threatened by a common danger; (2) the danger was real and substantial; (3) the cargo or ship was voluntarily sacrificed for the benefit of the cargo and the ship. As an effort to develop commonly accepted principles of general average, the ***York-Antwerp Rules***[2] were completed. The latest version was agreed to in 2016. The *York-Antwerp Rules* are not treaties or conventions, however, the rules have achieved widespread acceptance by maritime industry and have been incorporated into most of modern bills of lading. Ordinarily, the general average contribution will be covered by insurance. If it is not, however, the ship's crew will hold the goods belonging to a shipper until the contribution is paid.

Although total loss and general average are ordinarily covered by the insurance policy, special problems result from partial / particular average. Many insurance policies limit the insurer's liability for particular average. A policy designed as free from particular average (FPA) will not cover any particular average. A FPA policy, followed by certain specified losses, for example, "FPA fire", will not pay for any particular average of that nature. As such, the "FPA fire" will not pay for a particular average to the cargo due to fire.

B. Types of Marine Insurance Policies

Marine insurance is available either as a **special policy**[3] covering a single shipment or as an **open policy**[4] that insures all the cargo shipped by an exporter during a particular time period.

An open policy offers the convenience and protection of covering all shipments, whether by truck, rail, air or vessel, by the shipper of certain types of goods to certain destinations and over specified routes. With an open cargo policy, the exporter is authorized to issue a certificate of insurance on a form provided by the insurance company. However, the insurance company must be notified as soon as possible after the shipment under an open cargo policy. These certificates are negotiable and are transferred along with the bill of lading to the importer or the holder of the bill of lading. If a party is obliged to purchase insurance for an isolated sale, he can purchase a special cargo policy covering the single sale. However, in actual fact, parties involved in an isolated shipment often arrange to have their

---

1. general average contribution：共同海损分摊。共同海损发生后，所有受益方按各自的分摊比例分担共同海损的全部损失金额。

2. *York-Antwerp Rules*：《约克-安特卫普规则》。《约克-安特卫普规则》是有关共同海损的理算规则。虽然该规则不是具有法律约束力的国际条约，而仅具国际惯例性质，由当事人自愿选择适用，但一经采用即在当事人之间产生法律约束力。该规则历经一百多年的发展和完善，已为国际航运界、保险界普遍接受，成为国际上适用最广泛、最重要的共同海损理算规则。

3. special policy：特殊保险单、单独保险单。

4. open policy：开口保险单、预约保险单，即 open cover。保险公司与被保险人之间的货运保险合约的一种，其主要内容是：在双方约定的期限内，被保险人一切装运出口货物按约定的费率自动地得到保险。货物装运后，被保险人应立即通知保险人，由保险人签发保险单。被保险人先预缴一定金额的保险费，在货物价值确定以后再做调整。

goods covered by the open cargo policy of a **freight forwarder**[1] or **customs broker**[2].

C. Types of Insurance Coverage

Marine cargo insurance may be the most traditional and the most developed business of insurance. It is available for virtually any type of risk, for any cargo destined for almost any port. The insurers can choose different coverage according to their needs.

The two most internationally acknowledged marine cargo insurance clauses are ***Institute Cargo Clauses* (ICC)** [3] drafted by the Institute of London Underwriters and ***China Insurance Clauses* (CIC)** [4] drafted by the People's Insurance Company of China. Two of them are basically similar to each other, and the latter will be the focus of this section.

As is shown in **Exhibit 7-2**, CIC classifies insurance coverage into two main types: **Basic coverage**[5], which can be taken independently, and **additional coverage**[6], which should go with the basic coverage. Basic coverage can be classified into three categories: **Free From Particular Average (F. P. A.)**, **With Average or With Particular Average (W. A. or W. P. A)** and **All Risks**. Additional coverage includes **general additional coverage**, which covers 11 types of general extraneous risks, such as **TPND (Theft, Pilferage and Non-delivery)**[7], and **special additional coverage**, which covers 8 types of special extraneous risks, such as war risks.

Exhibit 7–2: Types of Insurance Coverage (according to CIC)

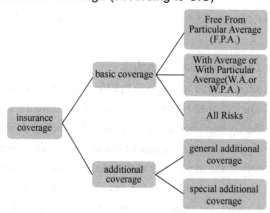

---

1. freight forwarder: 货物转运商。货物转运商是指介于运送人（比如轮船公司、航空公司、铁路公司等）与托运人（货主）之间，承揽国际贸易货物的转运业务，以收取佣金为业的货运承揽人（或公司）。

2. customs broker: 报关代理人。报关代理人是为船舶的进港或离港、货物的进口或出口准备相应文件、办理相关手续的代理人。

3. *Institute Cargo Clauses* (ICC):《协会货物条款》。《协会货物条款》由伦敦保险人协会最早制定于 1912 年，历史悠久，影响广泛，后经多次修订，最近版本为 2009 年版，是海上货物运输保险的基本条款，规定了保险人所负的责任，以作为保险人与被保险人相互约束的依据。

4. *China Insurance Clauses* (CIC):《中国保险条款》。《中国保险条款》是中国人民保险公司参照国际保险的习惯（主要是参照协会货物条款）并结合我国保险工作的实际于 1963 年制定的海上货物运输保险条款。该条款后经多次修订，最有影响力的版本为 1981 年版。

5. basic coverage: 基本险，也称主险，是指可以单独投保的险种，分为平安险、水渍险及一切险 3 种。

6. additional coverage: 附加险。在基本险别上附加承保的险别。这种险别不能单独承保，必须附属于基本险项之下。可分为一般附加险（承保由外来原因所引起的一般风险）和特殊附加险（承保与政治、军事、国家政策法令以及行政措施等因素相关联的特殊外来风险）两类。

7. TPND (Theft, Pilferage and Non-delivery): 盗窃和提货不着险。

With the original meaning that no particular average is covered, **Free From Particular Average (F. P. A.)** has the most limited scope of coverage, which includes the following.

(1) Total or Constructive Total Loss of the whole consignment hereby insured caused in the course of transit by natural calamities: heavy weather, lightning, tsunami, earthquake and flood.

(2) Total or Partial Loss caused by accidents the carrying conveyance being grounded, stranded, sunk or in collision with floating ice or other objects such as fire or explosion.

(3) Partial loss of the insured goods attributable to heavy weather, lightning and/or tsunami, where the conveyance has been grounded, stranded, sunk or burnt, irrespective of whether the event or events took place before or after such accidents.

(4) Partial or total loss consequent on falling of entire package or packages into the sea during loading, transshipment or discharge.

(5) Reasonable cost incurred by the insured on salvaging the goods or averting or minimizing a loss recoverable under the Policy, provided that such cost shall not exceed the sum insured of the consignment so saved.

(6) Losses attributable to discharge of the insured goods at a port of distress following a sea peril as well as special charges arising from loading, warehousing and forwarding of the goods at an intermediate port of call or refuge.

(7) Sacrifice in and Contribution to General Average and Salvage Charges.

(8) Such proportion of losses sustained by the shipowners is to be reimbursed by the Cargo Owner under the Contract of Affreightment Both to Blame Collision clause.[1]

Aside from the risks covered under F.P.A. as listed above, **With Average or With Particular Average (W.A. or W.P.A)** also covers partial losses of the insured goods caused by heavy weather, lightning, tsunami, earthquake and flood.[2] In other words, W. A. or W. P. A equals to F. P. A. plus partial loss due to natural calamities.

Besides the risks covered under the F. P. A. and W. A., **All Risks** also covers all risks of loss of or damage to the insured goods, whether partial or total, arising from external causes in the cause of transit. Among the three types of basic coverage, All Risks has the most comprehensive coverage, but actually it does not really cover all risks, as the term itself indicates. It excludes special additional coverage and exclusions. In other words, All Risks equals to W. A. or W. P. A plus general additional coverage.

The time of validity of a claim under CIC shall not exceed a period of two years counting from the

---

1. 平安险负责赔偿以下内容。（1）被保险货物在运输途中由于恶劣气候、雷电、海啸、地震、洪水自然灾害造成整批货物的全部损失或推定全损。（2）由于运输工具遭受搁浅、触礁、沉没、互撞、与流冰或其他物体碰撞以及失火、爆炸意外事故造成货物的全部或部分损失。（3）在运输工具已经发生搁浅、触礁、沉没、焚毁意外事故的情况下，货物在此前后又在海上遭受恶劣气候、雷电、海啸等自然灾害所造成的部分损失。（4）在装卸或转运时由于一件或数件整件货物落海造成的全部或部分损失。（5）被保险人对遭受承保责任内危险的货物采取抢救、防止或减少货损的措施而支付的合理费用，但以不超过该批被救货物的保险金额为限。（6）运输工具遭遇海难后，在避难港由于卸货所引起的损失以及在中途港、避难港由于卸货、存仓以及运送货物所产生的特别费用。（7）共同海损的牺牲、分摊和救助费用。（8）运输契约订有"船舶互撞责任"条款，根据该条款规定应由货方偿还船方的损失。

2. 除包括上列平安险的各项责任外，水渍险还负责被保险货物由于恶劣气候、雷电、海啸、地震、洪水自然灾害所造成的部分损失。

time of completion of discharge of the insured goods from the seagoing vessel at the final port of discharge.[1]

Chapter Summary

本章主要按照运输方式的不同，分别介绍各类国际货物运输法：

国际货物海上运输法：主要包括《海牙规则》《海牙-维斯比规则》以及《汉堡规则》，规定了提单项下承运人的义务、免责范围、责任限制，以及诉讼时效和第三方权利等。其中《海牙规则》历史悠久、影响深远，是《中华人民共和国海商法》制定的重要参考依据。

国际货物航空运输法：主要包括《华沙公约》(1929) 和《蒙特利尔公约》(1999)。根据后者的规定，国际航空承运人应当对旅客的人身伤亡、行李和货物损失，以及由于延误造成旅客、行李或货物的损失承担责任并予以赔偿。

国际货物铁路运输法：主要包括《国际铁路运输公约》和《国际铁路货物联运协定》，中国是后者的缔约国。

国际货物公路运输法：主要有《国际公路货物运输合同公约》，主要适用于欧洲国家，但仍不失为当前国际公路运输的一项重要的国际公约。

国际货物多式联运法：因 1980 年 5 月在日内瓦制定的《联合国国际货物多式联运公约》至今尚未达到该公约所要求的批准国家数量，目前国际上还没有统一的、规范多式联运的国际公约。

国际货物海上运输保险法：根据中国保险条款，海上货物运输保险主要分为基本险和附加险。其中，基本险是可以单独投保的险种，分为平安险、水渍险及一切险三种。附加险是在基本险别上附加承保的险别，可分为一般附加险和特殊附加险。

Exercises

Part Ⅰ. True or False Statements: Decide whether the following statements are True or False and explain why.

1. In international sales, a clean, on board and negotiable bill of lading will generally be required.

2. The original consignee may endorse the negotiable bill of lading either in blank by a bare signature of the endorser or by a special endorsement.

3. Under the *Hague Rules 1924*, the ocean carrier will be held liable for the damage or loss caused by the ocean carrier's actual fault.

4. China has ratified the *Montreal Convention 1999*, and its domestic transportation of cargo, luggage and passengers by air is also governed by the *Montreal Convention 1999*.

5. An open policy covers all shipments of the insured, whether by truck, rail, air or vessel, by the shipper of certain types of goods to certain destinations and over specified routes.

6. In the United States, *COGSA* applies to every bill of lading or document of title that evidences a contract for the transportation of goods by sea in domestic trade.

7. The *Hague Rules* limit the carrier's liability to a minimum of UK £ 100 per package or customary freight unit. The limits don't apply if the shipper has declared a higher value for the goods.

---

1. 索赔时效，从被保险货物在最后卸载港全部卸离海轮后起算，最多不超过 2 年。

8. Under a charter party if the charterer keeps the ship lying idle too long for loading or unloading, the ship owner will charge dead freight.

9. No bill of lading will be issued when the goods are transported under a charter party.

10. The *Warsaw Convention 1929* has been substituted by the *Montreal Convention 1999*, and thus ceased to be binding on its contracting states.

Part Ⅱ. Chapter Questions: Discuss and answer the following questions according to what you have learned in this chapter. You are encouraged to use your own words.

1. What are the purposes a bill of lading serve? Give your understanding on these purposes.

2. How many types of bills of lading are used in international sales? What are the usual circumstances under which they are used?

3. Compare the major changes in the provisions of the *Hague Rules*, the *Hague-Visby Rules* and the *Hamburg Rules*.

4. What are the basic duties of ocean carriers under bills of lading regulated by the *Hague Rules*?

5. To decide the seaworthiness of the ship provided by the ocean carrier, what factors should be taken into account?

6. What will regulate the obligations of shipper and ship owner under a charter party?

7. What's your understanding of the general average and the principle of general average contribution? Give an example to illustrate them.

8. What's the air carrier's liability for the death and bodily injury of passengers under the *Montreal Convention 1999*?

9. What is a consignment note?

10. What is a constructive total loss?

Part Ⅲ. Case Problem

1. The S.S. Eager was transporting goods to several ports on the east coast of Africa, including Beira in Mozambique. While still several miles at sea, the Eager learned that the rebel forces opposing the Mozambique government were attacking Beira. The ship then pulled into Beira and tied up at a pier. Immediately thereafter, it was struck by a mortar round. The goods in the ship's main cargo hold were destroyed.

Is the ship liable for the loss? Explain.

2. A shipper of fruits and vegetables delivered a refrigerated van of produce to the S.S. May Flower at the port of Elizabeth, New Jersey, on September 22 for the shipment to San Juan, Puerto Rico. The ship was supposed to sail that day but was unable to correct a boiler problem. Finally, the ship sailed on September 25 and arrived at the destination on September 27. The *Hague Rules* 1924 is incorporated into the bill of lading. Upon arrival, part of the produce was found to be rotten. The shipper claims that the carrier is liable.

（1）**Is the carrier liable for the damage to the shipment of produce? Why?**

（2）**If The *Hague Rules* 1924 isn't incorporated into the bill of lading, what law will apply to this case?**

Chapter 8
Payment in International Sale of Goods

 导读

本章主要介绍国际货物销售的各种支付方式及其基本法律知识，重点介绍在统一汇票和信用证的使用过程中涉及的国际公约和惯例。

 Warm-up Questions

(1) What are the difficulties for making payments for international sales?

(2) As far as you know, how many modes of payment are there for international sales?

(3) How much do you know about negotiable instrument, for example, check?

Like the international transportation of goods, the international payment is also an integral part of the international sale of goods. However, independent rules and trade customs have been developed to regulate and facilitate the international payment.

8.1   Modes of International Payment

In a sale of goods across national borders, the exporter (seller) and the importer (buyer) may not have previously dealt with each other, or each may know nothing about the other or the other's national legal system. Where the parties are strangers, these risks are significant, possibly overwhelming. Since they operate at a distance from each other, the seller and the buyer cannot concurrently exchange the goods for the payment funds without the help of third parties. On one hand, the seller does not know: Whether the buyer is creditworthy or trustworthy; whether related information, received from the buyer's associates and bankers, is reliable; whether exchange controls will hinder movement of the payment funds; how great the exchange risk is if payment in buyer's currency is permitted; and what delays may be involved in receiving payment from the buyer. On the other hand, the buyer does not know: Whether the seller can be trusted to ship the goods if the buyer prepays; whether the goods shipped will be of the quantity and quality as required in the contract; whether the goods will be shipped by an appropriate carrier and properly insured; whether the goods may be damaged in transit; whether the seller will provide the buyer with sufficient ownership documentation covering the goods (for example, a bill of lading) to allow the buyer to claim them from the carrier; whether the seller will provide the documentation necessary to satisfy export control regulations, import customs and valuation regulations (e.g., region of origin certificates, and inspection certificates); and what delays may be involved in receiving possession and use of the goods in the buyer's location.

Therefore, appropriate modes of payment are needed to distribute and reduce these potential risks to a considerable degree.

Although it is possible for the buyer to pay cash directly to the seller, the payment in international trade will usually involve banks located in the seller's region and in the buyer's region. However, the role of banks may be different in various modes of payment. The modes of remittance and collection involve the banks merely as intermediary. While under the payment by letter of credit, banks will be arranged to offer credit and finance for the parties.

A. Remittance[1]

It is a mode of international payment under which the buyer in international sales will voluntarily make payment to the seller via banks. The process is usually as follows: The buyer entrusts a local bank (buyer's bank) to make the payment, and the payment will then be forwarded to the seller through a seller's bank. Such a mode of payment is simple and cost saving. However, it will be agreed on by the parties only where the seller has great trust in the buyer, especially in the creditworthiness of the buyer.

If the buyer's bank transfers the instruction of payment to the seller's bank by mail, it is called **Mail Transfer (M/T)**[2]. If the instruction of payment is transferred by telegraph, the payment is **Telegraphic Transfer (T/T)**[3]. Where the buyer purchases a banker's draft and transfers the draft to the seller, the payment will be **Demand Draft (D/D)**[4]. In D/D, the draft is a sight draft with the buyer's bank to be a drawer, the seller's bank to be drawee and the seller to be a payee. These terms of the draft will be discussed in the following part of this chapter.

B. Collection[5]

Under this mode of payment, the seller issues a draft, appoints the buyer to be the payer (drawee),

---

1. remittance：汇付。汇付是国际贸易中的一种常见支付方式，指买方按合同约定的条件和时间，将货款通过银行主动汇寄给卖方。
2. Mail Transfer (M/T)：信汇。信汇是指买方将款项交给进口地银行，由其开具付款委托书。银行通过邮递交卖方所在地往来银行，委托其向卖方付款。
3. Telegraphic Transfer (T/T)：电汇。电汇是指进口地银行应买方之申请用电报向出口地往来行发出付款委托书，委托其向卖方付款。
4. Demand Draft (D/D)：票汇。票汇是指买方从进口地银行购买银行汇票邮寄给卖方，由卖方或其指定人持票从出口地相关银行取款。
5. collection：托收。出口人在货物装运后，开具以进口方为付款人的汇票（随附或不随附货运单据），委托出口地银行通过它在进口地的分行或代理行向进口方收取货款的一种结算方式。托收方式一般有光票托收和跟单托收两种。光票托收，是指出口商在出具汇票时不附带任何货运单据（如提单、发票等）。光票托收通常只用于收取货款的尾数、样品费、佣金等。跟单托收是指出口商将汇票连同所附货运单据一起交银行委托代收的托收方式。

forwards the draft (or together with some other documents) to banks, and entrusts banks to collect payment for the sale of goods from the buyer. In this process, the banking institutions serve as intermediaries between the seller and the buyer to handle the exchange of documents for payment. There are two types of collection: **clean collection** and **documentary collection**. In the event of a clean collection, only the draft will be used in the process, while under a documentary collection, other documents, including commercial invoice, bill of lading and insurance policy, etc. will be required. Compared with clean collection, documentary collection provides a safer alternative for payment, and therefore is more often used in international payment. The parties might indicate their desire for a documentary collection by specifying it in the payment terms of the international sales contract.

Typically, the documentary collection works like this: The seller places the goods in the hands of a carrier, and receives a bill of lading in return. The seller endorses the bill of lading and presents it to the bank (the seller's bank) for collection. Along with the **bill of lading**, the seller will include other essential documents such as a **marine insurance policy**, a **certificate of origin**, which may be required by customs regulations in the buyer's country, the **commercial invoice** describing the goods and showing the price to be paid, and finally a **draft**, used to make payment for the commercial invoice and the bill of lading. Other documents may be required as well, depending on the needs of the parties or the regulations on the import and export of their countries. The draft and documents are accompanied by a **collection letter** that provides instructions from the seller on such matters as who is responsible for bank collection charges, what to do in the event that the buyer dishonors the draft, and instructions for remittance of the proceeds back to the seller. The seller's bank forwards the draft and documents to a buyer's bank, also called collecting bank, with instructions that documents can be released to the buyer only upon payment of the draft. The collecting bank negotiates the documents to the buyer upon payment of the draft, and remits the money back to the seller's bank. Finally, the seller can get the payment from the seller's bank.

There are two types of documentary collection: **Document Against Payment (D/P)** and **Document Against Acceptance (D/A)**.[1] When D/P is used, the buyer shall not obtain the bill of lading and other documents until he has made the payment to the collecting bank. When D/A is used, the collecting bank will hand over the shipping documents to the buyer only upon the acceptance of the draft. Comparatively speaking, D/A may pose greater potential risks to the seller. For example, the buyer may refuse to pay the draft or has declared to be insolvent when the draft is mature.

As for the rules governing the collection, there is *Uniform Rules for Collection* **(URC522)**[2] published by the ICC. This version was published in 1995 and came into effect on 1 January 1996. URC522 is a codification of international customs and usages in international payment, and they are binding when the parties to a contract agree to apply them or don't expressly exclude the application of

---

1. 跟单托收分为付款交单和承兑交单两种方式。付款交单是指被委托的代收银行必须在进口商付清票款后才能将货运单据交给进口商的托收方式。承兑交单是指被委托的代收银行在付款人承兑汇票后即将货运单据交给付款人，付款人在汇票到期时履行付款义务的托收方式。

2. *Uniform Rules for Collection* (URC522)：《托收统一规则》。《托收统一规则》是国与国间托收结算业务应当遵循的基本做法和准则。它是由国际性民间商业组织国际商会根据国际上的一些习惯做法而制订的。《托收统一规则》522是从1996年开始生效的修订版。

them. In fact, the URC522 has achieved wide acceptance in international trade practice.

C. Letter of Credit[1]

As discussed in the preceding paragraphs, a seller will assume less credit risk in the documentary collection. Nevertheless, a seller still faces the possibility that the buyer will not honor the documentary draft when it is presented for payment. Ideally, the seller would prefer not to release the title to the goods until it is certain that he will be paid. The buyer would want to postpone payment, until it is assured that the goods are as required by the sales contract and are no longer subject to the seller's control or disposal. In order to reconcile these conflicting objectives and reduce the risks involved in an international sales transaction, the parties may arrange for payment under a letter of credit. Letters of credit are flexible commercial instruments adaptable to a broad range of commercial uses. They are the most common form of payment for the international sale of goods.

8.2   Fundamentals of Negotiable Instruments

In the previous discussion, the draft has been mentioned from time to time. It is a specialized negotiable instrument commonly used to expedite foreign money payment in many types of international transactions. The negotiable instruments can serve two purposes: (1) They act as a substitute for money; and (2) they act as a financing or credit device. Although it is beyond the scope of this chapter to offer a thorough discussion on the law of negotiable instruments, an overview understanding of the negotiable instruments, especially the draft, is essential to the study of international business law.

A. Bill of Exchange

A Bill of Exchange is often called a draft. The word "draft" is more frequently used in U.S. law and banking practice, while the term "bill of exchange" is more frequently used outside the United States, particularly in England. In this chapter, the term of "draft" and the term of "bill of exchange" are used as the equivalent of each other. The origin of the bill of exchange lies in the history of the merchants. As merchants began to buy and sell goods in the markets of distant cities, they sought a safer means of transferring money than by carrying it in their caravans. They invented a wiser method to make the payment. It might have worked like this: Assume Merchant A delivered goods to Merchant B in a distant city, who became indebted to A for the purchase. Later, Merchant A desired to purchase goods from Merchant C. Merchant A could pay Merchant C by writing a piece of paper—an order addressed by A to B to pay that amount of money to C. Since the 19th century, the practice has been widely recognized and improved by the modern law of countries. A bill of exchange is a **three-party instrument, which is an unconditional written order by one party, which orders the second party To pay money to a third party**. Three primary parties are involved in a bill of exchange: (1) drawer—the party who writes the order; (2) drawee—the party who must pay the money

---

1. letter of credit: 信用证。信用证是指银行或其他人应客户的请求或指示，向第三人签发的一种承诺性函件或文据，即，若该第三人能履行该函件或文据所规定的条件，则该第三人要按所载条件签发以该行或其指定的另一银行为付款人的汇票，并由其承担兑付责任。

stated in the draft (payer); (3) payee—the party who receives the money from a draft.[1]

Two types of bills of exchange or draft are often used in international payment: sight draft and time draft. **Sight draft**[2] is a draft that is to be paid upon presentation or demand. It is also called demand draft. **Time draft**[3] is a draft due at a future date or after a specified period of time. The time draft requires a procedure of acceptance by the drawee. Typically, the acceptance is done by stamping the date and the word "accepted" across the face of draft, together with the name and signature of the drawee. The acceptance indicates the drawee's unconditional obligation to pay the draft on the date due. A draft payable at "sixty days after date" is payable by the drawee sixty days after the original date of the instrument. A draft payable at "sixty days sight" means that it is due to be paid sixty days after the date of the acceptance. Thus the time draft can provide the seller and the buyer with a mechanism for financing the international sale. Considering the difference in its negotiation, there are **order draft**[4] and **bearer draft**[5]. The former is payable to a specific payee, while the latter is payable to the holder, not a specific payee. The order draft must be negotiated through proper endorsement, while the bearer draft may be negotiated just by delivery.

B. Check[6]

It is drawn on a financial institution (the drawee) and is payable on demand. Primary parties involved in a check are also three parties: drawer, drawee, and payee. Drawer is the customer who has the checking account and writes the check. Drawee is the financial institution, where the drawer has his or her account. Payee is the party to whom the check is written. Obvious differences between a check and a draft are (1) the drawee under a check is always the financial institutions, and (2) the check must be paid on demand, no "time check" exists.

C. Promissory note[7]

It is a two-party negotiable instrument that is an unconditional written promise by one party to pay money to another party. Only two primary parties are involved in a promissory note: the drawer and the drawee. Drawer is the party who makes the promise to pay (borrower). Payee is the party to whom the

---

1. 汇票：一人向另一人签发的、要求该人即期或远期向指定的人或持票人无条件支付一定金额的书面支付命令。汇票包括三方基本当事人，即出票人（drawer）、付款人（drawee）及受款人（payee）。

2. sight draft：即期汇票。出票人签发的要求付款人在见票的当日或提示时，无条件支付一定金额给收款人或持票人的书面支付命令。票面上注明"见票即付"字样，无须承兑。汇票上没有明确表示付款日期的，可视为见票即付的汇票。

3. time draft：远期汇票。付款人见到汇票后，可于约定的将来某一日期付款的汇票。远期汇票在到期以前可以转让、流通，如果持票人急需现金，也可以通过贴现成为融通资金的工具。

4. order draft：指示汇票、记名汇票。出票人在汇票上写明受款人的姓名或商号的一种汇票。这种汇票，出票人在出票后，应该将该汇票交给票面上载明的受款人，然后才产生票据的效力。同时，作为受款人的执票人，可以依法背书转让。

5. bearer draft：来人汇票、不记名汇票。票面没有记载受款人的姓名或商号，或者仅记载"来人"字样的一种汇票。这种汇票在完成交付行为之后，即可转让。《中华人民共和国票据法》规定：汇票没有记载收款人名称的，汇票无效。

6. check：支票。出票人向某一银行开出的汇票，指示该银行向票据载明的收款人或其指定的人无条件即期支付一定数额的款项。支票的签发一般是以出票人在银行有存款为条件。

7. promissory note：本票。由出票人签发的，承诺在指定的付款日期或见票时无条件向收款人或持票人支付确定金额的票据。

promise to pay is made (lender). The promissory note should be distinguished from an IOU (e.g., "IOU Adam Brown, $100"). In a promissory note, there is "a promise to pay" and it is an undertaking to pay, more than a mere acknowledgement of an existing debt.

8.3   The Bill of Exchange

Among the negotiable instruments, bill of exchange is more complex and more frequently used in international trade. Therefore, some special attentions should be paid to the bill of exchange.

A. Laws Governing the Bill of Exchange

Though until the middle of the seventeenth century, bills of exchange were governed by a single international law, the *lex mercatoria*. And the rise of national laws brought about differences in the rules governing bills of exchange. Currently, there is no uniform legal system governing the bills of exchange across the world.

In 1882, England enacted the *Bills of Exchange Act 1882*. Today this law continues in force in the United Kingdom and in virtually all of Britain's former colonies. In the United States, the bill of exchange or draft now falls within the province of *UCC* (Article 3 Commercial Papers). The German law of negotiable instruments was enacted in 1871. France incorporated its law of negotiable instruments into the *French Commercial Code of 1807*. On the European continent, there were calls throughout the late half of the nineteenth century for the creation of an international negotiable instruments law. Finally, in 1930, **Convention providing a Uniform Law for Bills of Exchange and Promissory Notes (ULB)**[1] was signed in Geneva. The following year, **Convention providing a Uniform Law for Cheques (ULC)**[2] was also signed in Geneva. Now the ULB and ULC have been ratified by most European continental countries as well as Japan and some Latin American countries. Following the *ULB* and *ULC*, China has enacted its *Negotiable Instruments Law*, being effective as of 1 January 1996. However, the Anglo-American common law countries have not ratified the *ULB* or *ULC*.

Efforts have been made in drafting a truly international convention governing bills of exchange. The UNCITRAL produced a text called the *United Nations Convention on International Bills of Exchange and International Promissory Notes*[3] in May 1988, which was approved by the UN General

---

1. *Convention providing a Uniform Law for Bills of Exchange and Promissory Notes* (ULB):《统一汇票本票法公约》。为了便于国际支付、统一各方票据制度，1930 年 6 月，国际联盟主持召开日内瓦会议签订了《统一汇票本票法公约》(以下简称《公约》)，并于 1934 年 1 月 1 日起生效。《公约》参加国多限于大陆法系成员，其规定与英美票据法不同。因此，自《公约》生效后，国际上形成了日内瓦票据法体系和英美票据法体系并存的局面。

2. *Convention providing a Uniform Law for Cheques* (ULC):《统一支票法公约》。为了便于国际贸易的票据支付，统一各方支票法，1931 年 3 月 19 日国际联盟主持召开了日内瓦会议，签订了《统一支票法公约》，并已于 1934 年生效。到目前为止，《统一支票法公约》在国际贸易支付中仍占有重要地位。

3. *United Nations Convention on International Bills of Exchange and International promissory Notes*:《联合国国际汇票与国际本票公约》。联合国国际贸易法委员会于 1988 年 12 月 9 日通过了《联合国国际汇票与国际本票公约》，旨在消除国际支付所用票据中现有的重大不一致和不确定之处，但由于迄今缔约成员极其有限，尚未生效。

Assembly and was open for ratification. Though only ten states must ratify the convention before it will come into effect, until January 2023 only 5 countries have ratified the convention, and it seems unlikely that it will be effective anytime soon.

B. Brief requirements of the Bill of Exchange

There are strict and formal requirements for the bill of exchange. Under *ULB*, a bill of exchange contains:

1. The term "bill of exchange" inserted in the body of the instrument and expressed in the language employed in drawing up the instrument;

2. An unconditional order to pay a determinate sum of money;

3. The name of the person who is to pay (drawee);

4. A statement of the time of payment;

5. A statement of the place where payment is to be made;

6. The name of the person to whom or to whose order payment is to be made;

7. A statement of the date and of the place where the bill is issued;

8. The signature of the person who issues the bill (drawer).[1]

A bill of exchange which does not conform to any of the above requirements is invalid and dishonored under *ULB*. Under the Anglo-American laws governing the bills of exchange, item 1 and item 7 are not required.

The bill of exchange should be an unconditional order to pay, and cannot be conditioned on the performance of some other obligation. The reason for this is basic to the nature of the negotiability of bills of exchange. If a holder of a bill of exchange has to determine whether a collateral obligation had or hadn't been fulfilled, the negotiability and the use of bills of exchange will be greatly reduced. A bill of exchange must be payable in money, which must be for a definite sum. Usually, the parties to bills of exchange will routinely define their money obligations by referring to money units of account, such as the European Union's euro.

For example, the bills of exchange containing any of the following statements are deemed to be invalid. (1) "ABC Corp. promises to pay $100,000 to the order of Johnson, provided that the helicopter sold meets all contractual specifications." (2) "Payable to the order of Ray Rodes 6 months after the death of Alber Olds." (3) "I wish you would pay to the order of Merry Smith $ 500 on Oct. 20." The reasons are (1) the statement of "provided that the helicopter sold meets all contractual specifications" indicates the instrument is not an "unconditional order"; (2) "the death of Alber Olds", though will come in the future, surely is not a fixed determinable future time; (3) expression of "I wish", or the like, does not indicate an order.

C. Negotiation of the bill of Exchange

Negotiation[2] is the transfer of an instrument from one party to another so that the transferee (holder) takes legal rights in the instrument. The rights that a holder acquires depend on the manner in

---

1.《统一汇票本票法公约》第 1 条。汇票应包含下列内容：1. 票据主文中列有"汇票"一词，并以开立票据所使用的文字说明之；2. 无条件支付一定金额的命令；3. 付款人（受票人）的姓名；4. 付款日期；5. 付款地；6. 受款人或其指定人的姓名；7. 开立汇票的日期和地点；8. 开立汇票的人（出票人）的签名。

2. negotiation：转让。由一人向另一人转移汇票或其他流通证券，从而使受让人成为票据持有人。

which the instrument was negotiated and the governing law. The correct **manner of negotiation** of the bill of Exchange depends on whether the instrument is a bearer instrument or an order instrument. Order bill of Exchange / draft is payable to a specific payee, often containing the words "pay to the order of Co. A" or "pay to Francis Madero". Order draft is negotiated by endorsement and delivery. While the bearer bill of Exchange / draft that is payable to the holder, not to a specific payee, often contains the words "pay the bearer" or the signature of the last endorsee. The bearer draft is negotiated by delivery alone.

Endorsement. An endorsement refers to the act of writing down signatures with or without additional statements on the back of the negotiable instrument. When endorsed, the amount of money stated in the bill of exchange is indivisible, i.e., a bill of exchange must be transferred as a whole, partial negotiation of the sum of payment is not allowed. As mentioned before in Chapter 7, there are **special endorsements** and **blank endorsements**. In blank endorsements, only the signature of the endorser appears on the instrument, for example, "Jane Austin (signed)". In special endorsements, the signatures of both the endorser and the endorsee appear, for instance, "Pay to William Kaiser (signed) Jane Austin (signed)".

By putting his signature on the bill of exchange, the endorser will be held secondarily liable to the subsequent holders for guaranteeing the acceptance or payment of the bill of exchange. That is, when the bill of exchange is dishonored by the drawee, the last holder has the right to require the endorser to reimburse the stated amount and relevant expenses of the bill of exchange.

8.4   Letters of Credit

A. Overview

A transaction of international sales typically involves at least three contracts: The sales contract between buyer and seller, the carriage contract, and the letter of credit contract by which the sale is financed. The use of the letter of credit as a tool to reduce payment risk has grown substantially over the past decade. Letters of credit facilitate international trade by substituting the credit of the bank for that of the buyer. Electronic communication has taken over some aspects of letters of credit practice, but not others. They dominate the issuance process in bank-to-bank communications, and are sometimes used by applicants to stimulate the issuance process. However, they have not been able to create an entirely paperless transaction pattern for many reasons. First, the beneficiary still wants a piece of paper committing the banks to pay upon specified conditions. Second, electronic bills of lading still are not accepted in most trades as transferable documents of title, for the reasons discussed in Chapter 7. Thus, in the collection of the letter of credit, physical documents will be forwarded, while funds settlement may be electronic.

There are mainly two types of letters of credit: **clean credit**[1] and **documentary credit**[2]. However,

---

1. clean credit: 光票信用证。又称"无跟单信用证"，与"跟单信用证"相对应，不必交付货运单据，仅凭汇票付款的信用证。光票信用证用以清算商品价款风险较大的非贸易性支出。

2. documentary credit: 跟单信用证。受益人支款时，除提交汇票外，还要提供规定的单据的信用证。跟单信用证是开证行有条件的付款承诺书，使受益人有收款保障。这个条件就是"单证相符"。跟单信用证一般是由银行根据进口商要求向出口商开立的，并在一定期限内由付款行凭单据付给出口商一定金额款项。国际贸易结算中使用的信用证基本上都是跟单信用证。

in business practice, letter of credit is generally referred to as documentary credit, thus in the following text the expression of letter of credit is equivalent to documentary credit.

The letter of credit can be defined as a conditional undertaking by a bank, issued in accordance with the instructions of the applicant (the buyer), in favor of the beneficiary (the seller), wherein the bank promises to pay, accept, or negotiate the beneficiary's draft up to the amount of the contract price within the prescribed time limit, upon the beneficiary's presentation of stipulated documents. According to *UCP*600, which will be introduced in detail in the following subsection, Credit means any arrangement, however named or described, that is irrevocable and thereby constitutes a definite undertaking of the issuing bank to honor a complying presentation.[1] A credit is irrevocable even if there is no indication to that effect.[2]

In a letter of credit transaction, the promise of an internationally recognized bank is substituted for that of the buyer. As long as the seller complies with all requirements in the letter of credit, such as tendering the documents called in the letter of credit (usually including bill of lading, draft, insurance policy, commercial invoice and other collateral documents) within the time allowed, the seller has more assurance of being paid than in any other mode of payment, except receiving cash in advance.

The use of the letter of credit in international payment is as follows.

If the sales contract requires the payment to be made by letter of credit, at first, there will be a contract between the buyer and the Buyer's Bank ("**issuing bank**"[3]). The buyer initiates the contract by applying to his own bank for the issuance of a letter of credit in favor of the seller (beneficiary), and thereby agrees to reimburse the issuing bank for payment of drafts presented with certain shipping documents (such as bills of lading, etc.) specified in the terms and conditions of the letter of credit. Thus the issuing bank undertakes the payment obligation to the seller (the beneficiary). If the seller requires an obligation of a bank in the seller's jurisdiction, the letter of credit must be confirmed by a Seller's Bank ("**confirming bank**"[4]). The Buyer's Bank (issuing bank) will forward its letter of credit to the seller through another bank, the Seller's Bank, which is usually a correspondent bank to the Buyer's Bank. By merely indicating "We confirm this credit", the Seller's Bank (confirming bank) makes a direct promise to the seller that it will assume the same obligation and liability as the issuing bank, and will pay the contract price to the seller if the seller presents the required documents to it. Confirmation of a letter of credit must be bargained for and specified in the sales contract. If no confirmation of the credit is required by the sales contract, Buyer's Bank can forward the letter of credit through a "notifying bank" or an "**advising bank**"[5], which is near the seller. This bank acts as the agent of the issuing bank and has only a duty to communicate the terms of the credit accurately. It is not obligated to the seller but will take the documents and forward them to the Buyer's Bank for collection purposes

---

1.《跟单信用证统一惯例 600》第 2 条定义：……信用证意指一项约定，无论其如何命名或描述，该约定不可撤销并因此构成开证行对于相符提示予以兑付的确定承诺。……

2.《跟单信用证统一惯例 600》第 3 条释义：……信用证是不可撤销的，即使信用证中对此未作指示也是如此。……

3. issuing bank：开证行，指应申请人要求或代表其自身开立信用证的银行。

4. confirming bank：保兑行，指应开证行的授权或请求对信用证加具保兑的银行。

5. advising bank：通知行，指应开证行要求通知信用证的银行。

only.[1] The issuing bank communicates the issuance of the letter of credit to the seller's bank, via the confirming or advising bank. The confirming bank or advising bank then informs the seller of the issuance of the letter of credit.

Upon receiving the letter of credit, the seller will prepare the necessary documents accordingly. For example, the seller will send the goods to the carrier, which issues a negotiable bill of lading as a combination of receipt and contract. After having the complete set of documents needed, the seller takes these documents to the Seller's Bank, which (as a confirming bank) is obligated to pay the seller the contract price upon presentation of the documents. To obtain payment, the seller attaches a "draft" to the documents, and in the letter of credit, the banks have promised to honor such a draft. If a "demand draft" is used, the confirming bank will pay the amount immediately, usually by crediting the seller's account either in the Seller's Bank or in some other bank designated by the seller. In the event that the draft is a "time draft" (e.g., "pay 30 days after sight"), the confirming bank need not pay upon the presentment of the draft and documents, but it must "accept" the time draft when it is presented. This "acceptance" creates an obligation on confirming the bank that it will pay at the later time stated in the draft.

In return for the bank's payment, the seller will endorse both the draft and the negotiable bill of lading to the Seller's Bank and transfer the other documents to it. The Seller's Bank, in turn, will endorse and forward the draft, with the required documents attached to the Buyer's Bank. It thus, presents the draft (with the accompanying documents) to the Buyer's Bank for payment. The Buyer's Bank is obligated under the letter of credit to honor the draft and to reimburse the Seller's Bank if the documents attached to the draft are conforming. Since there is already a correspondent relationship between the two banks, the Buyer's Bank will credit the Seller's Bank account with the amount of the draft.

The Buyer's Bank then advises the buyer that the documents have arrived and that payment is due. Since the buyer and the Buyer's Bank usually have an established relationship, the usual course of events will be for the bank to be authorized to charge the amount of the draft to the buyer's bank account, and to forward the documents to the buyer. If there was not an established relationship between the

---

1. 在信用证结算方式下，还可能涉及其他银行，如"被指定银行"（nominated bank，又称被指定行、被委托行或被授予行，指在信用证中被开证行指定代理该证业务的银行。被指定行一般是开证行的代理或账户行。被指定的身份多为通知行、议付行、付款行、保兑行、偿付行等。）"议付行"（negotiating bank，凭信用证承接出口商的汇票、货运单据并议付票款的银行。议付票款后，立即将单据寄出，向开证行、保兑行、付款行或偿付行追索垫款。议付行和开证行之间不是代理关系。议付行是根据信用证上开证行的付款承诺，向开证行索偿。开证行收到议付行寄来的单据，如发现单据不符合信用证条款，可以拒绝付款，议付行可据此向出口商追索票款。）、"偿付行"（reimbursing bank，开证行的代理人接受信用证开证行的委托，代开证行偿还议付行垫款的第三方银行。偿付行在以进口商或开证行为汇票付款人的信用证出现，凭议付行证明单证相符的索汇证明书，代开证行偿付货款。开证行收到单据，如发现不符，应向议付行追回已付款项，不能向偿付行进行追索，因为偿付行没有审单，不负单证不符之责。）、"付款行" [paying bank，信用证规定的汇票付款人。信用证以进口地货币开出时，开证行审单无误后付款给议付行，一经付款，则为最终付款，再无权向议付行追索。信用证以出口地货币开出时，付款行就是议付行，议付行审单无误后付款给出口商，一经付款，即无权向出口商追索。信用证以第三方货币开出时，付款行是第三方的银行，其地位与偿付行相似，都不凭单据而凭汇票和索汇证明信，履行汇票付款人的责任，将票款付给持票人（即议付行），一经付款，不得追索。]

buyer and its bank, the buyer would be required to pay or to arrange sufficient credit[1] for the draft before the documents were released to it. When the draft and documents are forwarded from the seller to the Seller's Bank to the Buyer's Bank to the buyer, each of these parties will endorse the bill of lading to the next party.

Once the buyer has paid or arranged to pay, the Buyer's Bank will obtain possession of the bill of lading, and only then will it be entitled to obtain the goods from the carrier. Note that the buyer has effectively paid for the goods while they were at sea, long before their arrival. In fact, the buyer is bound to pay for the goods as soon as the draft and required documents are presented to the Seller's Bank. If the goods fail to arrive, the buyer must look to its **Insurance Certificate**[2] for protection and reimbursement.

B. The Governing Rules: UCP600

Although there are national laws (e.g., Article 5 of the *UCC*) governing letters of credit, the *Uniform Customs and Practice for Documentary Credits* (commonly called "*UCP*")[3] published by the International Chamber of Commerce (ICC) is the most important rule governing letters of credit across the world. *UCP* is the codification of international trade customs and usages on bankers' dealing with letters of credit, offering a rather uniform and detailed manual of operations for banks. The *UCP* does not purport to be law, however, it is incorporated by reference in most international letters of credit.

The ICC published the first version of *UCP* in 1933 and has published a revision of the *UCP* about every ten years. The latest version is the sixth revision of the rules called *UCP*600. It is the fruit of more than three years of work by ICC's Commission on Banking Technique and Practice. The *UCP*600 came into effect on 1 July 2007. *The Uniform Customs and Practice for Documentary Credits*, 2007 Revision, ICC Publication no. 600 ("*UCP*") are rules that apply to any documentary credit ("credit") (including, to the extent to which they may be applicable, any **standby letter of credit**[4]) when the text of the credit

---

1. credit: 借款、贷款

2. Insurance Certificate: 保险凭证。又称为小保单。证明保险合同已经订立或保险单已经正式签发的一种书面凭证，是内容和格式简化了的保险单。保险人向投保人出具保险凭证是为了简化订立保险合同的单证手续。保险凭证一般不列明具体的保险条款，只记载投保人和保险人约定的主要保险内容。保险凭证虽未记载保险合同的全部内容，但与保险单具有相同的法律效力。保险凭证未列明的内容，以相应的保险单记载的内容为准，保险凭证记载的内容和相应的保险单列明的内容发生抵触时，以保险凭证的记载为准。保险凭证一般用于团体保险业务、货物运输保险业务和机动车责任保险业务中。

3. *Uniform Customs and Practice for Documentary Credits* (commonly called "*UCP*"): 《跟单信用证统一惯例》。该惯例是由国际商会制定公布的关于银行与商人之间信用证的运行或流通机制的出版物，1933年首次制定公布，后经多次修订。2007 年生效的版本亦称为 (《国际商会 600 号出版物》)。作为贸易惯例，《跟单信用证统一惯例》并不具有法律效力，却是全世界公认的、到目前为止最为成功的一套非官方规定。在当事人约定其信用证受《跟单信用证统一惯例》约束的情形下，《跟单信用证统一惯例》具有法律拘束力。

4. standby letter of credit: 备用信用证。备用信用证是指开证行根据开证申请人的指示，对受益人开立的承诺承担某些义务的保证，即开证行保证在开证申请人未能履行其义务时，受益人只要凭备用信用证的规定向开证行开具汇票 (或不要汇票)，并随附开证申请人未履行其义务的声明或证明文件，即可取得开证行的偿付。备用信用证广泛流行于美国和日本。因美国和日本两个国家的法律禁止银行开立保函，所以美国和日本的银行都以备用信用证来代替保函。

expressly indicates that it is subject to these rules. They are binding on all parties thereto unless expressly modified or excluded by the credit. (Article 1 of *UCP*600)[1] And a letter of credit must state the following terms: (1) The bank with which it is available or whether it is available with any bank; (2) whether it is available by sight payment, deferred payment, acceptance or negotiation; (3) an expiry date for presentation.[2]

*UCP*600 reduces the number of articles from 46 in *UCP*500 to 39. The new edition contains major changes that letter of credit practitioners will need to know. Among them are new articles on definitions and interpretations (Article 2 and Article 3), replacement of the term "reasonable time" with a maximum of five banking days for examining documents, and re-drafted transport articles aimed at resolving confusion over the identification of carriers, masters and agents. Also, available along with *UCP*600 is an updated version of ***International Standard Banking Practice for the Examination of Documents under Documentary Credits***[3], commonly called *ISBP*. The ISBP is a checklist of items that document checkers need to look for when examining documents presented under letters of credit. Since it was first published in 2002, the *ISBP* has been an indispensable companion to the *UCP*.

C. Basic Legal Principles

The *UCP*600 has established two basic legal principles of the letter of credit. One is the Principle of Independence and the other is the Rule of Strict Compliance.

1. The Principle of Independence[4]

The Principle of Independence, sometimes also called the autonomy of letters of credit, is intended to secure the wide use of letter of credit in international payment. Generally, it means that the bank's obligations under the letter of credit are independent of the buyer's and seller's obligations under the contract for the sale of goods. Such a principle is embodied in Article 4. It states: "A credit by its nature is a separate transaction from the sale or other contract on which it may be based. Banks are in no way concerned with or bound by such a contract, even if any reference whatsoever to it is included in the credit. Consequently, the undertaking of a bank to honor, to negotiate or to fulfill any other obligation under the credit is not subject to claims or defenses by the applicant resulting from its relationships with

---

1.《跟单信用证统一惯例 600》第 1 条 统一惯例的适用范围：跟单信用证统一惯例（2007 年修订本，国际商会第 600 号出版物）适用于所有在正文中标明按本惯例办理的跟单信用证（包括本惯例适用范围内的备用信用证）。除非信用证中另有规定，本惯例对一切有关当事人均具有约束力。

2.《跟单信用证统一惯例 600》第 6 条 有效性、有效期限及提示地点。a：信用证必须规定可以有效使用信用证的银行，或者信用证是否对任何银行均为有效。b：信用证必须规定它是否适用于即期付款、延期付款、承兑抑或议付。d. i：信用证必须规定提示单据的有效期限。

3. *International Standard Banking Practice for the Examination of Documents under Documentary Credits*：《关于审核跟单信用证下单据的国际标准银行实务》。提供了一套审核适用《跟单信用证统一惯例》的信用证项下单据的国际惯例，对于各国正确理解和使用《跟单信用证统一惯例》、统一和规范各国信用证审单实务、减少拒付争议的发生具有重要的意义。

4. Principle of Independence：（信用证的）独立性原则。（信用证的）独立性原则是指信用证一经开立，在银行与买卖双方之间即建立起一种独立于买卖合同的关系。开证行及其他参加信用证业务的银行处理与该信用证有关的业务时，只以信用证规定为准，银行无须过问买卖合同的内容，也无须关心买卖合同的履行情况，更无须对买卖合同的纠纷负责任。

the issuing bank or the beneficiary."[1] Article 5 of *UCP*600 furthers the Principle of Independence by stating: "banks deal only with documents, and not with the goods or any issues concerning the performance of the sale contract."[2]

That is to say, the issuing bank or confirming bank will perform its obligation of payment if the beneficiary (Seller) performs its obligations, i.e., presenting the documents as required by the irrevocable letter of credit, regardless of whether those obligations fulfill the sales contract obligations or not, even when the issuing bank or the confirming bank is notified that there is a breach of sales contract committed by the seller. In the event of a breach of sales contract committed by the seller, the proper redressing way for the buyer is to seek remedies for breach of contract from the seller.

To this Principle of Independence, there is one well-established exception. This exception provides that **fraud,** on the part of the seller/beneficiary brought to the issuing bank's attention before it has paid out against tender of apparently conforming documents, discharges the bank's absolute obligation to pay.

This exception was established in the United States in *Sztejn v. Henry Schroder Banking Corporation* (See Case 8-1).

【 Case 8-1 】

Sztejn v. Henry Schroder Banking Corporation
31 N.Y.S. 2d 631 (1941)

BACKGROUNDS AND FACTS

The Plaintiff contracted with Transea, an Indian company for the purchase of hog bristles. The Plaintiff contracted with Schroder Banking Corporation, a US bank, for the issuance of an irrevocable letter of credit providing: Schroder will pay once the shipment is made, and when the Commercial invoice and bill of lading made out to the order of Schroder is presented. Then the letter of credit was delivered to Transea through banking channels. Transea filled 50 cases with cow hair and other worthless rubbish and procured bill of lading from the shipping company and obtained the invoice, which shows the shipment of 50 cases of hog bristles ordered by the Plaintiff. The documents and the draft were presented to Schroder by the Chartered Bank of India, acting as an agent for Transea. The Plaintiff filed a complaint that Transea filled the fifty boxes with worthless junk to defraud, seeking to refrain the issuing bank from paying on the letter of credit.

SHIENTAG, JUSTICE

It is well established that a letter of credit is independent of the primary contract of sale between the buyer and the seller. The issuing bank agrees to pay upon presentation of documents, not goods. … However, I believe that a different situation is presented in the instant action. This is not a controversy

---

1.《跟单信用证统一惯例 600》第 4 条 信用证与合同。a：就性质而言，信用证与可能作为其依据的销售合同或其他合同，是相互独立的交易。即使信用证中提及该合同，银行亦与该合同完全无关，且不受其约束。因此，一家银行作出兑付、议付或履行信用证项下其他义务的承诺，并不受申请人与开证行之间或与受益人之间在已有关系下产生的索偿或抗辩的制约。……

2.《跟单信用证统一惯例 600》第 5 条。单据与货物/服务/行为：银行处理的是单据，而不是单据所涉及的货物、服务或其他行为。

between the buyer and seller concerning a mere breach of warranty regarding the quality of the merchandise; on the present motion, it must be assumed that the seller has intentionally failed to ship any goods ordered by the buyer. In such a situation, where the seller's fraud has been called to the bank's attention before the drafts and documents have been presented for payment, the principle of the independence of the bank's obligation under the letter of credit should not be extended to protect the unscrupulous seller. It is true that even though the documents are forged or fraudulent if the issuing bank has already paid the draft before receiving notice of the seller's fraud, it will be protected if it exercised reasonable diligence before making such payment. However, in the instant action, Schroder has received notice of Transea's active fraud before it accepted or paid the draft.

DECISION

The court held in favor of the plaintiff and enjoined the bank's payment.

The fraud exception is narrowly defined and incorporated into Article 5 of the *UCC*. Its application is subject to a lot of limitations such as "materially fraudulent", good faith holder of the draft, etc.

While *UCP*600 has no provisions concerning the fraud exception, the law of China has drawn on the provisions of *UCC* and expressed in a much clearer way. Provisions *on Adjudicating the Disputes Arising from Letters of Credit* were issued by the People's Supreme Court of PRC and came into effect on 1 January 2006. Article 8 provides four situations in which a fraud under a letter of credit transaction shall be deemed to exist: (1) The beneficiary forged the documents or tendered the documents containing fraudulent information; (2) the beneficiary intentionally failed to deliver the goods or deliver the worthless goods; (3) the beneficiary and the applicant or a third party colluded to tender fraudulent documents based on fictional underlying transaction; (4) other situations in which a fraud under the letter of credit was committed.[1]

When discovering any of the above situations and believing that irreparable harm may arise from the fraud, the issuing bank, the applicant or the other parties having an interest in the letter of credit transaction, may petition to the competent court for suspending the payment under the letter of credit. The court order for suspending the payment under the letter of credit shall be rendered within 48 hours and shall come into force upon its rendering. (Article 9 and Article 12)[2] However, even when a fraud under the letter of credit has been proved, the payment under the letter of credit shall not be suspended in any of the following circumstances: (1) A nominated person has made the payment in good faith according to the instruction from the issuing bank; (2) a nominated person has in good faith honored the draft drawn under the letter of credit; (3) the confirming bank has performed its duty of payment under the letter of credit in good faith; or (4) the negotiating bank has negotiated the draft drawn under the

---

1.《最高人民法院关于审理信用证纠纷案件若干问题的规定》第 8 条。凡有下列情形之一的，应当认定存在信用证欺诈：（一）受益人伪造单据或者提交记载内容虚假的单据；（二）受益人恶意不交付货物或者交付的货物无价值；（三）受益人和开证申请人或者其他第三方串通提交假单据，而没有真实的基础交易；（四）其他进行信用证欺诈的情形。

2.《最高人民法院关于审理信用证纠纷案件若干问题的规定》第 9 条和第 12 条。第 9 条：开证申请人、开证行或者其他利害关系人发现有本规定第 8 条的情形，并认为将会给其造成难以弥补的损害时，可以向有管辖权的人民法院申请中止支付信用证项下的款项。第 12 条：人民法院接受中止支付信用证下款项申请后，必须在 48 小时内作出裁定；裁定中止支付的，应当立即开始执行。人民法院作出中止支付信用证项下款项的裁定，应当列明申请人、被申请人和第三人。

letter of credit in good faith.[1]

2. The Rule of Strict Compliance[2]

Since banks may only deal with the documents, rather than the goods or services related to the letter of credit, in determining whether the documents submitted by the beneficiary are in order on their face, a bank under the obligation for payment, which may be the issuing bank, the confirming bank or a nominated bank, is entitled to apply the so-called Rule of Strict Compliance. In other words, the bank may reject documents that do not strictly comply with the terms specified in the letter of credit.

The Standard for Examination of Documents. Article 14 of *UCP*600 provides the standard for the examination of documents. "Data in a document, when read in context with the credit, the document itself and international standard banking practice, need not be identical to, but must not conflict with, data in that document, any other stipulated document or the credit."[3] And "In documents other than the commercial invoice, the description of the goods, services or performance, if stated, may be in general terms not conflicting with their description in the credit."[4] That is to say, data in documents are not required to be identical but no conflict is endured. And the primary document for describing the goods in a documentary sale transaction is the commercial invoice. The description in the commercial invoice must be specific and must correspond with the description in the credit, while descriptions in all other documents can be "in general terms not conflicting with" the description in the credit. Thus, where a credit called for "100% acrylic yarn" and the invoice merely stated "imported acrylic yarn", the credit was not satisfied, even though the packing list stated "100% acrylic yarn".

Many of the cases, which litigate issues concerning the strict compliance of documents, seem to revolve around discrepancies in transportation terms. Express conditions in the credit that loading, presentment or other acts must be performed by a certain time will be strictly enforced. Also, a discrepancy in the location of shipment or delivery will fail to comply with the terms of a credit. A credit calling for "**Full Set**[5] Clean On Board Bill of Lading" is not satisfied by a tender of "truckers bill of lading", even though evidence was presented that the bill of lading was in customary Mexican form and that Mexican truckers did not specify on the bill of lading that the goods were "on board". Nor is the "Full Set Clean On Board Bill of Lading" requirement satisfied by air waybill, even though air delivery

---

1. 《最高人民法院关于审理信用证纠纷案件若干问题的规定》第 10 条。人民法院认定存在信用证欺诈的，应当裁定中止支付或者判决终止支付信用证下款项，但有下列情形之一的除外：（一）开证行的指定人、授权人已按照开证行的指令善意地进行了付款；（二）开证行或者其指定人、授权人已对信用证项下票据善意地作出了承兑；（三）保兑行善意地履行了付款义务；（四）议付行善意地进行了议付。

2. Rule of Strict Compliance：（信用证的）严格相符原则。与信用证业务有关的银行只根据表面上符合信用证条款的单据付款、承兑或议付。"严格相符原则"就是要求单、证一致，单、单一致，即卖方提交单据的种类、份数及内容必须在表面上完全与信用证规定一致；各种单据同类项目的内容应相互一致，不能彼此矛盾。

3. 《跟单信用证统一惯例 600》第 14 条。审核单据的标准 d：单据中内容的描述不必与信用证、信用证对该项单据的描述以及国际标准银行实务完全一致，但不得与该项单据中的内容、其他规定的单据或信用证相冲突。

4. 《跟单信用证统一惯例 600》第 14 条。审核单据的标准 e：除商业发票外，其他单据中的货物、服务或行为描述若须规定，可使用统称，但不得与信用证规定的描述相矛盾。

5. full set：整套（提单）。根据法律规定或航运习惯，按托运人要求，承运人签发的一式数份的正本提单。通常提单上均注明"正本提单×份，凭其中一份完成交货责任后，其余无效"，目的在于防止货物关系人利用提单份数进行一物两卖，使提单的合法受让人了解全套正本提单份数的情况，防止因正本提单遗留在外而引起纠纷。

may be preferable. Recent cases often involve typographical errors. When the letter of credit mistakenly identified the beneficiary as Sung Jin Electronics, while the documents were correctly addressed to Sung Jun Electronics, the banks were allowed to refuse payment. But this decision has been criticized by practicing lawyers as being "too narrow".[1]

Period for Documents Examination. Banks, including a nominated bank, a confirming bank and the issuing bank, shall each have **a maximum of five banking days following the day of presentation to determine if a presentation is complying.**[2] The presentation of required documents must be made by or on behalf of the beneficiary not later than 21 calendar days after the date of shipment, but in any event not later than the expiry date of the credit.[3] For the presented documents not required by the letter of credit, the banks may just disregard them or return them to the beneficiary.[4]

Notice Procedures for the Dishonor. When an issuing bank, a confirming bank or a nominated bank determines that a presentation is complying, it must honor the payment under the letter of credit. However, when a nominated bank, a confirming bank, if any, or the issuing bank determines that a presentation does not comply, it may refuse to honor or negotiate.[5] Sometimes, the discrepancies between documents and the requirements of the letter of credit may be trivial or typographical, and the applicant—buyer, may want the payment made and the goods delivered, despite the discrepancy. Thus, before deciding to dishonor, an issuing bank may in its sole judgment, approach the applicant (the buyer) for **a waiver of the discrepancies**.[6] Quite frequently, applicants will in fact waive the discrepancies discovered by the bank. Thus, the system of honoring will continue to work.

When a nominated bank, a confirming bank, if any, or the issuing bank decides to refuse to honor or negotiate, it must give a single **notice** to that effect to the presenter. The notice must be given by telecommunication or, if that is not possible, by other expeditious means no later than the close of the fifth banking day following the day of presentation.[7]

If the issuing bank, the confirming bank, or the nominated bank dishonors the credit and refuses to pay when the documents are presented, the dishonor may be rightful or wrongful. If there truly are

---

1. See *Hanil Bank v. Pt. Bank Negara Indonesia (Persero)* (S.D.N.Y. 2000).

2.《跟单信用证统一惯例 600》第 14 条。审核单据的标准 b：按照指定行事的被指定银行、保兑行（如有）以及开证行，自其收到提示单据的翌日起算，应各自拥有最多不超过 5 个银行工作日的时间以决定提示是否相符。

3.《跟单信用证统一惯例 600》第 14 条。审核单据的标准 c：提示若包含一份或多份按照本惯例第 19 条、20 条、21 条、22 条、23 条、24 条或 25 条出具的正本运输单据，则必须由受益人或其代表按照相关条款在不迟于装运日后的 21 个公历日内提交，但无论如何不得迟于信用证的到期日。

4.《跟单信用证统一惯例 600》第 14 条。审核单据的标准 g：提示信用证中未要求提交的单据，银行将不予受理。如果收到此类单据，可以退还提示人。

5.《跟单信用证统一惯例 600》第 16 条。不符单据及不符点的放弃与通知 a：当按照指定行事的被指定银行、保兑行（如有）或开证行确定提示不符时，可以拒绝兑付或议付。

6.《跟单信用证统一惯例 600》第 16 条。不符单据及不符点的放弃与通知 b：当开证行确定提示不符时，可以依据其独立的判断联系申请人放弃有关不符点。然而，这并不因此延长 14 条（b）款中述及的期限。

7.《跟单信用证统一惯例 600》第 16 条。不符单据及不符点的放弃与通知 c：当按照指定行事的被指定银行、保兑行（如有）或开证行决定拒绝兑付或议付时，必须一次性通知提示人。……d：第 16 条（c）款中要求的通知必须以电讯方式发出，或者，如果不可能以电讯方式通知时，则以其他快捷方式通知，但不得迟于提示单据日期翌日起第 5 个银行工作日终了。

discrepancies between the specifications in the credit and the documents actually presented (and they are not waived), the banks are entitled to dishonor, although they must follow the above notice procedures specified in the *UCP*600 to protect themselves. If the issuer dishonors a presentation of documents, which do comply strictly with the letter of credit, that is a wrongful dishonor. It is also a breach of one or more contracts. First, it is a breach of the letter of credit contract, for which the beneficiary will have a cause of action. Second, it may be a breach of the credit application agreement between the applicant and the issuer, for which the applicant may have a cause of action. The applicant's right to sue the issuer for wrongful dishonor would arise out of the credit application agreement, and would be analyzed under ordinary contract law. It would also depend upon the terms of the credit application agreement, which might or might not include a clause disclaiming the liability of the issuers for wrongful dishonor.

Disclaimers of Banks. The banks enjoy some disclaimers under the *UCP*600. **First, the bank is not liable for "the effectiveness of documents".** A bank assumes no liability or responsibility for the form, sufficiency, accuracy, genuineness, falsification or legal effect of any document, or for the general or particular conditions stipulated in a document; nor does it assume any liability or responsibility for the description, quantity, weight, quality, condition, packing, delivery, value or existence of the goods, services or other performance represented by any document, or for the good faith or acts or omissions, solvency, performance or standing of the consignor, the carrier, the forwarder, the consignee or the insurer of the goods or any other person.[1] **Second, the Bank is not liable for the consequences resulting from transmission and translation problems of documents.** A bank assumes no liability for the consequences arising out of delay, loss in transit, mutilation or other errors arising in the transmission of any messages or delivery of letters or documents, when such messages, letters or documents are transmitted or sent according to the requirements stated in the credit, or when the bank may have taken the initiative in the choice of the delivery service in the absence of such instructions in the credit. If a nominated bank determines that a presentation is complying and forwards the documents to the issuing bank or confirming bank, whether or not the nominated bank has honored or negotiated, an issuing bank or confirming bank must honor or negotiate, or reimburse that nominated bank, even when the documents have been lost in transit between the nominated bank and the issuing bank or confirming bank, or between the confirming bank and the issuing bank. And a bank assumes no liability or responsibility for errors in translation or interpretation of technical terms and may transmit credit terms without translating them.[2] **Third, force majeure exemption.** A bank assumes no liability for the consequences arising out of the interruption of its business by Acts of God, riots, civil commotions,

---

1.《跟单信用证统一惯例 600》第 34 条。关于单据有效性的免责：银行对任何单据的形式、充分性、准确性、内容真实性、虚假性或法律效力，或对单据中规定或添加的一般或特殊条件，概不负责；银行对任何单据所代表的货物、服务或其他履约行为的描述、数量、重量、品质、状况、包装、交付、价值或其存在与否，或对发货人、承运人、货运代理人、收货人、货物的保险人或其他任何人的诚信与否，作为或不作为、清偿能力、履约或资信状况，也概不负责。

2.《跟单信用证统一惯例 600》第 35 条。关于信息传递和翻译的免责：当报文、信件或单据按照信用证的要求传输或发送时，或当信用证未作指示，银行自行选择传送服务时，银行对报文传输或信件或单据的递送过程中发生的延误、中途遗失、残缺或其他错误产生的后果，概不负责。如果指定银行确定交单相符并将单据发往开证行或保兑行。无论指定的银行是否已经承付或议付，开证行或保兑行必须承付或议付，或偿付指定银行，即使单据在指定银行送往开证行或保兑行的途中，或保兑行送往开证行的途中丢失。银行对技术术语的翻译或解释上的错误，不负责任，并可不加翻译地传送信用证条款。

insurrections, wars, acts of terrorism, or by any strikes or lockouts or any other causes beyond its control. A bank will not, upon resumption of its business, honor or negotiate under a credit that expired during such interruption of its business.[1] **Fourth, disclaimer for acts of an instructed party.** A bank utilizing the services of another bank for the purpose of giving effect to the instructions of the applicant does so for the account and at the risk of the applicant. An issuing bank or advising bank assumes no liability or responsibility should the instructions it transmits to another bank not be carried out, even if it has taken the initiative in the choice of that other bank.[2]

Chapter Summary

国际货物销售的主要支付方式有汇付（包括信汇、电汇、票汇）、托收和信用证。

国际货物销售中常用的流通票据有汇票、支票和本票。

《统一汇票本票法公约》是旨在统一国际贸易票据支付的最重要的国际公约。该公约规定汇票应包含下列内容：1. 票据主文中列有"汇票"一词，并以开立票据所使用的文字说明之；2. 无条件支付一定金额的命令；3. 付款人（受票人）的姓名；4. 付款日期的记载；5. 付款地的记载；6. 受款人或其指定人的姓名；7. 开立汇票的日期和地点的记载；8. 开立汇票的人（出票人）的签名。汇票可根据其转让方式的不同分为记名汇票和不记名汇票。记名汇票可以依法背书转让；不记名汇票可通过直接交付来转让。

信用证以银行的信用取代了商人的信用，是一种更为安全可靠的国际贸易结算方式。《跟单信用证统一惯例 600》是全世界公认的、到目前为止最为成功的一套关于信用证的运行和流通的非官方规定。信用证业务的基本原则有独立性原则和严格相符原则。

Exercises

Part Ⅰ. True or False Statements: Decide whether the following statements are True or False and explain why.

1. Direct payment by buyers such as M/T, T/T and D/D is the simplest mode of international payment and no bank is involved in the process of payment.

2. Documentary collections and documentary letters of credit belong to the documentary sale where documents of a bill of lading and a draft are often used.

3. Drafts, checks and promissory notes are all written and unconditional orders to pay a sum of money.

4. *Convention providing a Uniform Law for Bills of Exchange and Promissory Notes* (ULB) is the internationally uniform rules governing the Bill of Exchange and Promissory Note.

5. An advising bank is a bank that independently promises that it will pay, accept, or negotiate a

---

1.《跟单信用证统一惯例 600》第 36 条。不可抗力：银行对由于天灾、暴动、骚乱、叛乱、战争、恐怖主义行为或任何罢工、停工或其无法控制的任何其他原因导致的营业中断的后果，概不负责。银行恢复营业时，对于在营业中断期间已逾期的信用证，不再进行承付或议付。

2.《跟单信用证统一惯例 600》第 37 条。关于被指示方行为的免责 a：为了执行申请人的指示，银行利用其他银行的服务，其费用和风险由申请人承担。b：即使银行自行选择了其他银行，如果发出指示未被执行，开证行或通知行对此亦不负责。

letter of credit when the documents specified in the credit are presented to it and the other terms and conditions of the credit have been complied with.

6. According to the rule of strict compliance, the data in the documents must be identical to the requirements of the letter of credit.

7. Fraud is a well-established exception to the principle of independence under the *UCP*600.

8. The L/C calls for shipment of "1,000 bed pillows, size 20×26 in". The commercial invoice shows the shipment of "1,000 bed pillows, size 20×26 in", but the B/L describes the shipment as "1,000 pillows". In this way, the L/C is still satisfied.

9. Upon finding discrepancies, the issuing bank must send a waiver of discrepancy to the applicant of the letter of credit under *UCP*600.

10. A bank will not be held liable for the consequences arising from the interruption of its business by strikes.

Part Ⅱ. Chapter Questions: Discuss and answer the following questions according to what you have learned in this chapter. You are encouraged to use your own words.

1. How do you understand the importance of the draft in international payment? Consider the financing function of drafts and their roles in the documentary sale and the documentary credit.

2. How can the bill of exchange be classified?

3. What are the basic requirements of the bill of exchange?

4. Suppose you (the buyer) take part in an international sale of goods and the letter of credit is used as a tool of payment. If you hope to be protected from the potential fraud committed by the seller, what should you do?

5. Under what circumstances will the banks not be held liable under a letter of credit?

6. In case of discovering a discrepancy, how will the issuing bank act if the rules of *UCP*600 apply?

7. How do you understand the two basic principles for handling letters of credit under the *UCP*600?

8. How many categories of banks are involved in letter of credit transactions?

9. Under the law of China, what are the provisions on the fraud exception to the principle of independence in letter of credit transactions?

10. How do you understand the standard for the examination of documents stated in Article 14 of *UCP*600?

Part Ⅲ. Case Problem

1. Seller has a confirmed letter of credit it received from Buyer for the sale to Buyer of 1,000 bales of Grade A cotton. The letter of credit required the Seller to deliver a carrier's bill of lading and a certificate of inspection to the confirming bank before the bank was allowed to pay on the credit. The cotton that the Seller shipped was defective and the Seller had to bribe the carrier in order to obtain a clean bill of lading and the inspection service in order to get a satisfactory certificate. Because the Seller has a long-time relationship with the confirming bank, the Seller told the bank about the bribes. The confirming bank, which was depending on the Seller to receive the money from the sale of the cotton to pay off a debt the Seller owed to the bank, paid on the letter of credit anyway. (Actually, it took the credit as payment in full on the debt Seller owed it.) The confirming bank then forwarded the credit to

the issuing bank asking for reimbursement. The issuing bank, which had been tipped off about what had happened by an employee of the carrier, refused to pay. The confirming bank then sued the issuing bank, demanding reimbursement.

What should the court's decision be? Explain.

(1) What will be the confirming bank's argument for seeking reimbursement from the issuing bank?

(2) What will be the issuing bank's argument for not paying?

(3) Do you think the confirming bank can successfully obtain the reimbursement from the issuing bank? Explain.

(4) What legal or ethical responsibilities does the seller have to the confirming bank?

2. John Little (U.S. buyer) signed a contract to buy 1,000 "new VCRs with manufacturer's warranty" from Robin Hood (South Korea seller). Hood is shipping the VCRs C.I.F. San Francisco. The contract requires payment by an irrevocable letter of credit. And *UCC* is the governing law. At Little's request, Nottingham Bank has issued such a letter of credit on Little's behalf, promising to honor a draft accompanied by an invoice and clean, on board bill of lading for 1,000 "new VCRs with manufacturer's warranty". Little has been told by Scarlet (Little's friend and Hood's competitor) that although Hood obtained actual bills of lading describing the goods as 1,000 "new VCRs with manufacturer's warranty"; shipper's load, weight and count, the actual shipment are all used and inoperable junk VCRs.

(1) What should Little do? You are Little's Attorney and he asks you for help.

(2) Would it make a difference if Little was known to be very shaky financially, and likely to file a petition for bankruptcy at any time?

(3) Would it make a difference if Hood's Bank had confirmed the letter of credit and had already paid over the amount of the draft to Hood before you learned about the alleged defective shipments?

Part Ⅲ International Transfer of Intellectual Property Rights

Chapter 9
Intellectual Property Rights and Licensing

 导读

本章主要介绍和讨论知识产权和知识产权国际转让的相关概念和法律问题。主要包括：（1）知识产权的基础知识：概念、种类和基本法律规则；（2）著作权、专利权、商标权和商业秘密的内涵、权利内容、保护期限及其他法律问题；（3）主要知识产权国际组织和国际条约；（4）知识产权许可贸易——国际许可及国际许可协议的主要条款、国际特许经营、强制许可的含义及相关法律规定等。

 Warm-up Questions

(1) As you see it, what is the role of technology in the development of a nation?

(2) Can you name some types of intellectual property rights recognized under the law of China?

(3) What may be the difficulties in getting access to the advanced technologies owned by a foreign company?

(4) In what ways can intellectual property rights, e.g., a patent, be transferred from one country to another?

9.1   Fundamentals of Intellectual Property Rights

Intellectual property is a legal term that refers to creations of the human mind for which a monopoly is given to the owners by law. For the purpose of academic study, intellectual property is generally classified into two main types: copyright and industrial property. Industrial property is divided into two categories: patent and trademark. Besides, trade secret is also included in the realm of intellectual property rights.

Intellectual property is a creature of national law. International law does not create it, although it does establish rules and guidelines for its uniform definition and protection, and it sets up ways that make it easier for owners to acquire rights in different countries. National laws are also important in establishing the rules for assigning and licensing intellectual property. Before discussing the international transfer of intellectual property, this chapter shall begin with the fundamentals of intellectual property rights.

A. Copyright

Copyright protects the authorship of any work that can be fixed in a tangible medium for the purpose of communication, such as literary, dramatic, musical or artistic works; sound recordings; films; radio and television broadcasts; and computer programs.[1] Article 3 of *Copyright Law of the People's Republic of China* provides that for purposes of this law, the term "works" means intellectual achievements in the fields of literature, art and science, which are original and can be expressed in a certain form, including: (1) written works; (2) oral works; (3) musical, dramatic, quyi, choreographic and acrobatic art works; (4) works of the fine arts and architecture; (5) photographic works; (6) audiovisual works; (7) graphic works such as drawings of engineering designs, product designs, maps and sketches, and model works; (8) computer software; and (9) other intellectual achievements conforming to the characteristics of the works.[2]

Theoretically, **copyright includes pecuniary rights and moral rights.** The "pecuniary rights" inherent in copyright allow an author to exploit a work for economic gain. In particular, pecuniary rights include the right to reproduce the work, the right to distribute the work, and (depending on the nature of the work) the right to public performance. Moral rights are an author's personal rights to keep others from tampering with his works. The three basic moral rights are (1) the right to object to distortion, mutilation or modification, (2) the right to be recognized as the author, and (3) the right to control public access to the work. In a few countries, there is the fourth moral right: the right to correct or retract a work.[3] Moral rights are not recognized in the copyright laws of common law countries such as the U.K. and the United States. They claim that the author can bring an action against the distortion, mutilation or modification of his/her work according to contract law and tort law.

Copyrights can date back to the 15th century. It is recorded that the first known copyright was issued by the Duke of Milan in 1481. The first true *Copyright Act* was enacted in England in 1709. Later similar statutes appeared in Spain, the United States, France and Germany.

Unlike patent or trademark, copyright arises automatically upon the creation of work, and there is no registration process. Article 2 of *Copyright Law of the People's Republic of China* provides that works of Chinese citizens, legal persons or unincorporated organizations, whether published or not, shall have copyright in accordance with this Law.[4]

---

1. Copyright：著作权，有时也称版权，是指作者及其他权利人对文学、艺术和科学作品享有的人身权和财产权的总称。

2.《中华人民共和国著作权法》（2020 年 11 月修正）第 3 条：本法所称的作品，是指文学、艺术和科学领域内具有独创性并能以一定形式表现的智力成果，包括：（1）文字作品；（2）口述作品；（3）音乐、戏剧、曲艺、舞蹈、杂技艺术作品；（4）美术、建筑作品；（5）摄影作品；（6）视听作品；（7）工程设计图、产品设计图、地图、示意图等图形作品和模型作品；（8）计算机软件；（9）符合作品特征的其他智力成果。

3. 著作权包括人身权和财产权两类权利。著作权的人身权（又称精神权利）大致包括：发表权、署名权、修改权、保护作品完整权、收回已发表的作品权等。著作权的财产权是指著作权人通过复制、发行、出租、展览、表演、放映、广播、信息网络传播、摄制或者改编、翻译、汇编等方式使用作品并由此获得报酬的权利，以及许可他人以上述方式使用作品，并由此获得报酬的权利。

4.《中华人民共和国著作权法》（2020 年 11 月修正）第 2 条：中国公民、法人或者非法人组织的作品，不论是否发表，依照本法享有著作权。……

About **the duration** for which copyright may be granted, **TRIPs Agreement**[1] sets **the minimum time period of the life of the author plus 50 years.**[2] Some WTO members provide for longer terms of duration. For example, Germany, Austria, and Switzerland grant protection for the life of the author plus 70 years. Spain grants protection for the life of the author plus 60 years. And the United States grants 70 years after the mortality of the author.

B. Patent

Patent[3] is "**a statutory privilege granted by the government to inventors, and to others deriving their rights from the inventor, for a fixed period of years, to exclude other persons from manufacturing, using or selling a patented product or from utilizing a patented method or process.**"

There are two basic reasons why governments grant patents. One is that patent is a confirmation of the private property rights of the inventor. The second is that a patent is a grant of a special monopoly, which prevents others from utilizing the patentee's invention without his consent, to encourage invention and industrial development across the state. Sometimes these purposes are at odds with each other. On the private side, is the inventor's claim for recognition and economic advantage. On the public side, there is not only the interests of the government in promoting economic development but also the social benefits in encouraging intervention, as well as the desire of consumers to purchase goods at reasonable prices. Some legal writers have suggested that the function of the patent law is, therefore, to reconcile and satisfy the whole scheme of public and private interests pressing for recognition.

What are the inventions that qualify for patent protection? To acquire a patent, an inventor must show that a new product, method or process has **novelty, inventiveness, and utility.**[4] **Novelty** means that no other inventor can have obtained a patent for the same invention. The invention has not been made available to the public anywhere in the world by written or oral description, by use or in any other way.

---

1. *TRIPs Agreement* : *Agreement on Trade-Related Aspects of Intellectual Property Rights*，《与贸易有关的知识产权协定》。该协定是世界贸易组织下的一项多边贸易协定。《与贸易有关的知识产权协定》对"知识产权"及其保护做了集成性规定，所涵盖的知识产权形式包括：（1）著作权与邻接权；（2）商标权；（3）地理标志权；（4）工业品外观设计权；（5）专利权；（6）集成电路布线图设计权；（7）未披露的信息专有权。

2. 关于著作权的保护期限，《中华人民共和国著作权法》的规定与 TRIPs 一致。一般为作者终生加上其死亡后 50 年，截止于作者死亡后第 50 年的 12 月 31 日。但著作权中的人身权（署名权、修改权、保护作品完整权）的保护期不受限制。

3. Patent：专利权，简称专利，是指专利权人（发明创造人或权利受让人）对特定的发明创造在一定期限内依法享有的独占实施权。专利权具有排他性、时间性和地域性的法律性质。排他性是指专利权人对其拥有的专利权享有独占或排他的权利，未经其许可或者出现法律规定的特殊情况，任何人不得使用，否则即构成侵权。时间性指法律对专利权所有人的保护不是无期限的，而有限制，超过这一时间限制则不再予以保护，专利权随即成为人类共同财富，任何人都可以利用。地域性指依一国法律取得的专利权只在该国领域内受到法律保护，而在其他国家则不受该国家的法律保护，除非两国之间有双边的知识产权保护协定，或共同参加了有关保护知识产权的国际公约。

4. Novelty：新颖性。新颖性是指在申请日以前没有同样的发明在国内外出版物上公开发表过、在国内公开使用过或者以其他方式为公众所知。也没有他人就同样的发明向专利局提出过申请。

Inventiveness：创造性。创造性是指同申请日以前已有的技术相比，该发明有突出的实质性特点和显著的进步，不是现有技术通过简单地分析、归纳、推理就能够自然获得的结果。创造性的判断以所属领域普通技术人员的知识和判断能力为准。

Utility：实用性。实用性是指该发明能够制造或者使用，并且能够产生积极效果。它有两层含义：第一，该技术能够在产业中制造或者使用；第二，必须能够产生积极的效果，即同现有的技术相比，申请专利的发明能够产生更好的经济效益或社会效益。

Sometimes "great minds think alike" — two or more inventors may reach the invention at the same time and each file a patent application. Under such circumstances, the rule of "early coming, early serving" will apply in order to avoid granting the same patent to two patentees. That is, the early application is deemed to be the prior invention when considering the novelty of the latter application. **Inventiveness** means that the idea underlying an invention cannot have been obvious at the time the invention was made to a person having ordinary skill in the art. Here "a person having ordinary skill in the art" has been described as "a skilled technician who is well acquainted with workshop technique and who has carefully read all the relevant literature. He is supposed to have an unlimited capacity to assimilate the contents of, it may be, scores of specifications but to be incapable of a scintilla of invention." Utility means that the product or process is one that can be used in industry or commerce (capable of industrial application). Just by this nature can patents be expected to stimulate the economic development of a nation.

The patent application process varies from country to country. In some, it begins with a simple review of the application form to see if it is complete; in others, it starts with an extensive search of domestic and foreign materials to determine if the product or process is both novel and inventive. The next step is to publish the notice of the application. In most countries, the notice has to include all of the information contained in the inventor's application. The reason for doing this is to give interested third parties the opportunity to oppose the application. In developing countries, it also serves as a substitute for an examination of novelty and inventiveness by a patent office.

What are the inventions excluded from patent protection? Inventions that do not meet the qualifications will be denied patents. In addition, The *TRIPs Agreement* allows a WTO member to deny a patent to an inventor in order to protect the lives or health of humans, animals, or plants or to protect the environment from serious injury. Besides, the Agreement also allows the WTO member to deny a patent to an inventor in order to protect the order of the public or morality. The *TRIPs Agreement* allows countries to deny patents in the following situations: (1) diagnostic, therapeutic, and surgical methods for the treatment of humans and animals; (2) plants and animals other than microorganisms and plant varieties, and (3) essentially biological processes for the production of plants or animals.[1] In conformity with the *TRIPs Agreement, Patent Law of the People's Republic of China* provides that two types of inventions will not receive patent protection: (1) illegal inventions, and (2) non-patentable subject matters. The "illegal inventions" refers to the inventions whose purpose is contrary to laws, public policy or public interests. The non-patentable subject matters include: (1) scientific discoveries, (2) rules and methods of mental activities, (3) methods of diagnosis or treatment of disease, (4) new varieties of animals and plants, (5) Nuclear transformation methods and substances obtained by nuclear transformation methods, and (6) A design that mainly serves as a logo for the pattern, the color or combination of the two of the printed matter.[2]

---

1. 根据《与贸易有关的知识产权协定》第 27 条的规定，各成员可拒绝对下列内容授予专利权：人类或动物的诊断、治疗和外科手术方法；除微生物外的植物和动物，以及生产植物和动物的主要生物方法。

2. 根据《中华人民共和国专利法》（2021 年 6 月 1 日施行）第 5 条规定。对违反法律、社会公德或者妨害公共利益的发明创造，不授予专利权。对违反法律、行政法规的规定获取或者利用遗传资源，并依赖该遗传资源完成的发明创造，不授予专利权。第 25 条规定对下列各项，不授予专利权：（1）科学发现；（2）智力活动的规则和方法；（3）疾病的诊断和治疗方法；（4）新的动物和植物品种；（5）原子核变换方法以及用原子核变换方法获得的物质；（6）对平面印刷品的图案、色彩或者二者的结合做出的主要起标识作用的设计。对前款第（4）项所列产品的生产方法，可以依照本法规定授予专利权。

Duration of Patents. The *TRIPs Agreement* sets the minimum duration of patents at 20 years. The 20-year duration is followed by almost all WTO members.[1]

C. Trademarks

Trademarks are used by merchants and others to identify themselves and their products from similar goods or services supplied by others.[2] Now trademarks have become one of the core factors in the competitiveness of enterprises. In the broad sense, there are different kinds of trademarks. (1) A trademark, in common sense, is any word, name, symbol, device or any combination thereof adopted and used by a manufacturer or merchant to identify his goods and distinguish them from those manufactured or sold by others. (2) A trade name is the name of the manufacturer. (3) A service mark is a mark used in the sale or advertising of services to identify the services of one person and distinguish them from the services of another. (4) Collective marks are used by members of an association, collective or cooperative organization to identify their products or services to their members. (5) A certification mark is a mark used exclusively by a licensee or franchisee, to indicate that a product meets certain standards. Among the above kinds of trademarks, it should be noted that a trademark is different from a trade name. Once a trade name was used to denote any mark descriptive of a good or service, but today, it is a company business name. For example, "P&G" is a trade name for "P&G Inc". And "Rejoice" is one of the trademarks of its products.

Trademarks have several functions. From the perspective of an owner, a trademark is the fortune and the right to put a product, with this mark, into circulation. From the viewpoint of a consumer, a trademark serves to designate the origin or source of a service, indicate a particular standard of quality, protect the consumer from confusion and help the consumer to make a purchase decision among the various similar products or services. Trademark law seeks to prevent others from intentionally or unintentionally infringing on the owner's mark. The users may defend their use of a similar mark on the basis that such use will not create confusion in the consumer, either through the unrelated nature of the goods or markets or their geographic distance apart.

Acquiring Trademarks. Trademarks are acquired in two ways: by use and by registration. In either case, a person claiming a trademark must show that it does not infringe on any other mark and that it is distinctive. Distinctive means that the mark is such that it will distinguish the goods or services with which it is connected from other similar goods.

The Term of Registered Trademarks. The *TRIPs Agreement* requires that members of the WTO protect trademarks for terms of at least 7 years. Also, it provides for trademarks to be renewable indefinitely. Under the *Trademark Law of the People's Republic of China*, the duration term for a trademark is 10 years and renewable.[3]

---

1. 根据《中华人民共和国专利法》(2021 年 6 月 1 日施行)的规定，发明创造包括三类：发明、实用新型和外观设计。其中发明专利权的保护期限为 20 年，实用新型专利权的期限为 10 年，外观设计专利权的期限为 15 年，均自申请日起计算。

2. Trademark：商标。商标是商品的生产者、经营者在其生产、制造、拣选或者经销的商品上或者服务的提供者在其提供的服务上采用的，用于区别商品或服务来源的，由文字、图形、字母、数字、三维标志、声音、颜色组合，或上述要素的组合。商标包括商品商标、服务商标和集体商标、证明商标。

3. 关于商标的保护期限，《中华人民共和国商标法》(2019 年 11 月 1 日起施行)规定，注册商标的有效期为 10 年，自核准注册之日起计算。注册商标有效期满，需要继续使用的，应当在期满前 12 个月内申请续展注册；在此期间未能提出申请的，可以给予 6 个月的宽展期。宽展期满仍未提出申请的，注销其注册商标。每次续展注册的有效期为 10 年。

D. Trade Secrets

Trade secrets are confidential information that has commercial value and the owner has taken reasonable measures to protect them.[1] Unlike patents, copyrights and trademarks, trade secrets are protected by contract, tort and trade secrecy laws, rather than by particular statutory enactments.

The *TRIPs Agreement* requires the WTO members to protect what the Agreement calls "undisclosed information". That is, natural and legal persons must be given the legal means to prevent information from being disclosed to, acquired by, or used by others without their consent in a manner contrary to honest commercial practice. The information, however, must (a) be secret, (b) have commercial value because it is a secret, and (c) have been reasonably protected from disclosure by its owner. For example, the secret recipe of "11 herbs and spices" for Kentucky fried chicken lies in a bank vault. Few people know it, and they are contractually obligated to secrecy. In the manufacture process, the ingredients are mixed by two different companies in two different locations and then combined elsewhere in a third, separate location. To mix the final formula, a computer processing system is used to blend the mixtures together and ensure that no one outside KFC has the complete recipe. Such a recipe can be recognized as trade secret or undisclosed information under *TRIPs*.

In most cases, the legal protection given to trade secrets comes about in connection with their assignee, licensee, or employee. That is, the owner of trade secrets may prevent an assignee, licensee, or employee from disclosing secret information to third parties by agreements. Such agreements may take the forms of confidential agreements, non-competition agreements or confidentiality provisions in the franchise agreements. For example, a franchise agreement covers the following clauses:

"Franchisee shall not at any time, without franchisor's prior written consent, copy, duplicate, record, or otherwise reproduce in any manner any part of the manuals, updates, supplements, or related materials, in whole or in part, or otherwise make the same available to any unauthorized person.

The manuals at all times remain the sole property of franchisor; upon the expiration or termination, for any reason, of the franchise agreements, franchisee shall return to franchisor the manuals and all supplements thereto."

National laws provide legal liabilities for the infringement of trade secrets. For example, Article 9 of *Law of the People's Republic of China Aguinst Unfair Competition* provides: Business operators shall not commit the following acts that infringe on Trade Secrets: (1) Obtaining the trade secrets by theft, bribery, fraud, coercion, electronic intrusion or other improper means; (2) disclosing, using or allowing others to use the trade secrets obtained by the means mentioned above; (3) disclosing, using or allowing others to use the trade secrets in their possession in violation of the confidentiality obligation or the requirements for keeping the trade secrets; (4) instigating, enticing or aiding others to violate the

---

1. Trade secrets:商业秘密。商业秘密是指不为公众所知悉、能为权利人带来经济利益，并经权利人采取保密措施的技术信息和经营信息。和其他知识产权（专利权、商标权、著作权等）相比，商业秘密有着以下特点：非公开性、非排他性和保护期限的非法定性。商业秘密的前提是不为公众所知悉，而其他知识产权都是公开的。商业秘密是一项相对权利。如果其他人以合法方式取得了同一内容的商业秘密，他们就和第一个人有着同样的地位。商业秘密的拥有者既不能阻止在他之前已经开发掌握该信息的人使用、转让该信息，也不能阻止在他之后开发掌握该信息的人使用、转让该信息。商业秘密的保护期不是法定的，取决于权利人的保密措施和其他人对此项秘密的公开。一项技术秘密可能由于权利人保密措施得力和技术本身的应用价值而延续很长时间，远远超过专利受保护的期限。

confidentiality obligation or violate the requirements for keeping business secrets, and obtain, disclose, use or allow others to use the trade secrets. Any natural person, legal person or other organization other than the business operator who commits any of the illegal acts mentioned in the preceding paragraph shall be deemed to have infringed upon trade secrets. A third party who knowingly or should know that the employees, former employees or other units or individuals have committed the illegal acts mentioned in the first paragraph of this article and still acquires, discloses, uses or allows others to use the trade secret shall be deemed to have infringed the trade secret. The trade secrets mentioned in this Law refer to technical information, business information and other commercial information that is not known to the public and has commercial value and has been kept confidential.[1]

9.2   International Intellectual Property Organizations and Treaties

Lying at the heart of intellectual property protection are the national laws. In an effort to drive these national rules of application toward greater uniformity, states have established a variety of international organizations and international treaties. Among them, two international organizations currently play an active role in defining intellectual property rights and administering the international treaties that govern those rights.

A. World Intellectual Property Organization

The **World Intellectual Property Organization (WIPO)**,[2] created in 1967, is responsible for administering major international treaties on intellectual property protection as well as the global forum for intellectual property services. There are now more than 190 parties to this Organization, including China. One of WIPO's more important tasks is to facilitate the transfer of technology, especially to and among developing countries. Thus, WIPO has established two permanent committees: Committee for Development Cooperation Related to Industrial Property and Committee for Development Cooperation Related to Copyrights and Neighboring Rights responsible for helping countries modernizing their national intellectual property laws.

---

1. 参见《中华人民共和国反不正当竞争法》(2019 修正) 第 9 条: 经营者不得实施下列侵犯商业秘密的行为: (1) 以盗窃、贿赂、欺诈、胁迫、电子侵入或者其他不正当手段获取权利人的商业秘密; (2) 披露、使用或者允许他人使用以前项手段获取的权利人的商业秘密; (3) 违反保密义务或者违反权利人有关保守商业秘密的要求, 披露、使用或者允许他人使用其所掌握的商业秘密; (4) 教唆、引诱、帮助他人违反保密义务或者违反权利人有关保守商业秘密的要求, 获取、披露、使用或者允许他人使用权利人的商业秘密。经营者以外的其他自然人、法人和非法人组织实施前款所列违法行为的, 视为侵犯商业秘密。第三人明知或者应知商业秘密权利人的员工、前员工或者其他单位、个人实施本条第 1 款所列违法行为, 仍获取、披露、使用或者允许他人使用该商业秘密的, 视为侵犯商业秘密。本法所称的商业秘密, 是指不为公众所知悉、具有商业价值并经权利人采取相应保密措施的技术信息、经营信息等商业信息。

2. World Intellectual Property Organization (WIPO): 世界知识产权组织。这是一个致力于促进使用和保护人类智力作品的国际组织。总部设在瑞士日内瓦的世界知识产权组织, 是联合国组织系统中的 16 个专门机构之一。它管理着涉及知识产权保护各个方面的 24 项 (16 部关于工业产权, 7 部关于版权, 及《建立世界知识产权组织公约》) 国际条约。

B. Council for Trade-Related Aspects of Intellectual Property Rights

The Council for Trade-Related Aspects of Intellectual Property Rights (TRIPs Council)[1] was created in 1995 with the adoption of the Agreement Establishing the World Trade Organization (WTO Agreement). The Council is responsible for overseeing the *TRIPs*, which is an annex to the WTO Agreement. In particular, the Council is responsible for monitoring WTO member compliance with the *TRIPs Agreement*, for helping members consult with each other on trade-related aspects of intellectual property rights, and for assisting members in settling disputes. The Council consults with WIPO.

C. Intellectual Property Treaties

The principal comprehensive agreement establishing general intellectual property obligations for most countries of the world is the *Agreement on Trade-Related Aspects of Intellectual Property Rights* (*TRIPs Agreement*), which came into effect in 1995 with the adoption of the *Agreement Establishing the World Trade Organization* (*WTO Agreement*).

The goal of the *TRIPs Agreement* is to create a multilateral and comprehensive set of rights and obligations governing the international trade in intellectual property rights. To accomplish this goal, the Agreement establishes a common minimum of protection for intellectual property rights applicable within all the WTO members. This common minimum is given force in five ways.

a. The WTO members are required to be parties to the following conventions: (1) Paris *Convention for the Protection of Industrial Property* (*Paris Convention,* of 1883); (2) Berne *Convention for the Protection of Literary and Artistic Property* of 1887 as revised in 1971; (3) *International Convention for the Protection of Performers, Producers of Phonograms, and Broadcasting Organizations, or Rome Convention*, of 1961; and (4) the 1989 *Treaty on Intellectual Property in Respect of Integrated Circuits*.

b. The *TRIPs Agreement* fills in the gaps in many of these conventions. For example, it specifies the minimum duration of patents, copyrights, and trademarks. The *TRIPs Agreement* sets the minimum duration of patents at 20 years and sets the minimum time period for which copyrights may be granted at 50 years. The *TRIPs Agreement* requires that members of the World Trade Organization protect trademarks for terms of at least 7 years. Also, it provides for trademarks to be renewable indefinitely.

c. The WTO Dispute Settlement Body will govern the disputes arising from the *TRIPs Agreement*.

d. Transition periods are specified for when developed (1996), developing (2000), and the least developed countries (2006) must bring themselves fully into compliance with the *TRIPs Agreement*.

e. *The basic principles of the General Agreement on Tariffs and Trade*—such as national treatment and transparency are made applicable to the field of intellectual property rights.

The first international intellectual property treaty and the principal convention dealing with industrial property is the *Paris Convention for the Protection of Industrial Property*, or *Paris Convention*.[2] The *Paris Convention* was originally adopted in 1883 by 11 states and since has been

---

1. Council for Trade-Related Aspects of Intellectual Property Rights：与贸易有关的知识产权理事会，是世界贸易组织的内设机构，负责监督执行《与贸易有关知识产权协定》(TRIPs)。

2. *Paris Convention for the Protection of Industrial Property*:《保护工业产权巴黎公约》，简称《巴黎公约》，于 1883 年 3 月 20 日在巴黎签订，1884 年 7 月 7 日生效。巴黎公约的调整对象即保护范围是工业产权，包括发明专利权、实用新型、商标权、工业品外观设计、服务标记、厂商名称、货物标记或原产地名称以及制止不正当竞争等。巴黎公约的基本目的是通过确立国民待遇原则、优先权原则等保证成员方的工业产权在所有其他成员方都得到保护。1985 年 3 月 19 日中国成为该公约成员国。

revised for many times. The latest amendment was made in 1979. China became a signatory state to this Convention on March 19, 1985. It establishes a union of states responsible for protecting industrial rights. Three basic principles are incorporated in the convention: (1) National treatment, which requires members to give the same protection to the nationals of other states that it grants to its own nationals. In other words, the *Paris Convention* eliminated the potential discrimination against foreigners in obtaining patents and trademarks; (2) right of priority, which gives applicants who have filed for protection in one member a grace period of 12 months in which to file in another member. The Convention provides that the date of an applicant's foreign application is deemed the same as the date of the applicant's original application on the same invention within 12 months; and (3) common rules, which set minimum standards for the creation of intellectual property right. But the Convention does not require any minimum substantive standard of industry property protection.

In 1970, the *Patent Cooperation Treaty* (PCT) [1] supplemented the *Paris Convention* by establishing a centralized utility patent application process. The *PCT* application is filed on a standard form with the WIPO. The WIPO processes the common application and forwards it to the countries designated by the applicant.

Other industrial property treaties are the *Treaty on Intellectual Property in Respect of Integrated Circuits* of 1989, which is not currently in force, but which the *TRIPs Agreement* requires the WTO members to apply, the Agreement on Sources of Goods of 1891, which forbids the importation of goods bearing false or deception indications of their source, and the *Trademark Law Treaty* of 1994, which simplifies national trademark protection rules.

The principal convention dealing with artistic property is the *Berne Convention for the Protection of Literary and Artistic Property*, better known as the *Berne Convention*.[2] It deals with the granting of copyrights among signatory members. The signatory members are bound by four principles. These are (1) national treatment which requires members to afford the works of authors from other signatory states the same treatment as those of their own citizens. (2) unconditional protection and members must provide protection without any formalities. All an author needs to do is to affix the symbol © and the year of authorship to provide copyright protection throughout the world, and the Convention will grant national treatment to copyright holder from other signatory states automatically from the moment of creation rather than the time of filing. (3) protection independent of protection in the member of origin, which allows authors who are citizens of non-members to obtain protection within the Berne Union by publishing their works in a member. and (4) common rules, which are the establishment of minimum standards for granting copyrights which are common in all members.

Other conventions, which deal with artistic property are the *International Convention for the Protection of Performers, Producers of Phonograms, and Broadcasting Organizations* of 1961, better known as the Rome Convention, which protects artists from the making of unauthorized recordings and

---

1. *Patent Cooperation Treaty* （PCT）:《专利合作条约》, 主要涉及国际专利申请的提交、检索及审查的一个条约。该条约不对"国际专利授权": 授予专利的任务和责任仍然属于各个成员方的专利局或行使其职权的机构。

2. *Berne Convention for the Protection of Literary and Artistic Works*:《保护文学和艺术作品伯尔尼公约》, 简称《伯尔尼公约》, 是关于著作权保护的国际条约, 核心是规定了每个缔约方都应自动、平等保护在其他各缔约方中首先出版的作品。该公约 1886 年 9 月 9 日制定于瑞士伯尔尼。1992 年 10 月 15 日中国成为该公约成员方。

from the unauthorized use of authorized recordings, the *Phonogram Piracy Agreement* of 1971, which protects producers of phonograms from the unauthorized reproduction of their works, the *Agreement on Satellite Transmissions* of 1974, which outlaws unauthorized satellite transmissions, and the *WIPO Copyright Treaty* of 1996, which extends the provisions of the *Berne Convention* to computer programs and databases.

9.3   Regulations on International Licensing

Intellectual property rights may be transferred from one country to another in various ways.

Licensing[1] is most widely used in the international transfer of intellectual property rights. A license is a nonexclusive revocable privilege that allows a licensee to use a licensor's property. It means that an intellectual property rights owner (licensor) authorizes the use of such rights to a licensee, in exchange for an agreed payment, such as copying software or using a patented invention to manufacture products. That is, only the right of use, not the ownership of the intellectual property is transferred through licensing. A license is created by agreement, and usually, the standard-form agreement will be adopted. Under the licensing agreement of intellectual property right, the licensor wishes to transfer the exploitation of the intellectual property right, gaining the most return from the limited duration period of protection and trying to keep its dominant position in the corresponding field of technology as well. It is the licensee, which will exploit the intellectual property right and may be required by the licensing agreement to undertake considerable expenditure and accept some unreasonable restrictive clauses.

A. Typical Terms in International Licensing Agreements

These purposes of the licensor and licensee may find their expression in terms under a licensing agreement. The following list of terms in a licensing agreement is typical but not exhaustive.

1. Parties

The information of parties to the licensing agreement and accuracy is important for obvious reasons.

2. Definitions

It is required for ease of negotiation, drafting and later interpretation.

3. Date

Date of agreement and effective date of license, which may be the basis for calculating the duration of the license.

---

1. Licensing: 知识产权许可（简称"许可"），是指许可方将所涉知识产权的使用权授予被许可方按照约定使用，被许可方支付相应费用的交易安排。通常由知识产权许可方与知识产权被许可方，依法签订书面许可合同的形式来实现。知识产权许可一般分为3类：独占许可、排他许可、普通许可。普通许可（nonexclusive license）允许被许可人在规定的地域范围内使用在合同中所约定的知识产权内容，同时保留在该地域范围内许可人自己使用该项知识产权以及再授权第三方使用该项知识产权的权利。排他许可（exclusive license）仅允许被许可方在规定的地域范围内，拥有该项知识产权的使用权，任何第三方也包括许可方自己在内，均无权使用该项知识产权。独占许可（sole license）允许被许可方在规定的地域内独家使用其知识产权，而不再许可第三方在该地域内使用其知识产权，但仍保留许可方自己使用其知识产权的权利。

4. Grant

The specific description of the intellectual property under license, is often accompanied by annexes of drawings or images and the like[1].

5. Acknowledgement of title

Intellectual property belongs to the licensor. It remains so during and after the license and that licensee will not attempt to challenge that title.

6. Territory

The geographic area, customer groups, or industries in which the license may operate.

7. Exclusivity

The type of license — exclusive license, sole license or nonexclusive license.

8. Term

The duration of the licensing agreement within the protection period of the intellectual property.

9. Renewal

Whether the term of the licensing agreement is renewal and the way to renew.

10. Most favored treatment

Whether the licensee has the right to better terms as may be offered and granted to future licensees in other territories.

11. Royalties and payments[2]

Lump sums, one-time payments, periodic royalties, or sliding royalties based on performance. Basis for calculation: sales, net accounting, exclusive of taxes, duties, freight, returns or rejected goods.

12. Accounts and inspection

Whether the licensor has the right to inspect the accounts or plants of the licensee.

13. Information sharing

Whether the licensor and licensee shall share any information of technical advance related to the intellectual property under the license.

14. Technical assistance

In the process of the licensee exploiting the intellectual property right, whether the licensor is under the obligation to provide technical assistance and training.

15. Confidentiality

Requirements for nondisclosure of employees, assignees, and sublicensees. Time limits for nondisclosure beyond the term of the license.

16. Rights to sublicense[3]

Whether sublicense is permitted or on approval.

---

1. 实施许可的具体知识产权，应用简洁的专业术语、图表等描述该知识产权的内容和实质特征。

2. royalties and payments：使用费及其支付方式。有一次性支付、分期支付等多种方式。许可使用费的费率可以是固定的也可以是浮动的。

3. sublicense：分许可，指获得许可的被许可方，在指定的地域范围内又向他人授权使用该知识产权。

17. Termination

By the licensor: on notice, on anniversary date, for cause, or where licensee in breach of a material obligation.

By licensee: on notice, on anniversary date, for cause, or on payment of penalty.

18. Choice of law

Forum selection, applicable procedure and substantive law.

19. Arbitration

Whether available, selection of arbitration institution, the composition of the tribunal, and applicable arbitration rules.

20. Force majeure

List of events agreed to excuse nonperformance of the licensing agreement.

21. Other clauses

B. Regulating the Anti-competitive Aspects of International Licensing

International Licensing of intellectual property is subject to two conflicting sets of legal rules. One is the statutory rules creating intellectual property monopolies. The other is unfair competition laws.[1] In balancing these two rules, most countries have adopted rules to regulate the anti-competitive aspects of intellectual property licensing in their regulations for the transfer of technologies or competition laws. The international law also approves such regulations on intellectual property licensing. Article 40 of the *TRIPs Agreement* provides: Nothing shall prevent members from specifying in their national legislation licensing practices or conditions that may in particular cases constitute an abuse of intellectual property rights having an adverse effect on competition in the relevant market. As provided above, a member may adopt, consistently with the other provisions of this Agreement, appropriate measures to prevent or control such policies, which may include, for example, exclusive grant-back conditions, conditions preventing challenges to validity, and coercive package licensing, in the light of the relevant laws and regulations of that member.

Such unfair competition rules are found in unfair competition legislation, such as the *Sherman Antitrust Act* or the European Union's *European Community Treaty*. These rules declare illegal any agreement or arrangement that adversely affects competition within the national state or, in the case of the EU, within the common market or any conduct that tends to monopolize trade. However, these rules, at the same time, declare some exemptions of licensing agreements. The EU Commission, for example, may do so either through block grants that apply to a particular category of agreements or on a case-by-case basis when the overall effect of a license "contributes to improving the production or distribution of goods, or to promoting technical or economic progress, while allowing consumers a fair share of the resulting benefit." The U.S. courts arrive at the same end by applying a "rule of reason." Thus except for certain agreements, such as horizontal price fixing, which the courts regard as illegal, the courts will consider what overall impact a particular agreement will have on the competition before declaring it invalid.

According to *Civil Code of the People's Republic of China*, technology contracts that illegally

---

1. 知识产权的正当行使不需受反垄断法的调整，但如果滥用知识产权产生排除、限制竞争的效果，则应该适用反垄断法来予以规制。

monopolize technology or infringe upon the technological achievements of others shall be invalid (Article 850). And *Anti-monopoly Law of the People's Republic of China* shall apply to govern the acts of business operators abusing intellectual property rights to exclude or restrict competition (Article 68). The *Foreign Trade Law of the People's Republic of China* 2004 (amended in 2016) provides that in the international licensing agreement if the intellectual property right owner is involved in any one of such practices as preventing the licensee from challenging the validity of the intellectual property right in the licensing contract, conducting coercive package licensing or incorporating exclusive grant-back conditions in the licensing contract, which impairs the fair competition order of foreign trade, the Ministry of Commerce, People's Republic of China may take measures as necessary to eliminate such impairment (Article 30).[1] And China prohibits the transfer of technologies relating to fissionable materials or the materials from which they are derived as well as the import or export relating to arms, ammunition and implements for war.

C. Compulsory Licenses[2]

A compulsory license is to work a patent or use copyright without the consent of the owner but based on a license that is issued by a government. Compulsory licenses are common in most countries of the world, especially in developing countries. They arise when the owner of the intellectual property, in particular patents, refuses or is unable to work the property in a particular country within a certain period of time. In such a case, a third party may apply for a compulsory license, which will be issued by the government without the consent of the owner.

The *Paris Convention for the Protection of Industrial Property* (the Paris Convention) recognizes the right of countries to impose compulsory licenses on patents with certain limitations. It states as follow.

(1) Members may legislate measures providing for the grant of compulsory licenses to prevent abuses of the exclusive rights conferred by the patent, for example, for failure to work.

(2) Forfeiture of the patent will not be provided for except where the grant of compulsory licenses is not sufficient to prevent abuses. Forfeiture or revocation of a patent will not be instituted before the expiration of three years from the grant of the first compulsory license.

(3) A compulsory license may not be applied for on the ground of failure to work or insufficient working before the expiration of three years from the date of application for the patent, or four years from the date of the grant of the patent whichever period expires last. It shall be refused if the patentee justifies his inaction by legislating reasons. Such compulsory license shall be nonexclusive and shall not be transferable even in the form of the grant of a sublicense except with that part of the enterprises of goodwill, which exploits such license.

---

1. 关于我国对知识产权相关限制竞争性行为的规制，相关规定可参见我国的《民法典》《反垄断法》《对外贸易法》《技术进出口管理条例》等法律法规。

2. compulsory license：强制许可，指国家专利行政部门根据具体情况，可以不经专利权人的同意，通过行政申请程序直接允许申请者实施专利。强制许可也是一种实施专利的许可，是对专利权人权利的一种限制。但强制许可实施人不能无偿实施专利，他必须向专利权人支付合理的使用费。对于强制许可，世界各国特别是发展中国家的专利法中都有相应的规定。《巴黎公约》第5条A款也规定了缔约国有权采取立法措施，规定强制许可。规定强制许可的主要目的是防止专利权人对专利权进行垄断，并且加以滥用，从而损害国家或者民众的利益。因此，对不愿实施，或者在一定期限内不实施专利的专利权人，采取强制许可的措施是合适的，也是合理的。

9.4 Regulations of International Franchising

Franchising[1] constitutes a rapidly expanding form of doing business abroad. Now it even becomes a business model in which many different owners share a single brand name. A parent company allows the franchisee to use the company's strategies and trademarks; in exchange, the franchisee pays an initial fee and royalties based on revenues. The parent company also provides the franchisee with support, including advertising and training, as part of the franchising agreement. For the franchisor, the franchise is a faster, cheaper form of expansion than building "chain stores" to distribute goods and avoid investment and liability over a chain. For the franchisee, the franchisor's success is the success of the franchisees. The franchisee is said to have a greater incentive than a direct employee because he or she has a direct stake in the business. Thus hundreds of multinational companies have developed tens of thousands of foreign franchises, e.g. MacDonald's maybe one of the most successful ones.

Under the intellectual property law, franchise is a specialized license in which the licensor (franchiser) permits the licensee (franchisee) to work the licensor's intellectual property under the supervision and control of a franchiser. A license allows a licensee to use intellectual property, usually a trademark, for the licensee's own purposes. Depending on the licensing agreement between them, the licensee may use the intellectual property as a component of its own products, and it may sell the products derived from it under the licensor's name or under its own name. Sometimes the licensee may even sell the intellectual property or the products derived from it in direct competition with the licensor. However, a franchisee has more limited rights. The key difference is that a franchisee is regarded as a unit or element of the franchiser's business.

Three types of franchises have evolved since the beginning of the twentieth century: distributorships, chain-style businesses, and manufacturing or processing plant. A distributorship franchise exists when a manufacturer licenses a dealer to sell its products. The automobile dealership is an example. A chain-style business franchise is an arrangement in which a franchise operates under a franchiser's trade name and is identified as a part of the franchiser's business chain. Most of the foreign fast-food restaurants are operated in this way. A manufacturing or processing plant franchise exists when a franchiser provides the franchisee with the formula or the essential ingredients to make a popular product. The franchisee then wholesales or retails the product according to the standards established by the franchiser. Examples of this kind are Coca-Cola and other soft-drink firms.

Although the franchisee has more limited rights than a licensee, the regulations governing international franchising agreements are the same as those governing licenses. Competition laws will greatly affect the legal issue arising out of the franchising agreement. For example, the EU has invalidated franchisers' "quality assurance" provisions when they are deemed unduly restrictive of the franchisee's ability to compete. Tied-purchase clauses that require the franchisee to buy certain goods from the franchiser are sometimes difficult to justify on quality control grounds. And geographic exclusivity provision will not be permitted if it unduly restricts competition within the host country.

Most franchisers have standard contracts, which are used in their home markets and have them

---

1. Franchising：特许经营，是指特许人以合同约定的形式，允许被特许人有偿使用其商标、专利、产品及运作管理经验等从事经营活动，被特许人按合同规定，在特许人统一的业务模式下从事经营活动，并向特许人支付相应费用的商业经营模式。在法律性质上，特许经营是知识产权许可的一种变体。

revised and adapted to international franchising without significantly altering the franchiser's successful business formula. Under an international franchising agreement franchise fees and royalties must be specified, the provision of services, training and control by the franchiser are detailed, the term and area of the franchise, accounting procedures agreed on, business standards and advertising selected, insurance obtained, taxes and other liabilities allocated, dispute settlement procedures should be decided. A trademark licensing clause lies at the heart of all international franchising agreements conveying the local trademark rights of the franchiser to the franchisee in return for royalty payment. Case 9-1 illustrates some legal problems in franchising.

【 Case 9-1 】

Dayan v. McDonald's Corp.
466 N.E. 2d 958 (1984)

BACKGROUNDS AND FACTS

Dayan, the Plaintiff, received an exclusive franchise to operate McDonald's restaurants in Paris in 1971. The franchise agreement required that the franchise should meet all quality, service, and cleanliness (QSC) standards set by McDonald's. And the franchise agreement stated the rationale for maintaining QSC standards was that: "a departure of restaurants anywhere in the world from these standards impedes the successful operation of restaurants throughout the world, and injures the value of McDonald's patents, trademarks and property." Dayan agreed to maintain these standards and also agreed not to vary from QSC standards without prior written approval. After several years of QSC standards violations by Dayan, McDonald's sought to terminate the franchise and Dayan brought this action to enjoin the termination. The lower court found that good cause existed for the termination and Dayan appealed.

BUCKLEY, PRESIDING JUSTICE

Dayan argued that McDonald's was obliged to provide him with the operational assistance necessary to enable him to meet the QSC standards. He verbally asked Sollars (a McDonald's manager) for a French-speaking operations person to work in Paris for 6 months. Sollars testified that he told Dayan it would be difficult to find someone with such appropriate background but that McDonald's could immediately send him an English-speaking operations man. The idea was summarily rejected by Dayan as unworkable even though Sollars had informed Dayan that sending operations person who did not speak the language to a foreign country was very common and very successful in McDonald's international system. Nonetheless, Sollars agreed to attempt to locate a qualified person as requested by Dayan. Through Sollars' efforts, Dayan was put in contact with Michael Maycock, an operations person speaking French. Dayan testified that he hired Michael Maycock sometime in October 1977 and placed him in charge of the training, quality control and equipment.

As the trial court correctly realized: "It does not take a McDonald's-trained French-speaking operations person to know that grease dripping from the vents must be stopped and not merely collected in a cup hung from the ceiling, that dogs are not permitted to defecate where food is stored, that insecticide is not blended with chicken breading; that past-dated products should be discarded."

The finding that Dayan refused non-French-speaking operational assistance and that McDonald's fulfilled Dayan's limited request for a French-speaking operational employee is well supported by the record. Accordingly, we find McDonald's fulfilled its contractual obligation to provide a requested operational assistance to Dayan.

In view of the foregoing reasons, the judgment of the trial court denying the plaintiff's request for a permanent injunction and McDonald's properly terminating the franchise agreement is affirmed.

DECISION

Judgment was affirmed for McDonald's. McDonald's had fulfilled all of its responsibility under the agreement to assist the plaintiff in complying with the provisions of the license. The plaintiff had violated the provisions of the agreement by not complying with the QSC standards. The plaintiff is permitted to continue the operation of his restaurants but without the use of McDonald's trademarks or name.

 Chapter Summary

当今知识产权贸易已成为国际贸易的重要组成部分。因此，本章重在对知识产权及知识产权贸易的相关法律知识和法律问题加以介绍和讨论。著作权、专利权、商标权和商业秘密是为各国国内法及国际条约所确认的主要的知识产权类型。著作权是指作者及其他权利人对文学、艺术和科学作品享有的人身权和财产权的总称。专利权是发明创造人或其权利受让人对特定的发明创造在一定期限内依法享有的独占实施权。商标是用以区别商品和服务不同来源的商业性标志，由文字、图形、字母、数字、三维标志、颜色组合、声音或者上述要素的组合构成。商标权指商标主管机关依法授予商标所有人对其注册商标受国家法律保护的专有权。商标权人拥有依法支配其注册商标并禁止他人侵害的权利。商业秘密是指不为公众所知悉、能为权利人带来经济利益、并经权利人采取保密措施的技术信息和经营信息，如管理方法，产销策略，客户名单、货源情报等经营信息；生产配方、工艺流程、技术诀窍、设计图纸等技术信息。

知识产权的保护具有地域性，主要是各国国内法确认的产物，但国际条约对统一、协调知识产权的保护和实施也起到了重要作用。一些重要的知识产权国际条约包括《巴黎公约》《伯尔尼公约》《专利合作条约》《与贸易有关知识产权协定》和世界知识产权组织等国际组织在促进知识产权保护和贸易方面也发挥着重要作用。

知识产权贸易包括知识产权转让和知识产权许可。知识产权的国际许可是指许可方将所涉知识产权的使用权授予被许可方按照约定使用，被许可方支付相应费用的交易安排。在实践中，知识产权的国际许可包括独占许可、排他许可、普通许可等多种类型。知识产权国际许可通常由许可方与被许可方依法签订书面许可合同的形式来实现。国际许可协议的主要条款一般包括：当事人名称或姓名及住所；名词与术语的解释；许可使用的知识产权名称和内容；实施许可的范围、期限和类型；技术情报和资料及其保密事项；技术服务的内容；使用费及其支付方式；后续改进成果的归属和使用；违约金或者损失赔偿的计算方法；争议的解决方式；法律选择条款；不可抗力条款；其他条款。对于知识产权许可协议中限制竞争的条款，其合法性则可能受到各国反垄断法的调整。与一般的知识产权许可不同，强制许可是一种非自愿许可，是国家专利行政部门依照专利法规定，不经专利权人同意，直接允许其他单位或个人实施其发明创造的一种许可方式。国际特许经营则是知识产权国际许可的一种变体，现已发展成为一种商业经营模式。在该模式下，特许人以合同约定的形式，允许被特许人有偿使用其商标、专利、产品及运作管理经验等从事经营活动，被特许人按合同规定，在特许人统一的业务模式下从事经营活动，并向特许人支付相应费用。

Exercises

Part I. True or False Statements: Decide whether the following statements are True or False and explain why.

1. International treaties such as the *Paris Convention* and the *Berne Convention* created some new types of intellectual property.

2. Under the *Copyright Law of the People's Republic of China*, oral works will not be protected by copyrights.

3. The *TRIPs Agreement* sets the uniform time period for which copyrights shall be protected for 50 years.

4. The inventions whose purpose is contrary to public policy or public interests will not be granted patents in China.

5. The *Berne Convention* allows members to establish certain formalities such as the requirement that the word copyright or its abbreviation appear on the work as a prerequisite to granting protection.

6. After the *TRIPs Agreement* came into effect, the *Berne Convention* and the *Paris Convention* have ceased to be effective.

7. National treatment shall be followed in the protection of foreign intellectual property rights among the WTO members.

8. The laws of China prohibit such clauses in international licensing agreement as preventing the licensee from challenging the validity of the intellectual property right, conducting coercive package licensing or stating exclusive grant-back conditions.

9. If the state has granted compulsory license on a patent to a third party, then the third party need not to pay the patentee a royalty.

10. A franchise is a specialized license and the franchisee has more limited rights in using the intellectual property right.

Part II Chapter Questions. Discuss and answer the following questions according to what you have learned in this chapter. You are encouraged to use your own words.

1. What are the conditions for an invention to be granted a patent?

2. How do you understand the pecuniary rights and moral rights of a copyright's owner?

3. In a broad sense, how many kinds of trademarks are there? Give an example for each kind.

4. What are the legal requirements for the information to be regarded as trade secret?

5. In your eyes, what is the purpose of the *TRIPs Agreement* in the field of intellectual property? Can you feel the influence of this Agreement on China?

6. In international licensing agreements, the licensee usually will impose some unfair restrictive provisions on the licensee. Name and describe one of them.

7. How does it differ among exclusive-license, sole-license and non-exclusive license?

8. In your point of view, what may be the reason or reasons justifying compulsory license?

9. What are the limitations for a state to grant compulsory licenses under the *Paris Convention*? Are these limitations binding on China?

10. Explain the differences between a franchise and a license in terms of intellectual property transfer.

Part Ⅲ Case Problem

1. The Little Company, based in the United States, owns several patents, which are essential both to the manufacture of xerographic copiers and to the manufacture of photographic developing machines. Little Company has entered into a licensing agreement with the Great Company, a China's company. The agreement contains the following clauses:

(1) The licensee may use the technology only for the manufacture and sale of xerographic equipment;

(2) The license may sell the products made with the technology only in Mexico;

(3) The licensee must grant to the licensor all technological improvements it makes in connection with the licensed technology. The licensee is expressly forbidden from applying for patents in its own name on any improvements to the licensed technology;

(4) The licensee may not disclose to any other party any trade secret provided by the licensor to the licensee;

(5) The licensee may not use any of the licensor's patented technology for a period of 3 years following the expiration of the last patent.

Comment on the validity of these clauses under the law of China.

2. Murphy (Plaintiff) slipped and fell on water that had accumulated on a motel floor. Holiday Inn (Defendant) had licensed the motel to the operator, who operated it under the terms of Holiday Inns' franchise agreement. Under the franchise agreement, Holiday Inn provides its trade name and trademark to the operator. To achieve system-wide standardization of business identity and uniformity of commercial service, some regulatory provisions are contained in the franchise agreement. These regulatory provisions do not interfere with the daily maintenance of the operator's premises, set standards for employee skills or productivity or determine employee wages or working conditions. Holiday Inn submitted a motion for a summary judgment that no principal-agent or master-servant relationship existed with the operator, thus they would not be liable for Murphy's injuries.

Was there an agency relationship between Defendant and the operator that could make Defendant liable for Plaintiff's injuries?

Part Ⅳ. Further reading

FORM OF INTELLECTUAL PROPERTY TRANSFER AGREEMENT

THIS INTELLECTUAL PROPERTY TRANSFER AGREEMENT (the "Agreement") is made on [date], 2015

BETWEEN

REUTERS S.A., a company incorporated in Switzerland, whose principal office is at 153 route de Thonton, 1245 Collonge-Bellerive, Geneva, Switzerland ("Reuters"); and

BRIDGE TRADING COMPANY, a corporation organized under the laws of the State of Delaware, whose principal office is at 788 Office Parkway, Creve Couer, Missouri (the "Company").

WHEREAS

(A) Reuters has agreed to sell and/or transfer all of its and its applicable affiliates' right, title and interest in the Intellectual Property (as defined below) to the Company, and

(B) The Company has agreed to purchase and accept the same for the Consideration (as defined below).

NOW, IT IS AGREED as follows.

1. Definitions and Interpretation

1.1 In this Agreement:

Business Day means a day (other than a Saturday or Sunday) on which banks generally are open in New York, USA for the transaction of a full range of business.

Buyer means Instinet Group Incorporated.

Completion means completion of the transfer hereunder in accordance with Section 3.

Intellectual Property means the software applications (together with all source and object code and documentation related thereto and all intellectual property rights therein) and other intellectual property rights described on Schedule A.

Transfer Time means the close of the Business Day on the date of this Agreement.

1.2 In this Agreement:

(a) the headings are inserted for convenience only and shall not affect the construction of this Agreement;

(b) a reference to sell or purchase or transfer includes a reference to procure the sale of or procure the purchase of or procure the transfer of, as the case may be; and

(c) general words introduced by the word other shall not be given a restrictive meaning by reason of the fact that they are preceded by words indicating a particular class of act, matter or thing, nor by the fact that they are followed by particular examples intended to be embraced by the general words.

2. The Transfer

2.1 Effective as of the Transfer Time, Reuters hereby sells and transfers and the Company hereby purchases all of Reuters and its applicable affiliates' right, title and interest in the Intellectual Property.

2.2 The price for the sale and transfer in Section 2.1 shall be the sum of $350,000, as outlined in Schedule A (the "Consideration").

2.3 If any sales tax, value added tax or other transfer tax is properly chargeable in respect of the sale and purchase in Section 2.1, the Company shall pay to Reuters the amount of such tax in addition to and at the same time as the Consideration. Reuters will issue the Company a proper tax invoice in respect thereof.

2.4 THE COMPANY HEREBY ACKNOWLEDGES THAT REUTERS MAKES NO REPRESENTATION OR WARRANTY TO THE COMPANY UNDER THIS AGREEMENT, EITHER EXPRESS OR IMPLIED, WITH RESPECT TO THE INTELLECTUAL PROPERTY, AND THAT THE ABOVE SALE AND TRANSFER IS MADE TO THE COMPANY ON AN "AS IS" BASIS.

3. Completion

3.1 The sale and purchase of the Intellectual Property shall be completed, and legal title and ownership in respect of the Intellectual Property shall be deemed to pass to the Company, in each case, with effect from the Transfer Time.

3.2 Reuters shall:

(a) Cause to be delivered or made available to the Company such additional documents as the Company may reasonably require to complete the sale and purchase of the Intellectual Property; and

(b) do such other things reasonably necessary to give full effect to this Agreement.

3.3 The Company shall:

(a) Timely pay or cause to be paid the Consideration in cash to Reuters or to whom and in the manner as Reuters may direct;

(b) cause to be delivered or made available to Reuters such additional documents as Reuters may reasonably require to complete the sale and purchase of the Intellectual Property; and

(c) do such other things reasonably necessary to give full effect to this Agreement.

4. Licenses

4.1 The Company acknowledges that, as a current affiliate of Reuters, it has a royalty-free, non-exclusive, non-transferable and non-sublicensable right and license to use the third-party software set forth on Schedule B in connection with its business, pursuant to agreements between Reuters and/or an affiliate (other than the Company) and the applicable third parties. The Company covenants that it shall use all such software in compliance with all terms and conditions of such agreements to the extent that Buyer and/or the Company has been given access to a copy of such agreements.

4.2 Reuters grants to the Company a perpetual, royalty-free, non-exclusive license to use all know-how, techniques, ideas, processes and similar intellectual property that (i) was created, invented or developed by Reuters (or its applicable affiliates) prior to the Transfer Time and (ii) relates to the business of the Company, but is not included in the Transferred Know-How (as defined in Schedule A). The Company may sublicense this license solely in connection with the operation of its business, and not for the independent use of any third party. The Company may assign this license only in connection with the merger, reorganization or sale of the business of the Company to which this license relates. Any purported sublicense or assignment by the Company in violation of the foregoing shall be null and void and of no force or effect. To the extent Reuters or any affiliate (other than the Company), on the one hand, and the Company or any current or future affiliate, on the other hand, enter into any future agreement governing a party's use of specific items of intellectual property of the other party, such specific provisions (and the term of any such permitted use) shall be deemed to supersede and modify accordingly the above general license.

4.3 The Company grants to Reuters and its affiliates (other than the Company) a perpetual, royalty-free, non-exclusive license to use all Transferred Know-How that has a relation or application to the business of Reuters or any affiliate other than the Company. Reuters and its affiliates may sublicense this license solely in connection with the operation of their businesses, and not for the independent use of any third party. Reuters and its affiliates may assign this license only in connection with the merger, reorganization or sale of any of their businesses to which this license relates. Any purported sublicense or assignment by Reuters or an applicable affiliate in violation of the foregoing shall be null and void and of no force or effect. To the extent Reuters or any affiliate (other than the Company), on the one hand, and the Company or any current or future affiliate, on the other hand, enter into any future agreement governing a party's use of specific items of intellectual property of the other party, such specific provisions (and the term of any such permitted use) shall be deemed to supersede and modify accordingly the above general license.

5. Enter Agreement

This Agreement (including the Exhibits, which are hereby incorporated in the terms of this Agreement) sets forth the entire understanding and agreement among the parties as to matters covered herein and therein and supersedes any prior understanding, agreement or statement (written or oral) of intent among the parties with respect to the subject matter hereof.

6. Counterparts

This Agreement may be executed in any number of counterparts, each of which shall be deemed to be an original and all of which together shall be deemed to be one and the same instrument.

7. Variation (*omitted*)

8. Notices (*omitted*)

9. Costs (*omitted*)

10. Governing Law

THE AGREEMENT SHALL BE GOVERNED BY, AND CONSTRUED IN ACCORDANCE WITH, THE LAWS OF THE STATE OF NEW YORK. Each party hereby irrevocably agrees that any legal action or proceeding against it arising out of this Agreement or the transactions contemplated hereby shall be brought only in the Supreme Court of the State of New York in and for the County of New York or the U.S. District Court for the Southern District of New York, preserving, however, all rights of removal to a federal court under 28 U.S.C. §1441. Reuters hereby designates, appoints and empowers Reuters America Holdings, Inc., with offices currently at 3 Times Square, New York, New York 10036, as its lawful agent to receive for and on its behalf service of process in the State of New York in any such action or proceeding and irrevocably consents to the service of process outside the territorial jurisdiction of said courts in any such action or proceeding by mailing copies thereof by registered United States mail, postage prepaid, to its address as specified in or pursuant to Section 8. Any service made on any such agent or its successor shall be effective when delivered regardless of whether notice thereof is given to the affected party. If any person or firm designated as agent hereunder shall no longer serve as agent of such party to receive service of process in the State of New York, the party so affected shall be obligated promptly to appoint a successor to so serve; and, unless and until such successor is appointed and the other parties notified of the same in writing, service upon the last designated agent shall be good and effective. Reuters hereby agrees to at all times maintain an agent to receive service of process in the State of New York pursuant to this Section 10.1. The foregoing provisions of this Section 10.1 shall not affect, limit or prevent the parties from serving process in any other manner permitted by law.

11. Taxes (*omitted*)

12. U.S. Bankruptcy Code (*omitted*)

AS WITNESS, this Agreement has been signed by or on behalf of the parties the day and year first above written.

SIGNED

_____

for and on behalf of Reuters S.A.

SIGNED

----

for and on behalf of Bridge Trading Company

Part Ⅳ Settlement of International Commercial Disputes

Chapter 10
International Commercial Arbitration

 导读

国际商事交易往往伴随着国际商事争端，因此国际商事争端的解决也是学习国际商法需要关注的重要内容。本章主要介绍和讨论：（1）解决国际商事争议的一般方法：替代性争端解决方法、仲裁和诉讼；（2）国际商事仲裁的基础问题：国际商事仲裁的界定、历史以及国际商事仲裁机构；（3）国际商事仲裁的主要法律问题：国际商事仲裁协议、国际商事仲裁程序以及国际商事仲裁裁决的承认和执行。

 Warm-up Questions

(1) Compared with domestic business disputes, what are the difficulties for settling cross-border ones?

(2) As you see it, how many methods are used to resolve the disputes arising from international business?

(3) What's the final resort to resolve international commercial disputes?

(4) When choosing the method of dispute resolution, what factors will you take into account?

(5) Give your suggestions on how to avoid disputes in international transactions.

10.1 Methods of International Commercial Dispute Settlement

An inevitable consequence of increased trade is increased business disputes. In attempting to settle those disputes, many questions that are relevant to a domestic commercial dispute are equally relevant to an international commercial dispute, but they become more complex in the international context. In international commercial transactions, the parties usually live and work oceans away. They look, speak and act differently from each other. The domestic laws of their jurisdictions governing such commercial transactions may be divergent and unfamiliar to each other. In one word, the business transactions that span continents and cultures raise many complicated legal and tactical problems.

This chapter presents several alternatives for international commercial dispute resolution, including Alternative Dispute Resolution, arbitration, and litigation. These methods may be used individually or in a combined way.

Alternative Dispute Resolution

Alternative Dispute Resolution (ADR) [1] offers an amicable method of dispute resolution through voluntary consultation. It has become popular for its flexible procedure, and the least harm to the long-term business relationships between parties. However, the agreement for dispute resolution reached through ADR is not legally binding. If any of the parties refuses to fulfill the above agreement, such dispute may still have to resort to other methods, that is, arbitration or litigation. To some degree, ADR may be regarded as the "screening procedure" for arbitration or litigation. ADR is usually thought to cover all the methods of dispute resolution but arbitration and litigation, although some argue it should also include the method of arbitration.

Negotiation, as its name implies, is the process of reaching an agreement by the parties through oral or written discussion. Despite its simplicity, negotiation is an important tool in the process of dispute settlement, and undoubtedly the one most commonly relied on. It is used not merely to resolve disputes but to prevent them from arising in the first place and to lay the groundwork for other forms of dispute settlement. Negotiation is carried out voluntarily between the parties without the involvement of any third party. It is much more flexible in the procedure and form. One obvious advantage of negotiation is time-saving and money-saving. However, the potential shortcoming is that the agreement reached through negotiation highly depends on the bargaining power of the parties, which may put the economically weaker party in a disadvantaged position. Moreover, if negotiation fails, the parties may still have to resolve their disputes through other methods.

Mediation[2] is a voluntary, nonbinding, and conciliation process. The parties agree on an impartial third party (mediator) who helps them amicably reach a solution. The mediator may be an individual or an institution. It is private and there are no public court records. The mediator will see each party privately and listen to their respective viewpoints, trying to ensure that each party understands the other's point of view and helping them to achieve a compromise solution. A mediator cannot compel the parties to arrive at a settlement and the final decision to settle rests with the parties themselves. The parties reserve all the rights to resort to binding arbitration or litigation. Mediation is a method of resolving disputes originating from the oriental countries. Now it has won increasing popularity as a way of settling international commercial disputes among private parties in other parts of the world.

Mini-trial[3] is a method often used to resolve disputes between corporations. The dispute will be submitted to a mini-trial panel which is composed of a third party (Chairman) and a senior member of management from each of the parties in dispute. The parties meet to agree with the basic rules of the

---

1. Alternative Dispute Resolution（ADR）：替代争议解决方式又称选择性的争议解决方式，是非诉讼、非仲裁的选择性争议解决方式的概括性的统称。它指可以被法律程序接受的，通过协议而非强制性的有约束力的裁定解决争议的任何方法。主要方法包括：协商、调解、小型审理、简易陪审团审判等。替代争议解决方式具有非正式性、非强制性、广泛性、灵活性的特点，是对诉讼和仲裁的辅助手段，是社会有机体自我完善机制的表现。

2. 调解是指争端的当事人就争议的实体权利、义务，在第三方的组织和主持下，以法律、法规、商业惯例、政策以及社会公德为依据，自愿进行协商，达成协议、解决纠纷的办法。近年，国际商事争议解决领域有重要国际规则进展。

3. 小型审理是一种集协商、调解、仲裁各部分特点于一身的非诉讼性、混合性纠纷解决程序。在小型审理中，由第三方和当事人各自的管理人员组成审理小组，然后按照各方合意的程序来解决商业纠纷。

process including the number of documents to be disclosed, the time for each party to prepare the brief and the date to present the case. On the appointed date for the hearing, each party will make a presentation of the case. Following the presentations, the management representatives of each party will meet by themselves in an effort to reach a settlement. If no settlement can be made, the Chairman may put forward his/her proposal for resolution of the disputes. The proceedings are confidential and may not be referred to in any subsequent litigation.

10.2   Settlement of International Commercial Disputes through Arbitration

Dispute resolution in international commercial transactions runs from friendly negotiation to litigation. In between lies international commercial arbitration, a binding alternative to litigation. Parties to the contracts for the international sale of goods often agree that potential disputes concerning the contract will be settled through arbitration. The volume of international commercial arbitration has grown enormously in recent decades around the world. Thus, a clear understanding of the arbitration is necessary.

A. Overview of Arbitration and International Commercial Arbitration

Arbitration implies that the parties agree to submit a dispute for settlement to private persons, which results in a binding award that will be enforced by the court. In other words, **arbitration**[1] is an out-of-court proceeding in which a neutral third party called an arbitrator hears evidence and then makes a binding decision. Arbitration has two dimensions: contractual and judicial. On one hand, arbitration is based on the agreement between parties. No Arbitration is possible without such an agreement. On the other hand, the arbitrator exercises a judicial task. Arbitration is based on arbitration law laying down the rules for arbitration procedure and the legal effects of the award. The court can enforce a correct award or annul an incorrect award.

A distinction is usually made between national arbitration and international arbitration. For national arbitration, all elements (parties, dispute, place of arbitration) are located within one legal system. In case of international arbitration, these elements have gone beyond one legal system. According to Article 1.3 of **UNCITRAL Model Law on International Commercial Arbitration**[2] (1985, With amendments as adopted in 2006), an arbitration is international if: (a) the parties to an arbitration agreement have, at the time of the conclusion of that agreement, their places of business in different States; or (b) one of the following places is situated outside the State in which the parties have their places of business: (i) the place of arbitration if determined in, or pursuant to, the arbitration agreement; (ii) any place where a substantial part of the

---

1. Arbitration：仲裁是指当事方在争议发生之前或发生之后，签订书面协议，自愿将其争议提交由非司法机构的仲裁员组成的仲裁庭进行裁判，并接受该裁判约束的一种制度。仲裁在性质上是兼具契约性、自治性、民间性和准司法性的一种争议解决方式。

2. *UNCITRAL Model Law on International Commercial Arbitration*：《联合国国际贸易法委员会国际商事仲裁示范法》（1985 年制定，2006 年修订）。该示范法旨在协助各国考虑国际商事仲裁的特点和需要，改革其仲裁程序法并使之现代化。该示范法涵盖了仲裁过程的所有阶段，从仲裁协议、仲裁庭的组成和管辖权、司法审查，到仲裁裁决的承认和执行。

obligations of the commercial relationship is to be performed or the place with which the subject-matter of the dispute is most closely connected; or (c) the parties have expressly agreed that the subject-matter of the arbitration agreement relates to more than one country. As for the term "commercial", *UNCITRAL Model Law on International Commercial Arbitration* (1985,With amendments as adopted in 2006) gives the following interpretation: "commercial" should be given a wide interpretation so as to cover matters arising from all relationships of a commercial nature, whether contractual or not. Relationships of a commercial nature include but are not limited to, the following transactions: Any trade transaction for the supply or exchange of goods or services; distribution agreement; commercial representation or agency; factoring; leasing; construction of works; consulting; engineering; licensing; investment; financing; banking; insurance; exploitation agreement or concession; joint venture and other forms of industrial or business cooperation; carriage of goods or passengers by air, sea, rail or road.

In a nutshell, international commercial arbitration is given a wide interpretation: If any of the elements of a commercial dispute connects with more than one legal system, including the party's place of business, the place of arbitration, the place of performance, the place with which the dispute is most closely connected and the subject matter, it will be regarded as an **international commercial arbitration**.[1]

There are two distinct types of international commercial arbitration: **ad hoc and institutional arbitration**.[2] Ad hoc arbitrations involve selection by the parties of the arbitrators and rules governing the arbitration. The classic formula involves each side choosing one arbitrator who in turn chooses a third arbitrator. The ad hoc arbitration panel selects its procedural rules. Ad hoc arbitration can be agreed upon in advance or, quite literally, selected ad hoc as a dispute arises. Institutional arbitration involves selection of a specific arbitration center, often accompanied by its own rules of arbitration.

There are numerous competing centers of arbitration. Some centers are long-standing and busy, such as the International Chamber of Commerce, while other centers are recent in time and still struggling for clients such as the Commercial Arbitration and Mediation Center for the Americas (CAMCA). Some of the leading arbitral organizations for the arbitration of commercial disputes are as follows:

•**China International Economic and Trade Arbitration Commission**[3]

---

1. International commercial arbitration:国际商事仲裁。广义而言，国际商事仲裁是指双方当事人的营业地、仲裁地、仲裁裁决的履行地等位于不同国家的商事仲裁。国际商事仲裁广泛运用于解决：国际货物买卖合同中的争议；国际货物运输中的争议；国际保险中的争议；国际贸易、支付结算中的争议；国际投资争议；国际知识产权保护的争议；海上碰撞、救助和共同海损中的争议；国际环境污染争议等。

2. ad hoc and arbitration institutional arbitration：临时仲裁与机构仲裁。临时仲裁也称特别仲裁，它是一种在事先并不存在仲裁组织的情况下，当事人根据仲裁协议，将他们之间的争议交给临时组成的仲裁庭进行审理并做出裁决的仲裁。这种类型的仲裁活动不设任何常设仲裁机构或组织，仲裁庭的成员由当事人协商选定，仲裁庭因审理案件而成立，争议解决之后，仲裁庭即告解散。临时仲裁庭是仲裁的初始形态，目前仍有一些国家继续使用。所谓机构仲裁，又称制度仲裁，是指依照当事人双方的协议将争议交由一定的常设仲裁机构并依该机构所制定的现存仲裁规则所进行的仲裁。机构仲裁具有两大优势：一是它依据仲裁机构既定的仲裁规则进行仲裁，程序较为严格；二是它有现存的固定管理机构和合格可信的仲裁人员。机构仲裁是当今世界最主要的仲裁方式。

3. China International Economic and Trade Arbitration Commission（CIETAC）：中国国际经济贸易仲裁委员会（2000年，同时启用中国国际商会仲裁院的名称），是世界上主要的常设商事仲裁机构之一。中国国际经济贸易仲裁委员会在国内推出独具特色的行业争议解决服务，为不同行业的当事人提供适合其行业需要的仲裁法律服务，如粮食行业争议、工程建设争议、金融争议等服务。除传统的商事仲裁服务外，还为当事人提供多元争议解决服务，包括域名争议解决、网上仲裁、调解、投资争端解决等。

- **China Maritime Arbitration Commission**[1]
- **American Arbitration Association**[2]
- **International Chamber of Commerce**[3]
- **London Court of International Arbitration**[4]
- **Arbitration Institute of the Stockholm Chamber of Commerce**[5]
- St. Petersburg International Commercial Arbitration Court
- Hong Kong International Arbitration Center and the Hong Kong Mediation and Arbitration Center
- Singapore International Arbitration Centre
- Japan Commercial Arbitration Association
- World Intellectual Property Organization (WIPO) Arbitration and Mediation Center

Ad hoc arbitration presupposes a certain amount of goodwill and flexibility between the parties. It can be speedy and less costly than institutional arbitration. Institutional arbitration offers ease of incorporation in an international business agreement, supervisory services, a stable of experienced arbitrators and a fixed fee schedule.

B. Advantages and Disadvantages of Arbitration

Arbitration is usually faster, less informal, more neutral and more flexible for scheduling than litigation. **The arbitration proceedings are usually faster than court proceedings.** It may take several months or even years to bring the case through court proceedings. With the chance of an appeal by the losing party, the court settlement of the dispute may be further considerably delayed. It is obvious that this delay is damaging trade where quick access to money due is desired.

In arbitration there is in principle only a first instance procedure and therefore no time should be lost in appeal procedures. The informality of arbitration proceedings also enhances the speed of settlement. A hearing is generally more quickly arranged in arbitration proceedings. If the arbitrators make it clear to the parties in an earlier stage that they understand the essence of their dispute, the parties

---

1. China Maritime Arbitration Commission（CMAC）：中国海事仲裁委员会。中国海事仲裁委员会下设航空争议仲裁中心、计量争议仲裁中心、建设工程争议仲裁中心、海事调解中心、航空争议调解中心、救助打捞争议调解中心、物流争议解决中心、渔业争议解决中心等业务中心。

2. American Arbitration Association（AAA）：美国仲裁协会。美国仲裁协会成立于 1926 年，是美国最主要的国际仲裁常设机构，总部设在纽约。1996 年，美国仲裁协会设立了国际争端解决中心，旨在为全球 80 多个国家和地区提供 12 种语言的争端管理服务。美国仲裁协会受案范围广泛，包括商事仲裁，建筑、房地产及环境仲裁，劳动、雇佣及选举仲裁，政府及消费者仲裁几大类别。

3. International Chamber of Commerce（ICC）：国际商会仲裁院，成立于 1923 年，附属于国际商会，总部设在巴黎，是世界上主要的国际争端仲裁机构之一。国际商会仲裁院的仲裁员来自世界各国，能够使用多种语言进行工作。国际商会仲裁院最初受理的案件主要是有关货物买卖合同和许可证贸易的争议。

4. London Court of International Arbitration（LCIA）：伦敦国际仲裁院，是国际上最早成立的常设仲裁机构，也是英国最主要的国际商事仲裁机构，现由伦敦市、伦敦商会和女王特许协会三家共同组成的联合管理委员会管理。伦敦国际仲裁院受理的案件类型广泛，覆盖国际商事的方方面面，包括电信通讯、保险、石油及天然气开发、建筑等行业，其中尤其擅长国际海事案件的审理。

5. Arbitration Institute of the Stockholm Chamber of Commerce（SCC）：斯德哥尔摩商会仲裁院，成立于 1917 年，是瑞典最重要的常设仲裁机构。由于瑞典的仲裁历史悠久，体制完善，因此斯德哥尔摩商会仲裁院成为受理国际经济争议的一个重要场所。近年来，受理的国际案件比率近 50%，受理的案件语言包括英语、瑞典语、俄语、西班牙语及德语。

do not need to spend more time repeating their arguments but can direct their attention to the points which are still unclear to the arbitrators, thus saving time.

The arbitration proceedings are less formal than court proceedings. Arbitrators don't wear gowns. Advocates of the parties don't plead from the bench like attorneys in court. On the contrary, arbitrators, parties and lawyers often sit around one big conference table. The statements in arbitration are usually alternated in open discussions, with the parties contributing and putting their arguments forward. The informal atmosphere enhances the chance of an amicable settlement.

Although occasionally time is lost in the appointment of arbitrators because the opposing party is intent on delaying the arbitration in bad faith and therefore does not appoint an arbitrator, such loss of time can be avoided when the claimant is not deceived by this conduct and requests the arbitration institution to appoint the arbitrator.

Arbitration proceedings are usually confidential to outsiders. The proceedings of the court are public with a few exceptions. This public nature of the court is not always welcome: A competitor may hear the arguments in court and draw confidential information from this; newspapers may give the dispute unnecessary publicity, etc. Businessmen who need a confidential settlement may opt for arbitration because arbitration is not public: Only the parties and their advocates have access to the meetings, the arbitrators are bound to secrecy and the award can only be published with the content of the parties.[1]

Arbitration is usually regarded as more neutral than national courts. One of the parties is often not willing to submit to the jurisdiction of a court in the country of the other party for fear of being at a disadvantage. Arbitration permits the resolution of the case in a third "neutral" country, rather than in the country of one of the parties. The parties are generally free to choose the place of arbitration that is mutually convenient. For example, a dispute between a Canadian company and a Russian company might be arbitration in Beijing or Paris. Moreover, the arbitrators may be chosen by the parties from a roster of impartial commercial professionals and legal professionals, who may also be from a third country. And the case may be resolved using the impartial arbitration rules of the arbitrating tribunal, rather than the procedure buried in the statutes of the country of one party.

However, arbitration is not free from any **disadvantage**. Firstly, the costs involved in arbitration can be significant in some cases. Some argue arbitration costs are far less than litigation, but such a conclusion is not true in every case. Parties in a dispute need to pay not only administrative costs and their own attorney fees but also the arbitrators for their services. Arbitrators can be paid on a time basis: They are compensated for the time spent on the arbitration. Sometimes the importance of the dispute determines the remuneration: For example, in the International Chamber of Commerce, the arbitrators are to a large extent paid according to the monetary value of the claim. For a $100,000 claim, the arbitration cost would be closer to 13 percent.

Secondly, the enforcement or annulment of arbitration awards needs judicial confirmation. [2]Arbitration

---

1. 仲裁程序具有保密性的特点，而诉讼程序以公开为原则。在实践中，仲裁程序的保密性是当事人选择仲裁而不是诉讼的一个重要因素。

2. 仲裁裁决的强制执行和撤销需要司法协助和司法审查。因为仲裁庭的权力基于当事人之间的仲裁协议，而不是来源于国家的司法主权，因此仲裁庭本身并没有强制性的权力，也缺乏强制性的手段保障仲裁程序的执行，需要法院给予必要的支持与协助；同时仲裁的一裁终局制度虽然体现了效率优势，但也是仲裁遭到诟病的缺陷之一。为了体现公平与效益的平衡，防止和减少仲裁裁决的错误，仲裁除了需要法院的支持与协助外，还需要有必要的监督和控制。

only works efficiently when the arbitrators have actually solved a dispute. It is a fact that arbitral awards are generally fulfilled voluntarily. According to reports, 90 percent of the International Chamber of Commerce awards are honored by the losing party without any problems. However, there is always a risk that the losing party refuses to abide or apply for nullity of the arbitral award. In that case, a court procedure must decide on the enforcement or the annulment of the award. Generally, such enforcement or annulment proceedings have a limited scope and courts only examine the procedure problems for making the award. For instance, the scope is limited to the extent that whether there exists an invalid arbitration agreement, whether the arbitrator awards more than asked for (an **ultra petita award**[1]), whether the rights of the defense are violated or whether an award is contrary to the public policy.

C. Arbitration Agreement

The arbitration process requires at the outset an arbitration agreement has been reached. According to *UNCITRAL Model Law on International Commercial Arbitration* (1985, with amendments as adopted in 2006), the arbitration agreement is an agreement by the parties to submit to arbitration all or certain disputes, which have arisen or which may arise between them in respect of a defined legal relationship, whether contractual or not. An arbitration agreement may be in the form of an arbitration clause in a contract or in the form of a separate agreement. And the **arbitration agreement**[2] shall be in writing.

The arbitration agreement is not only the basis for arbitration, it often gives the arbitration shape as well. An arbitration clause must be carefully structured and worded. Generally speaking, the parties may arrange everything in the arbitration clause through mutual agreement on the condition that such arrangements are not contrary to the applicable law.

If the drafters of a contract do not have the necessary expertise, they do better to incorporate one of the available ready-made arbitration clauses. Many arbitration institutions offer suitable draft arbitration clauses. They may possibly offer sufficient inspiration for the drafting of an appropriate arbitration clause. Hereafter follows the arbitration clauses recommended by ICC and UNCITRAL for submission of disputes to arbitration by the respective institutions.

The arbitration clause of the ICC reads in English:

"All disputes arising in connection with the present contract shall be finally settled under the Rules of Conciliation and Arbitration of International Chamber of Commerce by one or more arbitrators appointed in accordance with the said Rules."

The arbitration clause of the UNCITRAL reads in English:

"Any dispute, controversy or claim arising out of or relating to this contract, or the breach, termination or invalidity thereof, shall be settled by arbitration in accordance with the UNCITRAL Arbitration Rules as at present in force."

---

1. ultra petita award：超出当事人约定仲裁范围的裁决。

2. arbitration agreement：仲裁协议（仲裁条款），是指双方当事人在自愿、协商、平等互利的基础之上将他们之间已经发生或者可能发生的争议提交仲裁解决的书面文件，是申请仲裁的必备材料。《中华人民共和国仲裁法》第 16 条规定，仲裁协议包括合同中订立的仲裁条款和以其他书面方式在纠纷发生前或者纠纷发生后达成的请求仲裁的协议。

They are concise ones. And sometimes parties may wish to consider adding:

"The number of arbitrators shall be … (one or three); The place of arbitration shall be … (city or country) and The language(s) to be used in the arbitral proceedings shall be …".

The validity of arbitration agreement in international commercial arbitration is governed by the law chosen by the parties. In case that the parties do not choose the governing law but choose a seat of arbitration, the law of the seat of arbitration is applicable; where no governing law or a seat of arbitration is chosen, the *lex fori* [1] shall apply.

However, it may be that one party claims that the contract, which contains the arbitration clause, is invalid as a whole for a reason unrelated to the arbitration clause. The arbitration clause then is protected against the alleged invalidity of the contract as a whole, because the nullity of the contract does not necessarily result in the invalidity of the arbitration clause (the so-called "autonomy of the arbitration clause").

A valid arbitration agreement/ arbitration clause will exclude the jurisdiction of the court over the dispute to the extent covered by the arbitration agreement or arbitration clause. Now it is generally accepted. But in the early development of international arbitration, this is not so clear.

Read the following case: *Scherk V. Alberto-Culver* in case 10-1.

【Case 10-1】

SCHERK v. ALBERTO-CULVER CO. [2]
417 U.S. 506 (1974)

BACKGROUND AND FACTS

ALBERTO-CULVER CO. (Respondent), an American manufacturer based in Illinois, in order to expand its overseas operations, purchased from SCHERK (Petitioner). SCHERK was a German citizen, and he owned three enterprises organized under the laws of Germany and Liechtenstein, together with all trademark rights of these enterprises. The sales contract, which was negotiated in the United States, England, and Germany, signed in Austria, and closed in Switzerland, contained express warranties by petitioner that the trademarks were unencumbered and a clause providing that "any controversy or claim

---

1. lex fori:（拉丁文）the laws of the forum，法院地法；诉讼地法；审判地法。在冲突法中，对于诉讼程序、证据规则和所采用的法律救济做出规定的诉讼所在地的法律。

2. 在该案中被上诉人 Alberto-Culver Co.是主营业地在伊利诺伊州的美国公司。它生产和销售化妆品。上诉人 Fritz Scherk 是一个德国人，他是依据德国法和列支敦士登法设立的三个相互关联的商业实体的所有人。在 20 世纪 60 年代，Alberto-Culver 开始与 Fritz Scherk 商洽交易。在欧洲和美国进行会谈后，双方在奥地利的维也纳签署了合同，合同规定 Scherk 将其拥有的企业和这些企业拥有的所有有关化妆产品的商标权转让给 Alberto-Culver。此外，合同包含了一个仲裁条款，规定"任何因本合同或其中的违约引起的争议或请求"应提交法国巴黎的国际商会仲裁，"合同及对合同的解释和履行适用美国伊利诺伊州法。"在交易完成约一年后，Alberto-Culver 声称发现其购买的合同下商标权存在第三方的权利请求。据此，Alberto-Culver 在伊利诺伊州北部管区联邦地区法院提起要求损害赔偿和其他救济的诉讼，主张 Scherk 对商标权状况的欺诈陈述违反 1934 年《证券交易法》的§10（b）及证券交易委员会的 10b-5 规则。作为回应，Scherk 请求在依当事人的协议于巴黎仲裁前中止诉讼。Alberto-Culver 反驳了该项请求。地区法院以 Wilko v. Swan 案为依据，驳回 Scherk 中止诉讼的请求，并且作出禁止 Scherk 进行仲裁的初步禁令。Scherk 不服地区法院的裁决，向第七巡回上诉法院提起上诉。上诉法院在一个法官反对的情况下，作出维持地区法院裁决的判决。Scherk 不服向美国联邦最高法院提出上诉。最高法院在审理本案时，对国际证券争议和国内证券争议作了区别，确认在国际领域，证券争议可以基于仲裁协议通过仲裁解决。

[that] shall arise out of this agreement or the breach thereof" would be referred to arbitration before the International Chamber of Commerce in Paris, France, and that Illinois laws would govern the agreement and its interpretation and performance. Subsequently, after allegedly discovering that the trademarks were subject to substantial encumbrances, the respondent offered to rescind the contract, but when the petitioner refused, the respondent brought suit in District Court for damages and other relief, contending that the petitioner's fraudulent representations concerning the trademark rights violated 10 (b) of the Securities Exchange Act of 1934. The petitioner moved to dismiss the action or alternatively to stay the action pending arbitration, but the District Court denied the motion to dismiss and arbitration was enjoined. The Court of Appeals affirmed.

JUSTICE STEWART

The Federal Arbitration Act, now 9 U.S.C. 1 et seq., reversing centuries of judicial hostility to arbitration agreements, was designed to allow parties to avoid "the costliness and delays of litigation, " and to place arbitration agreements "upon the same footing as other contracts ... " Accordingly, the Act provides that an arbitration agreement such as is here involved "shall be valid, irrevocable, and enforceable, save upon such grounds as exist at law or in equity for the revocation of any contract." 9 U.S.C. 2.

In *Wilko v. Swan*, this Court acknowledged that the Act reflects a legislative recognition of the "desirability of arbitration as an alternative to the complications of litigation.

Alberto-Culver's contract to purchase the business entities belonging to Scherk was a truly international agreement. Alberto-Culver is an American corporation with its principal place of business and the vast bulk of its activity in this country, while Scherk is a citizen of Germany whose companies were organized under the laws of Germany and Liechtenstein. The negotiations leading to the signing of the contract in Austria and to the closing in Switzerland took place in the United States, England, and Germany, and involved consultations with legal and trademark experts from each of those countries and from Liechtenstein. Finally, and most significantly, the subject matter of the contract concerned the sale of business enterprises organized under the laws of and primarily situated in European countries, whose activities were largely, if not entirely, directed to European markets.

Such a contract involves considerations and policies significantly different from those found controlling in Wilko. In Wilko, quite apart from the arbitration provision, there was no question but that the laws of the United States generally, and the federal securities laws in particular, would govern disputes arising out of the stock-purchase agreement. The parties, the negotiations, and the subject matter of the contract were all situated in this country, and no credible claim could have been entertained that any international conflict-of-laws problems would arise. In this case, by contrast, considerable uncertainty still existed, concerning the law applicable to the resolution of disputes arising out of the contract.

Such uncertainty will almost inevitably exist with respect to any contract touching two or more parties, each with its own substantive laws and conflict-of-laws rules. A contractual provision specifying in advance the forum in which disputes shall be litigated and the law to be applied is, therefore, an almost indispensable precondition to the achievement of the orderliness and predictability essential to any international business transaction. Furthermore, such a provision obviates the danger that a dispute under the agreement might be submitted to a forum hostile to the interests of one of the parties or unfamiliar with the problem area involved.

A parochial refusal by the courts of one party to enforce an international arbitration agreement would not only frustrate these purposes but would invite unseemly and mutually destructive jockeying by the parties to secure tactical litigation advantages. In the present case, for example, it is not inconceivable that if Scherk had anticipated that Alberto-Culver would be able in this country to enjoin resort to arbitration he might have sought an order in France or some other country enjoining Alberto-Culver from proceeding with its litigation in the United States. Whatever recognition the courts of this country might ultimately have granted to the order of the foreign court, the dicey atmosphere of such a legal no-man's-land would surely damage the fabric of international commerce and trade, and imperil the willingness and ability of businessmen to enter into international commercial agreements …

For all these reasons, we hold that the agreement of the parties in this case to arbitrate any dispute arising out of their international commercial transaction is to be respected and enforced by the federal courts in accord with the explicit provisions of the Arbitration Act.

DECISION

The judgment of the Court of Appeals is reversed and the case is remanded to that court.

D. Arbitration Proceedings

The arbitration proceedings are relatively straightforward. In its simplest form, the parties begin the process by the selection of an arbitrator or arbitrators. If they have agreed upon a place for arbitration to take place, the location is decided; otherwise, the arbitrator or tribunal may fix the location. The parties then exchange statements of claim and defense and any further statements, including any pleas as to the jurisdiction of the arbitration tribunal. The next step in the process is the hearing itself, where the arbitrator or arbitration tribunal will hear the evidence of the parties, any expert testimony, and final arguments. The arbitrator or arbitration tribunal will then deliberate and issues an award. Generally, if the parties have selected an arbitration institution, rules of the arbitration institution shall apply to the process of arbitration, unless the parties agree to be bound by other arbitration rules. For example, *UNCITRAL* rules cover the appointing authority, notice requirements, representation of the parties, challenges of arbitrators, evidence, hearings, statements of claims and defenses, pleas to the arbitrator's jurisdiction, provisional remedies, experts, default, rule waivers, the form and effect of the award, applicable law, settlement, interpretation of the award and costs. ***Arbitration Rules of China International Economic and Trade Arbitration Commission*** (2015) cover similar items.

1. Appointment of arbitrators

An arbitration tribunal consists of one or three arbitrators. When only one arbitrator has to adjudicate on a dispute, the parties usually have no difficulty over this appointment. In case of three arbitrators, each of the parties, within 7 business days upon receiving the notice of arbitration, appoints an arbitrator and a third arbitrator is then appointed jointly by the parties or by the arbitration institution based on the authorization of the parties. The third arbitrator is the presiding arbitrator. The nominated arbitration institution is also competent to appoint an arbitrator if one of the parties refuses to cooperate. The arbitrator appointed by one party cannot consider himself as an agent of that party: He must have an independent and impartial view. If this independence and impartiality are compromised, the arbitrator must refuse or hand back the appointment. Arbitrators must, in any event, disclose to the parties all instances, such as conflict of interests, financial ties, personal ties, etc. that could jeopardize their independence and impartiality. And the parties are entitled to challenge the independence and impartiality of arbitrators with cause.

2. Arbitration hearing[1]

Parties have a wide range of options for setting up proceedings of arbitration hearing. If they don't make use of these options, it is up to the arbitration institution to direct the proceedings. *Arbitration Rules of China International Economic and Trade Arbitration Commission* (2015) require a fundamental condition for the arbitration procedure that every party is entitled to an equal and fair trial. A breach of the fundamental rule of the right to an equal and fair trial results in the award set aside by the court of China.

The parties state the claims and defenses, submit evidence and debate. The arbitrators can order an expert assessment, a local visit, hear parties or witnesses and decide which evidence will be considered sufficient proof. If one of the parties does not cooperate without legal reasons, the arbitrators have jurisdiction to make an award by default. The arbitrators are required to make their award within six months, and at the due request of arbitrators, the Director of China International Economic and Trade Arbitration Commission may grant an extension.

E. Enforcement of Arbitral Awards: New York Convention

The enforcement of an international commercial arbitration award is obviously of critical importance to the winner of the award. Parties are deemed to be bound by the arbitral award unless the award has been annulled. As for international commercial arbitration, often the losing party gives effect to the arbitral award voluntarily. Because there is frequently social and commercial pressure from the commercial sector to abide by the arbitral award, an enterprise known for defaulting on arbitral awards looses credibility.

However, the arbitral award can be enforced where necessary through a court order. Necessarily, this requires a mechanism by which the award of a private adjudicator becomes enforceable by public authorities — the award must be recognized and enforced by states. The award is enforceable where the losing party has assets located or where that party resides. To overcome the problems of enforcing an international arbitral award in another country, an important international treaty has been adopted — the *Convention on the Recognition and Enforcement of foreign Arbitral Awards* (**New York Convention 1958**).[2] This convention, improves the enforcement of international commercial arbitration awards considerably. The *New York Convention* (1958) has been praised to be "the single most important pillar

---

1. arbitration hearing：仲裁开庭审理。

2. *Convention on the Recognition and Enforcement of foreign Arbitral Awards* （New York Convention 1958）：《承认及执行外国仲裁裁决公约》[简称《纽约公约》（1958）]。该条约规定各缔约方应承认外国仲裁裁决具有约束力，并依援引裁决地之程序规则及本条约的条款予以执行。

on which the edifice of international arbitration rests."

The *New York Convention* (1958) applies to the recognition and enforcement of arbitral awards, which are rendered in another member. Such arbitral awards are intended to settle disputes between private parties, not states. The *New York Convention* (1958) commits the courts in each contracting members to recognize and enforce (under local procedure rules) the awards of arbitration tribunals under arbitration clauses and arbitration agreements, which are valid and capable of being performed. Among contracting states of the *New York Convention* (1958), the party seeking enforcement of an arbitral award only needs to submit the arbitration agreement and the award to a court of the forum state. The burden of proof rests on the defendant to show that the award cannot be enforced by the court. The *New York Convention* (1958) sets forth the limited grounds under which recognition and enforcement of arbitral awards may be refused:

(1) incapacity of a party to the agreement containing the arbitration clause or the invalidity of the arbitration agreement under the law applicable to a party to the agreement;

(2) lack of proper notice of arbitration proceedings, the appointment of arbitrators or other reasons denying an adequate opportunity to present a defense;

(3) failure of the arbitral award to restrict itself to the terms of the submission to arbitration, or decision of matters not within the scope of that submission;

(4) composition of the arbitral institution not according to the arbitration agreement or applicable law;

(5) non-finality of the arbitral award under applicable law.

In addition to these grounds for refusal, recognition or enforcement of arbitral awards may also be refused if it would be contrary to the public policy of the member in which enforcement is sought; or if the subject matter of the dispute cannot be settled by arbitration under the law of that member. To some degree, the connotation of public policy is not so clear. Generally, it is thought to be the most basic and material morality and public interests. Courts in the United States have taken the position that the "public policy limitation on the *New York Convention* (1958) is to be construed narrowly and to be applied only where enforcement would violate the forum state's most basic notions of morality and justice."

People's Republic of China has adopted the *New York Convention* (1958), while two reservations to the *New York Convention* (1958) are made:

(1) China will apply the New York Convention (1958) to the recognition and enforcement of arbitral awards rendered in the territory of another contracting member only on the basis of reciprocity;

(2) China will apply the *New York Convention* (1958) only to the disputes arising from the contractual and non-contractual commercial relationships defined by the laws of China.

The *New York Convention* (1958), subjecting to the above reservations, became legally effective in China on 22 April 1987. That is, China applies the *New York Convention* (1958) to the recognition and enforcement of arbitral awards rendered in the territory of another contracting member. And China applies the *New York Convention* (1958) to disputes arising from commercial relationships defined by the laws of China. (See 10.2 A of this Chapter)

【Case 10-2】
Flexo Label Printing Machine Case [24 July 2007][1]
(Arbitration Award made by China International Economic and Trade Arbitration Commission CIETA)

I. PROCEDURE

The China International Economic and Trade Arbitration Commission South China Sub-Commission (hereinafter referred to as "SCCIETAC", or the "Arbitration Commission") accepted the case (Case No. SHEN M2006127X) according to:

The arbitration clause in Contract No. 040816 (hereinafter referred to as the "Contract"), signed by the Claimant, Shandong H Ltd. (hereinafter referred to as the [Buyer]) and the Respondent, N Corp. of the Kingdom of Denmark (hereinafter referred to as the [Seller]); and

The Request for Arbitration submitted by the [Buyer] on 28 August 2006.

The "China International Economic & Trade Arbitration Commission Arbitration Rules" (hereinafter referred to as the "Arbitration Rules"), which took effect on 1 May 2005, apply to this case.

On 21 September 2006, the Secretariat of SCCIETAC (hereinafter referred to as the "Secretariat") sent the Notice of Arbitration, the Arbitration Rules, and the Panel of Arbitrators to both parties via express mail service. Meanwhile, the Secretariat of SCCIETAC sent the Request for Arbitration submitted by the [Buyer] and its annexes submitted by the [Buyer] to the [Seller].

In accordance with the Arbitration Rules, the [Buyer] appointed Mr. W as arbitrator in this dispute. The [Seller] nominated Mr. C to the tribunal. Since the parties did not appoint the presiding arbitrator jointly, or entrust the Chairman of SCCIETAC to make this appointment within a specified time, the Chairman of SCCIETAC, pursuant to the Arbitration Rules, appointed Ms. L to be the presiding arbitrator. On 24 November 2006, the presiding arbitrator together with the arbitrators appointed by the parties formed the Arbitral Tribunal to hear the case. On the same day, the Secretariat sent the Notice of Composition of the Arbitral Tribunal to the parties.

The Secretariat arranged for an oral hearing to be held on the morning of 9 January 2007. On 5 December 2006, the Secretariat sent the Notice of the Oral Hearing to the parties. The [Seller] requested a postponement of the oral hearing for the reason that the original oral hearing date was in the Christmas season in the United States and Denmark, during which the [Seller] could not send representatives to participate in the oral hearing. The Secretariat forwarded these documents to the [Buyer].

After discussion, the Tribunal postponed the oral hearing from 9 a.m. on 9 January 2007 to 9 a.m. on 25 January 2007 with no alteration to other proceedings.

The Tribunal held the first oral hearing on 9 a.m. 25 January 2007 in the Shenzhen Special Economic Zone. Representatives of the [Buyer] and the [Seller] participated. At the hearing, the parties made presentations and debates, examined the evidence, and answered questions of the Tribunal. The Tribunal investigated and verified the facts of the case. Finding that the parties had the desire for

---

1. 本案的双方当事人是中国山东某公司（买方）和丹麦某公司（卖方），双方之前签订了一份柔版标签印刷机买卖合同。后在合同履行过程中，双方就柔版标签印刷机的质量问题引发争议，而将该争议提交当时的中国国际经济贸易仲裁委员会华南分会仲裁。中国国际经济贸易仲裁委员会华南分会依据相应仲裁规则做出了该仲裁裁决。阅读该案例，有助加深对仲裁程序的理解。

conciliation, the Tribunal sought to conciliate the case at the hearing and set a time limit for the parties to arrange a settlement.

On 28 March 2007, the Tribunal held a second oral hearing. At this hearing, the parties arrived at a tentative settlement and drafted a written Settlement Agreement. The representative of the [Buyer] signed the Settlement Agreement while the representative of the [Seller] needed to confirm with his client. The Tribunal then withheld further hearings pending the parties reaching their final Settlement Agreement. However, the [Seller] elected not to sign the Settlement Agreement and the conciliation between the parties failed.

In accordance with Article 42(2) of the Arbitration Rules, considering the request as truly necessary and the reasons for the extension truly justified, the Chairman of SCCIETAC extended the time period to 24 July 2007.

On 9 a.m. 4 July 2007, the Tribunal conducted the third oral hearing on the [Buyer]'s amended arbitral claims. At the hearing, the [Buyer] presented facts and issues for the amended arbitral claims and the [Seller] made its response. The parties also debated with each other. On the basis of the "Acceptance Report" and its annexes, the "Meeting Minutes" and other important evidentiary materials sealed by the parties, the Tribunal made inquiries to the parties. At the end of the hearing, the parties submitted their final opinions. The Tribunal specified a time period of three days after the hearing for the parties to submit any further written material to the Secretariat. Any material submitted beyond that specified time period would be refused. On the day the hearing ended, the [Seller] submitted its Counsel's Opinion and supplementary evidence. After the hearing, the [Buyer] submitted two Counsel's Opinion documents with evidence on 6 July 2007. The Secretariat forwarded the said materials to each party promptly. On 12 July 2007, the [Seller] submitted its Reply to the Counsel's Opinion and annexes of the [Buyer].

This case is now closed. The Tribunal, after discussing jointly, based upon the written documents and the facts identified in the oral hearing, rendered its arbitral award.

II. FACTS AND ISSUES

A. Facts

On 27 August 2004, the [Buyer] and the [Seller] concluded the disputed Contract in China, stipulating that the [Buyer] purchased a nine color Flexo label printer (the "Machine") from the [Seller] for US $954,932. The price was paid in full by the [Buyer]. After the printing Machine arrived at the destination, it was installed and the acceptance test had been carried out. Then, a dispute arose relating to the quality of the Machine. The parties could not reach a resolution of this dispute by negotiation, thus, the [Buyer] submitted the dispute to SCCIETAC according to the arbitration clause of the Contract.

B. Position of the parties

I. The [Buyer's] position

On 1 March 2005, the Machine was loaded on a ship and left the port in the United States. In the last third part of March, the Machine arrived at H port in Shandong, China. The customs were cleared and the price was paid in full. The Guarantee Period of the Machine was from 1 March 2005 to 1 September 2006. The parties carried out the preliminary check and acceptance on 15 June 2005. The

Acceptance Report provided that "all the functions of the Machine were checked and accepted, other related issues see the annex notes. " The annex explained that "insofar there are some unsettled problems of the Flexo label printing machine as the follows:

First, the overprint precision of the print unit and mould-cutting unit had not been checked;

Second, the irregular wine label underlying die mould-cutting, emission and collecting labels still needed to be solved in the next stage of performance by the [Seller] with comprehensive technology support.

[Seller] replied that the mould-cutting unit problem could be tested again when the accessory blade roller arrived. However, after this, the [Buyer] found the Machine had serious defects and could not be put into normal use.

First, the axial overprint of the printing unit was inaccurate (beer label overprint error was 0.3-0.5mm), article 6 of the Annex II of the Contract regulating the printing acceptance check criteria provides that the printing Machine overprint precision should be ±0.1mm;

Second, the printing and mould-cutting precision was inaccurate (the errors are 0.5mm), article 6 of the Annex II of the Contract regulating the printing acceptance check criteria provides that the printing machine overprint mould-cutting precision should be ±0.15mm;

Third, when the print speed was over 90 m/min, there would be a paper jam, article 6 of the Annex II of the Contract regulating the printing acceptance check criteria provides that the print speed should be 175 m/min;

Last, there existed some problem with the designation of the oven structure causing the plate to be overly dry and the hot air drying of the unit is inefficient.

Centering on the defects of the Machine, the parties carried out several negotiations and made a full record of the process of acceptance and adjustment in the form of "Meeting Minutes", which the [Seller]'s staff affirmed by signature. In the middle ten days of July 2006, the [Seller] sent its Chief Technology Officer in the Asian-Pacific Area (OEM foreign nationality engineer) to repair and adjust the Machine. However, the defects of the Machine were not solved in the end. On 25 July 2006, the [Buyer] applied to the T City Entry-Exit Inspection and Quarantine Bureau of the People's Republic of China (hereinafter referred to as "T City Entry-Exit Inspection and Quarantine Bureau") for technological performance authentication of the printing Machine. On 27 July 2006, the T City Entry-Exit Inspection and Quarantine Bureau issued an "Identification Report" (Tribunal's note: It should be "Certificate of Inspection").

According to the Contract concluded by the parties, if during the Guarantee Period, the goods were damaged due to design or manufacturing defects, or the quality and function did not conform with the contract provisions, the Buyer would entrust the China Commodity Inspection Bureau for inspection, and claim damages from the Seller (including replacement of goods) based on China Commodity Inspection Bureau's inspection certificate. All the costs would be assumed by the Seller.

The [Buyer] in its Request for Arbitration requested the following.

1. The [Seller] should replace the unqualified Flexo label printing machine with a qualified Flexo label printing machine within sixty days after the arbitral award was rendered. The Guarantee Period should be of 12 months after the new Flexo label printing machine was accepted. If the [Seller] could

not deliver the new qualified machine or the delivered machine could not pass the acceptance check, the Contract should be cancelled. The [Buyer] should return the delivered machines to the [Seller] and the [Seller] should return the price paid by the [Buyer] after the cancellation of the Contract.

2. The [Seller] should pay the damages. The damages should be calculated on the base number of US $954,932, the Contract price of the Flexo label printing machine, and at the rate of 5%.

3. The [Seller] should be responsible for the Arbitration Fees.

To support these arbitral requests, the [Buyer] submitted to the Tribunal the following evidence: a. The Contract and the Annexes Ⅰ and Ⅱ; b. The Machine Acceptance Report and its annexes; c. The Meeting Minutes of the four meetings the parties had; d. The Inspection Certificate provided by the T City Entry-Exit Inspection and Quarantine Bureau; e. The Catalog of Entry-Exit Commodities Inspected and Quarantined by the Competent Entry-Exit Inspection and Quarantine Authority issued by the General Administration of Customs and State Administration for Entry-Exit Inspection and Quarantine of the People's Republic of China.

Ⅱ. The [Seller's] position

On 18 December 2006, the [Seller] submitted to SCCIETAC a Dissent against the T City Entry-Exit Inspection and Quarantine Bureau's Inspection Certificate of the People's Republic of China (hereinafter referred to as the "Dissent"). The [Seller] provided the invoices, the bills of lading, the list of the goods, the Reply to the Problems Concerning the Flexo Label Printing Machine (hereinafter referred to as the "Reply to the Problems"), the No. 122 Announcement of the General Administration of Quality Supervision of the People's Republic of China of 2003 and other evidentiary materials to support its requests.

The [Seller] requested the Tribunal to find the following.

1. There were no quality problems with the disputed Machine for the following reasons.

a. The printing Machine was a qualified product. The disputed Machine belonged to the schedule of must-be-inspected commodities of the China Commodity Inspection Bureau. Necessary inspections had been carried out when the Machine entered into China and was delivered to the [Buyer].

b. The printing Machine had been checked and accepted by the parties and was accepted as a qualified product. According to the Acceptance Report provided by the [Buyer], the Machine was accepted on 25 June 2005. The [Buyer] affirmed that the Machine was installed and adjusted and functioned well. Therefore, the [Buyer] affixed its seal to the Acceptance Report.

c. From the evidence provided by the [Buyer], the Machine had been used all the time. In the course of use, damages caused by improper operation could not be excluded. At the same time, whether the [Buyer] properly operated the Machine, whether the appropriate materials were used or whether the printed products met the requirements of the [Buyer]'s client, all need to be verified by further evidence provided by the [Buyer]. The [Seller] maintained that there were improper operations and inappropriate materials used in the course of using the Machine by the [Buyer].

d. There were contradictions between the inspection time of the T City Entry-Exit Inspection and Quarantine Bureau's Inspection Certificate and the Acceptance Report signed by the [Buyer]. According to the Acceptance Report, all the functions of the Machine were accepted. However, the T City Entry-Exit Inspection and Quarantine Bureau's Inspection Certificate directly deemed the Machine to be badly designed or badly manufactured only because of the print precision and speed, two causes which were not existent. The contradicted identification was not in compliance with the facts.

2. All of the [Buyer's] arbitral claims including the amended ones should be dismissed.

III. OPINION OF THE ARBITRAL TRIBUNAL

A. The applicable law

The Contract has no choice of law clause. However, the arbitration institution and the Arbitration Rules chosen, as well as the citation of the Chinese laws in the written arbitration documents submitted by the parties demonstrate that the parties had impliedly chosen Chinese laws as the applicable law in this case. The Tribunal respects the will of the parties and their expression of intent. At the hearing, the Tribunal confirms with the parties that Chinese laws and regulations apply to this case at hand. Meanwhile, since the places of business (China and Denmark) of the parties are in two different Contracting States of the *United Nations Convention on Contracts for the International Sale of Goods* (hereinafter referred to as the "*CISG*"), and the parties do not expressly opt out the *CISG* regime, the Tribunal finds that the *CISG* applies to the present dispute. This is confirmed by the parties. Therefore, the Tribunal finds that the parties have expressly chosen the Chinese law and *CISG* as the applicable laws of the present case.

B. Regarding the Contract and its Annexes

The Contract is an international sales contract concluded by the [Buyer] and the [Seller] on 27 August 2007. The whole Contract consists of two parts, i.e., the Contract and Annexes I & II. The original Contract has two copies concluded in Chinese and English; both versions are equally authentic. The Contract provides that the [Seller] hereby sells to the [Buyer] an FBZ4200 nine color Flexo label printing Machine of [Seller] for a total price of US $954,932.00 CIF Qingdao, China. The origin and manufacturer should be [Seller] in the United States. The shipment is to be four and a half months after the advance payment is received. The Contract also gives clear and concrete provisions on the terms of payment, bills of payment, loading, quality guarantee, inspection and claim, force majeure, installation and adjustment, late delivery penalty, etc.

Article 19 of the Contract is the arbitration clause, which provides that, any dispute, controversy or claim arising out of, relating to or in connection with this contract and its performance, shall be settled through friendly negotiation. If no settlement can be reached, the dispute shall be submitted to the China International Economic and Trade Arbitration Commission Shenzhen Sub-Commission (SCCIETAC) for arbitration in accordance with the current effective arbitration rules. The arbitral award is final, and binding on both of the parties. The arbitration and execution fees should be borne by the losing party.

Article 20 of the Contract (Supplement condition) provides that: "If there are any supplement conditions of the Contract, the supplement conditions should be automatically preferred in the performance. If there are any conflicts between the contract provisions and the supplement conditions, the supplement conditions prevail. The contract has two annexes. Annex I sets out the specification list of the Machine. Annex II prescribes the acceptance check standards of the Machine on the quality and delivery time."

The two Annexes are supplement conditions of the Contract. The acceptance check standards that are set out in Annex II require that when used with stable raw material, printing ink and favorable print environment, the overprint precision should be "print to print ±0.1mm", "print to mould-cutting ±0.15mm", "print speed 175m/min". The following analysis will show that the above-mentioned is the most important contractual base for solving the disputed quality problems.

To conclude, the Tribunal finds that the disputed Contract consists of two parts, the Contract and the two annexes. The provisions included in the annexes are supplemental conditions. Both the Contract and the annexes reveal the true intent of the parties. The content of the two parts is legal and valid with complete formal elements. The Contract binds the parties since signature. The supplemental conditions prevail over the Contract provisions.

C. Regarding the Acceptance Report and its Annex

On June 2005 the parties signed an Acceptance Report for the Machine (hereinafter, referred to as the "Acceptance Report"). It states as follow.

"FBZ4200 Flexo label printing machine of the 040816 Contract, Machine No. 09122004, arrived safely at the H Ltd. in Shandong. After installation and adjustment, the Machine functions well. All the functions of the Machine were checked and accepted, other related issues see the annex notes."

The "annex notes" referred to in the Certificate of Acceptance, are formally named Annex of the Acceptance Report for the Machine (hereinafter referred to as the "Annex"). The Annex said that "After installation and adjustment, the Machine works orderly", and that "the Guarantee Period is 18 months from 1 March 2005 to 1 September 2006". Several quality problems were unsettled at the time of acceptance and the reply and promises of the [Seller] are recorded thereto. The main problems are: The problem with the ninth color ink stick; The stability of the auto-overprint system to be observed; The overprint precision of the print unit and mould-cutting unit has not been checked; The irregular wine label underlying die mould-cutting, emission and collecting labels is unsolved; The cold-hot unit film-mulching function is unsettled; and The problem of the locker of the flexo roller of the first print suit.

For the last problem, the [Seller] admitted it to be a damage of two flexo rollers resulting from a defect in the design of the first color suit [Translator's note: The "first color suit" means the "first print suit" judging from the context]. The [Seller] also promises to provide long-term technology support for all the existing problems. The Annex has the parties' signatures and seals on it.

The Report and its Annex were submitted by the [Buyer] to prove that the Machine has quality defects. The Tribunal observes that the [Seller] argues that "this is direct effective evidence that the disputed Machine was ratified by the parties and involves no dispute. " [See the Dissent against the T City Entry-Exit Inspection and Quarantine Bureau's Inspection Certificate of the People's Republic of China.] However, as a matter of fact, the parties hold totally contrary assertions as to the provable purpose of this evidence. Citing a series of records of the quality defects in the Annex of this evidence, the [Buyer] contends that the acceptance check carried out on 25 June 2005 was an incomplete or preliminary acceptance check. The [Buyer] submitted that the contention of the [Seller] that the Machine had been inspected and accepted at an earlier time could not stand. [See the Counsel's Opinion submitted by the [Buyer] on 20 June 2007.]

But, the [Seller] cites the following sentences as its defense that "after installation and adjustment, the Machine functions well. All the functions of the Machine were checked and accepted." The [Seller] contended that these words from the Inspection Report demonstrate that the Machine is qualified. But the [Seller] neglects the problems recorded in the Annex which are confirmed by the signatures and seals of the parties. In terms of the discrepancy of the quality assessments of the same machine, while the Inspection Report says the Machine functions well, the Annex says the Machine basically works orderly. It should be noted that the Annex also provides that there are still many quality defects of the Machine unsettled and that some functions fall short of the most important acceptance criteria. In light of these facts, the Machine does not conform to the Annex Ⅱ provisions, which prevail over the Contract provisions.

The Tribunal finds that there are conflicts between the Inspection Report and its Annexes. The problems listed in Annex Ⅱ, e.g., "the overprint precision of the print unit and mould-cutting unit has not been checked", are concerned with the most important content of the Contract relating to the quality requirements made by the parties. The specific problems listed in Annex Ⅱ have actually overturned the non-objective conclusion in the Report that the Machine functions well. Hence, the Tribunal finds that the Inspection Report on which the [Seller] based its defense cannot prove that the Machine is up to standard. The Tribunal further notes that, before the signing date of the Inspection Report and its Annexes, the parties had several meetings about the defects of the Machine found in the installation and adjustment. The [Seller] also promised to fix some of these problems. All of this was supported by the Meeting Minutes signed by the parties. However, some of the core problems such as the precision of the print to mould-cutting and the print speed have been unsettled for over nine months after the [Seller] promised to fix them at the acceptance. For that reason, the Meeting Minutes of 1 April 2006, confirmed by the parties, note that "the error of the overprint unit is 0.3-0.5mm, the production yield is 60%-70%"; and "when the print speed was over 80m/min, the stability of the Machine declines. "

The [Buyer] said that its company could not carry out production for two months and wanted to negotiate with the [Seller] about the assumption of the damages. Till July 2006, the [Seller] sent its Chief Technology Officer of Asian-Pacific Area and other members of [Seller's] staff to repair and adjust the Machine. But the problems remained unsettled. All these facts do not support the [Seller]'s contention that the Machine had been inspected and accepted and is up to standard. The Tribunal holds that the problems listed in the Annex confirmed by the parties can fully prove the fact that the Machine has quality defects.

D. The [Seller's] Dissent is dismissed

After examining the relative laws and regulations, the Tribunal finds that the Dissent of the [Seller] has no legal basis and should be dismissed. The reasons are as follows: (omitted)

E. Regarding the liability for breach of the Contract

After signing the Contract, the [Buyer] paid the contract price as provided and fulfilled its contractual obligations. The Machine supplied by the [Seller] does not conform to the Contract. This is supported by the Meeting Minutes signed by the parties, the Annexes and the Certificate of Inspection issued by the T City Entry-Exit Inspection and Quarantine Bureau.

The above conclusion demonstrates that the [Seller] failed to fulfill its quality guarantee obligation under Article 14 of the Contract; the nine color Flexo label printing machine it sold to the [Buyer] does not conform to the Contract. Article 25 of the *CISG* provides that: "A breach of contract committed by one of the parties is fundamental if it results in such a detriment to the other party as substantially to deprive him of what he is entitled to expect under the contract unless the party in breach did not foresee and a reasonable person of the same kind in the same circumstances would not have foreseen such a result."

The facts of the present case are as follow.

In the 18 months Guarantee Period from 1 March 2005 to 1 September 2006, the [Buyer] informed the [Seller] several times about the non-conformity of the Machine and required the [Seller] to take make-up measures. The [Seller] also promised to solve the problems many times and sent technology staffs to adjust and repair the Machine with which the [Buyer] actively cooperated. However, the quality defects cannot be eliminated in the end which reflects that the quality defects of the Machine cannot be made up for within a reasonable time with reasonable efforts. Hence, the [Buyer] cannot realize its purpose of the Contract, i.e., the contractual expectations of the [Buyer] are deprived of. This result could be fairly foreseen by the [Seller] because the parties have made express requirements of the core characteristics such as the overprint precision and the speed. And the [Seller] cannot claim he can not foresee such a detriment to the buyer. All of the above facts are supported by the Meeting Minutes of 21 April 2005, 28 April 2005 and 26 May 2005 signed by the parties, the Annexes of the Inspection Report of 25 June 2005, and the Meeting Minutes of 1 April 2006.

According to the *CISG* and the facts, the Tribunal determines that the [Seller] breached the Contract by providing a non-conforming Machine. The non-conformity of the Machine substantially deprived the [Buyer] of what is expected under the Contract. Hence, the breach is a fundamental breach. The [Seller] is responsible for the liability for the breach in accordance with the *CISG* and Chinese law and the Contract.

F. Regarding the [Buyer]'s claims

1. The claim that the [Seller] should replace the original Machine or the Contract should be avoided. The Tribunal finds in favor of this claim for the following reasons.

First, Article 46 (2) & (3) of the *CISG* stipulate the following.

"(2) If the goods do not conform with the contract, the buyer may require delivery of substitute goods only if the lack of conformity constitutes a fundamental breach of contract and a request for substitute goods is made either in conjunction with notice given under article 39 or within a reasonable time thereinafter.

"(3) If the goods do not conform to the contract, the buyer may require the seller to remedy the lack of conformity by repair, unless this is unreasonable having regard to all the circumstances. A request for repair must be made either in conjunction with notice given under article 39 or within a reasonable time thereinafter."

After the [Seller] breached the Contract, the [Buyer] gave notice within the period provided in Article 39 of *CISG* and Articles 15 and 17 of the Contract. Therefore, the [Buyer] is entitled to require replacement of the Machine, i.e., the [Buyer] is entitled to require the [Seller] to replace the non-conforming Flexo label printing machine (hereinafter referred to as the "Original Machine") with a conforming Flexo label printing machine (hereinafter referred to as the "New Machine").

The second arbitral claim made by the [Buyer] is that: "The [Seller] should pay the damages. The damages should be calculated on the base amount of US $954,932, the Contract price of the Flexo label printing machine, and at the rate of 5%."

The facts of the present case demonstrate that the Original Machine which was being adjusted or repaired all the time fails to meet the requirements of acceptance. This not only deprived the [Buyer] of what he is entitled to expect under the Contract but also cost a lot of labor and material loss during the two years of repeated adjustment. As for the [Buyer]'s right to damages when the Machine fails to meet the requirements of acceptance, Article 17 of the Contract expressly stipulates the following.

"The Seller should solve the problems within four weeks if the Machine cannot work in an orderly manner and the production cannot be carried out after the installation and adjustment. After four weeks, if the Machine still cannot work in an orderly manner, penalties should be paid by the Seller to the Buyer. The penalty should be 0.5% of the total contract price for every seven working days with a maximum limit of 5% of the total contract price.

"The [Buyer] is entitled to request replacement of a new machine or avoid the Contract and get an indemnity of 5% of the total contract price if after eight weeks of the installation and adjustment, the Machine fails to meet the requirements of acceptance due to design and/or manufacturing defects of the Machine itself."

On the basis of the facts and the Contract, the Tribunal determines that the [Buyer's] second arbitral claim is justified.

2. The claim that the [Seller] should be responsible for the arbitration fees

The Tribunal determines that the dispute is caused by the fundamental breach of the [Seller] deemed by the Tribunal to be the losing party. It is expressly provided in the Arbitration Clause, i.e., Article 19 of the Contract that "The arbitration and execution fees should be borne by the losing party."The Tribunal accepts this claim.

Ⅳ. AWARD

According to the above opinion, the Tribunal renders the following award:

(1) The [Seller] should replace the unqualified Flexo label printing Machine with a qualified Flexo label printing machine within sixty days after the arbitral award is rendered. The Guarantee Period should be of 12 months after the new Flexo label printing machine was accepted. If the [Seller] could not deliver the new qualified machine or the delivered machine could not pass the acceptance check, the Contract should be cancelled. The [Seller] should return the price paid by the [Buyer] and withdraw the machine delivered.

(2) The [Seller] should pay the damages of US $47,746.60, i.e., 5% of the total price of the Contract in the amount of US $954,932.

(3) The [Seller] is responsible for the Arbitration Fees. The Arbitration Fee for this arbitration is RMB 184,027. Since the [Buyer] has paid the entire sum in advance, the [Seller] should make payment of RMB 184,027 to the [Buyer].

The [Buyer] should pay for the travel expenses for the out-of-town arbitrator in the amount of RMB 12,076. Since the [Buyer] has paid RMB 14,000 in advance, the [Buyer] should be refunded for RMB

1,924 by the SCCIETAC.

The above payments should be made within twenty days from the date this award is handed down.

This award is the final decision and shall come into effect upon being handed down.

Chapter Summary

国际商事争议可通过协商、调解、小型审理（替代性争端解决方法）、仲裁和诉讼等方式谋求解决。每一种方式都各有特点，旨在满足当事人的不同需要，但仲裁无疑是其中一种颇受欢迎的国际商事争议解决方式。国际商事争议的当事方在争议发生之前或发生之后，通过签订书面协议（仲裁协议），自愿将其争议提交由非司法机构的仲裁员组成的仲裁庭进行裁判，并受该裁判约束。相较于诉讼，国际商事仲裁具有更加高效、私密、灵活的特点。国际商事仲裁存在临时仲裁和机构仲裁两种类型，目前国际范围内有众多仲裁机构提供国际商事仲裁服务，竞争日趋激烈。

有效的仲裁协议是仲裁机构获得管辖权的基本前提。国际商事争议的当事方，如欲将争议提交仲裁，必须在争议发生前在合同中约定仲裁条款或在争议发生后达成仲裁协议。国际商事仲裁程序一般依据各仲裁机构的具体仲裁规则执行，相较于诉讼，仲裁程序具有一定的灵活性。在国际商事仲裁裁决的承认和执行方面，《纽约公约》（1958）发挥了重要的保障和促进作用。在国际商事调解达成的和解协议的跨境执行方面，2019 年 9 月 12 日，《联合国关于调解所产生的国际和解协议公约》生效，将推动把调解作为一种解决国际贸易争端的有效替代方法。

Exercises

Part Ⅰ True or False Statements: Decide whether the following statements are True or False and explain why.

1. To resolve an international commercial dispute, the parties must first submit it to arbitration.

2. If the party did not obtain a satisfactory award through mediation, he/she may continue to bring the same dispute to a court with jurisdiction for resolution.

3. According to the laws of China, an arbitration clause taking the form of e-mail is deemed to be invalid.

4. If the contract, which contains the arbitration clause, is invalid as a whole for a reason unrelated to the arbitration clause, the arbitration clause then is invalid and parties cannot resort to arbitration.

5. A court of China may refuse to enforce a foreign arbitral award rendered by American Arbitration Association on the basis that the award contradicts the public policy of China.

6. An arbitration agreement must be made before a dispute arising between the parties.

7. Arbitration proceedings are usually publicly held. The public can have an access to arbitration hearing.

8. China will not apply the *New York Convention* (1958) to the recognition and enforcement of arbitral awards rendered in the territory of a non-contracting member.

9. Arbitration awards are final and binding. In case that an award is not voluntarily obeyed by the losing party, the arbitration institution can enforce the award by itself.

10. A contracting state of *New York Convention* (1958) can refuse to recognize and enforce a foreign arbitral award rendered in another contracting member on the ground that the arbitrators took bribery.

Part Ⅱ　Chapter Questions: Discuss and answer the following questions according to what you have learned in this chapter. You are encouraged to use your own words.

1. How many methods of dispute resolution in international commercial transactions? Give the list.

2. How do you understand the relationship between ADR and arbitration?

3. What is the essential difference between mediation and arbitration?

4. What are the advantages and disadvantages of resolving international commercial disputes by arbitration?

5. Suppose two parties to a sales contract agree to submit any dispute arising from the performance of the contract to China International Economic and Trade Arbitration Commission. Try to draft the arbitration clause for them.

6. How would a choice of law clause in the contract help to address some of a party's concerns?

7. In accordance with the *New York Convention* (1958), what are the grounds under which recognition and enforcement of foreign arbitral awards may be refused?

8. Will a Chinese court enforce a Mexico judgment dealing with a loan agreement on a promissory note if the note contradicts the relevant provisions in *Negotiable Instruments Law of China*? Suppose there is no treaty in this aspect but reciprocity between China and Mexico.

9. Compared with settling domestic business disputes through litigation, what legal problems may arise from settling international business disputes in such a way?

10. Do you agree with the statement that arbitration is a better method for settling international commercial disputes compared with litigation?

Part Ⅲ. Case Problem

You have started a small Hi-tech company in Guangzhou, China. Your competitor, a corporation based in New York is using your trade secrets and your patents without your permission or payment, which has vaporized your great fortune. How will you act to stop it and get compensation? Explain.

Part Ⅳ. Further reading

The following is an excerpt of *UNCITRAL MODEL LAW ON INTERNATIONAL COMMERCIAL LAW* (1985, with amendments as adopted in 2006).

CHAPTER Ⅲ. COMPOSITION OF ARBITRAL TRIBUNAL

Article 10. Number of arbitrators

(1) The parties are free to determine the number of arbitrators.

(2) Failing such determination, the number of arbitrators shall be three.

Article 11. Appointment of arbitrators

(1) No person shall be precluded by reason of his nationality from acting as an arbitrator, unless otherwise agreed by the parties.

(2) The parties are free to agree on a procedure of appointing the arbitrator or arbitrators, subject to the provisions of paragraphs (4) and (5) of this article.

(3) Failing such agreement,

(a) in an arbitration with three arbitrators, each party shall appoint one arbitrator, and the two arbitrators thus appointed shall appoint the third arbitrator; if a party fails to appoint the arbitrator within thirty days of receipt of a request to do so from the other party, or if the two arbitrators fail to agree on the third arbitrator within thirty days of their appointment, the appointment shall be made, upon request of a party, by the court or other authority specified in article 6;

(b) in an arbitration with a sole arbitrator, if the parties are unable to agree on the arbitrator, he shall be appointed, upon request of a party, by the court or other authority specified in article 6.

(4) Where, under an appointment procedure agreed upon by the parties,

(a) a party fails to act as required under such procedure, or

(b) the parties, or two arbitrators, are unable to reach an agreement expected of them under such procedure, or

(c) a third party, including an institution, fails to perform any function entrusted to it under such procedure,

any party may request the court or other authority specified in article 6 to take the necessary measure, unless the agreement on the appointment procedure provides other means for securing the appointment.

(5) A decision on a matter entrusted by paragraph (3) or (4) of this article to the court or other authority specified in article 6 shall be subject to no appeal. The court or other authority, in appointing an arbitrator, shall have due regard to any qualifications required of the arbitrator by the agreement of the parties and to such considerations as are likely to secure the appointment of an independent and impartial arbitrator and, in the case of a sole or third arbitrator, shall take into account as well the advisability of appointing an arbitrator of a nationality other than those of the parties.

Article 12. Grounds for challenge

(1) When a person is approached in connection with his possible appointment as an arbitrator, he shall disclose any circumstances likely to give rise to justifiable doubts as to his impartiality or independence. An arbitrator, from the time of his appointment and throughout the arbitral proceedings, shall without delay disclose any such circumstances to the parties unless they have already been informed of them by him.

(2) An arbitrator may be challenged only if circumstances exist that give rise to justifiable doubts as to his impartiality or independence, or if he does not possess qualifications agreed to by the parties. A party may challenge an arbitrator appointed by him, or in whose appointment he has participated, only for reasons of which he becomes aware after the appointment has been made.

Article 13. Challenge procedure

(1) The parties are free to agree on a procedure for challenging an arbitrator, subject to the provisions of paragraph (3) of this article.

(2) Failing such agreement, a party who intends to challenge an arbitrator shall, within fifteen days after becoming aware of the constitution of the arbitral tribunal or after becoming aware of any

circumstance referred to in article 12(2), send a written statement of the reasons for the challenge to the arbitral tribunal. Unless the challenged arbitrator withdraws from his office or the other party agrees to the challenge, the arbitral tribunal shall decide on the challenge.

(3) If a challenge under any procedure agreed upon by the parties or under the procedure of paragraph (2) of this article is not successful, the challenging party may request, within thirty days after having received notice of the decision rejecting the challenge, the court or other authority specified in article 6 to decide on the challenge, which decision shall be subject to no appeal; while such a request is pending, the arbitral tribunal, including the challenged arbitrator, may continue the arbitral proceedings and make an award.

Article 14. Failure or impossibility to act

(1) If an arbitrator becomes de jure or de facto unable to perform his functions or for other reasons fails to act without undue delay, his mandate terminates if he withdraws from his office or if the parties agree on the termination. Otherwise, if a controversy remains concerning any of these grounds, any party may request the court or other authority specified in article 6 to decide on the termination of the mandate, which decision shall be subject to no appeal.

(2) If, under this article or article 13(2), an arbitrator withdraws from his office or a party agrees to the termination of the mandate of an arbitrator, this does not imply acceptance of the validity of any ground referred to in this article or article 12(2).

Article 15. Appointment of substitute arbitrator

Where the mandate of an arbitrator terminates under article 13 or 14 or because of his withdrawal from office for any other reason or because of the revocation of his mandate by agreement of the parties or in any other case of termination of his mandate, a substitute arbitrator shall be appointed according to the rules that were applicable to the appointment of the arbitrator being replaced.

CHAPTER Ⅳ. JURISDICTION OF ARBITRAL TRIBUNAL

Article 16. Competence of arbitral tribunal to rule on its jurisdiction

(1) The arbitral tribunal may rule on its own jurisdiction, including any objections with respect to the existence or validity of the arbitration agreement. For that purpose, an arbitration clause which forms part of a contract shall be treated as an agreement independent of the other terms of the contract. A decision by the arbitral tribunal that the contract is null and void shall not entail ipso jure the invalidity of the arbitration clause.

(2) A plea that the arbitral tribunal does not have jurisdiction shall be raised not later than the submission of the statement of defense. A party is not precluded from raising such a plea by the fact that he has appointed, or participated in the appointment of, an arbitrator. A plea that the arbitral tribunal is exceeding the scope of its authority shall be raised as soon as the matter alleged to be beyond the scope of its authority is raised during the arbitral proceedings. The arbitral tribunal may, in either case, admit a later plea if it considers the delay justified.

(3) The arbitral tribunal may rule on a plea referred to in paragraph (2) of this article either as a preliminary question or in an award on the merits. If the arbitral tribunal rules as a preliminary question that it has jurisdiction, any party may request, within thirty days after having received notice of that ruling, the court specified in article 6 to decide the matter, which decision shall be subject to no appeal;

while such a request is pending, the arbitral tribunal may continue the arbitral proceedings and make an award.

Article 17. Power of arbitral tribunal to order interim measures.

Unless otherwise agreed by the parties, the arbitral tribunal may, at the request of a party, order any party to take such interim measure of protection as the arbitral tribunal may consider necessary in respect of the subject-matter of the dispute. The arbitral tribunal may require any party to provide appropriate security in connection with such measure.